My Life with

Verbal Bean

The Man –The Minister

Nita Bean Hodges

Biblical references cited: *The Holy Bible*: King James Version (KJV)

Visit www.verbalbean.com to listen to inspiring messages from Verbal Bean, including his teachings on ***Prayer*** and the ***Works of the Holy Ghost***.

To order additional copies, contact
Rev. Joel Bean
life@verbalbean.com

Second printing 2024
Printed in the United States of America

Dedication

I lovingly dedicate this book to the three wonderful children God gave to Verbal and me: Jana, Jennifer, and Joel. This book was written to share the extraordinary and miraculous story of your father, Verbal Winston Bean. He loved you unreservedly, and though he was taken early from us, the light of his love still glows brightly in all our lives. You three are the inspiration behind every word in these pages. Your love, laughter, and endless support have given me the strength to follow my dreams. This book is for you, with all my love.

Jana Kay and Calvin Wayne Bass
Lana Faye and Derek Walter Kreuger
Kaytlyn Jenee
Claire and Chapelle LaVon Bell
Jeremiah LaVon
Isaiah Wayne
Tessa Kay
Emma Novelle and Caleb Duane Herring

Jennifer Ellen Paroly
Hannah Noel and Uriah Chaz Blackmon

Joel Winston and Aileena Sheree Bean
Alyssa KayLin
Alivia Sheree
Amelia Kate
Asher Jon Winston Bean

Contents

Preface

I was invited by Bro. and Sis. Clifford Clark to speak in their church on Mother's Day in May 2021. My daughter, Jana Bass, joined me on that special day. The service was remarkable, and the Clarks were the epitome of welcoming hospitality to both of us.

After the service, we were invited to join Bro. and Sis. Clark and their family at the church event center. It was a beautiful facility, and they brought in delicious food for us all to enjoy. When dinner was finished, Bro. Clark said to me, "Sis. Hodges, did you know that Bro. Verbal Bean, your late husband, was my hero, and I was never privileged to meet him?"

I replied that I had never heard that, but it was gratifying to realize Verbal's ministry lived on in his life. Bro. Clark went on to explain, "I have read both books, *Prayer* and the *Works of the Holy Ghost,* so many times they are falling apart. I have listened to every recorded message of his I have been able to get my hands on. No one has had a greater impact on my ministry than Verbal Bean." I was touched to hear this testimony; it never fails to bless me when I am reminded that Verbal's ministry through his lessons on *Prayer* and the *Works of the Holy Ghost* still lives on today in printed and audio form.

We spent the rest of the afternoon discussing Verbal, his life, and ministry. Bro. and Sis. Clark asked various questions regarding Verbal and the life we had shared for fifteen years. It was a lovely day, and bringing up the memories I had cherished and held close for so long was an unexpected joy.

As we were getting ready to leave, Bro. Clark said, "Sis. Hodges, have you ever thought of writing a book about Bro. Bean?"

I replied, "I would love to; it's a marvelous story, but I'm not a writer and certainly not qualified to write that book."

Bro. Clark persisted, "You could do it. Please pray about it, and if God opens that door, I want to give you the first thousand dollars to finance the manuscript. In fact," he continued, "I'm going to give you that check today before you leave." I was astounded and touched by this generous gift.

On our way home, Jana said, "Mom, I hadn't heard about many of those experiences you shared today. They were new to me." I was amazed to think that so much of Verbal's life was unknown to Jana. I had thought that every aspect of our time together had been discussed and recounted to my children. It was a disturbing revelation, and I purposed in my heart that I would write Verbal's story for my children if for no one else.

I knew that doing justice to Verbal and his ministry was far beyond my capabilities, and I would need help. God sent that help in the beautiful person of Nila Ballestero Marxer. She has helped me through every paragraph and chapter in this book. We've laughed, cried, prayed together, and discussed whether the sentence really needed five commas. Nila's help and abilities have propped me up, and her encouragement has sustained me when I was ready to call it quits. She firmly told me her name was not to be mentioned in the creation of this book, but, as you can see, I had the last word.

I give heartfelt thanks and credit to my children, Jana, Jennifer, and Joel, who have patiently listened to my thoughts and memories and helped me separate the wheat from the chaff. They have been kind, loving, clear-eyed, and determined to see this manuscript through to the last period.

My humble thanks and gratitude go out to the Creator of all things good. Jesus Christ has been close and dear to me through the many pages of this manuscript. As I have recalled the revivals, prayer meetings, miracles, trials, and supernatural events that have made up the ministry of my late husband, I have relived those priceless days in awe of God's handiwork. The Spirit of our eternal Savior has overshadowed me and given me courage, and I believe, anointing to finish this beloved book.

Thank you for allowing me to express my heartfelt emotions regarding the formation of this story, *My Life with Verbal Bean, The Man–The Minister.* I wrote this book from a heart filled with gratitude for the life I was privileged to share with my loving husband, Verbal Winston Bean.

Foreword

This manuscript might as easily be called a compilation as a book. I have included many testimonies, stories, quotes, and events shared by multiple friends and ministers. This endeavor has been rewarding and sometimes heart-wrenching.

I regret that, as a young wife, I neglected to keep a journal of my life with Verbal. I didn't consider how valuable a record of our revivals and travels would have been. Many of the events we shared have vanished with time, and sadly, those years passed very swiftly. However, I am not completely bereft; my heart is filled with countless remaining memories of the weeks, months, and years we shared. They shine in my heart as the treasures they truly are.

It has been my deepest desire to tell, to the best of my ability, the story of Verbal Bean and the life I shared with him. Because of the need for clarity, I have also attempted to give voice to his early life and ministry before I was privileged to know him. I have learned many things about Verbal and his ministry that were new to me and added to the wealth of knowledge I already possessed. Often, I have been brought to tears by the accounts of the power and effectiveness of his ministry.

I have had first-hand knowledge of Verbal and the high calling of Christ Jesus in his life and ministry. The various accounts I have accumulated during the process of writing this book have only emphasized the things

I saw and experienced during the years of our marriage. While I was going through the few papers I had of Verbal's ministry, I found the letter from the young lady who had been healed of blindness when he prayed for her. I had never heard about or seen that testimony before this time.

Many stories of personal encounters with Verbal have been given to me through the months I have worked on this book. Often, the accounts begin something like this: "I attended a revival service where Bro. Bean was preaching, and while the Word was going forth, God showed me I was backslidden in heart." I have listened to or read with joy the reports of deliverance and miraculous healing. Then, usually, the ending included these words, "Bro. Bean's ministry has changed my life."

I have been acutely aware of the necessity of truthfully describing Verbal, his life, and ministry. Verbal's ministry stands on its own with no need for exaggeration or embellishment. However, some details have become hazy after these many years, so I have tried to be as exact as possible.

My strong resistance to taking on the task of authoring this book was the knowledge I am not a gifted writer. However, I have humbly come to understand that this wonderful story needs to be told. It is too valuable to disappear into the back roads of time. So, while the words I have written sometimes seem to me to be mundane and repetitive, the story is of utmost value and holds priceless truths that should never be ignored or overlooked. If we lose the knowledge of the ministry of Verbal Bean, who demonstrated to us what it means to walk with God, it will be a terrible loss.

Thank you for your forbearance and patience. May the words in this amazing story of a life well-lived bring hope and joy, and may the memory of Verbal Bean's lifespan and ministry be a light that will help guide you to your everlasting reward.

Chapter 1

The Introduction

"You're going to love my evangelist!" Uncle James said with a smile. These were the first words I ever heard spoken about Bro. Verbal Bean. My parents and I had made a trip to San Antonio, Texas, to visit my grandfather, Rev. C. P. Kilgore, who was in the hospital after suffering a heart attack. We learned the prognosis was not promising, seeing his heart was damaged, and no assurances were given to hope for a good recovery. Grandmother Kilgore had died three years earlier with cancer of the stomach. It had been a heartbreaking time for the Kilgore family. She was the angel of the family and the heart of the home, and now Granddad, the pillar of the family, was seriously ill.

Uncle James, Mother's younger brother, had driven from Houston, where he had assumed the pastorate of Life Tabernacle Church. He and Aunt Imogene were some of my favorite people on earth. After visiting with the family and spending time with Grandad, Uncle James was returning to Houston because they were in revival services. He then told us about his evangelist, Bro. Verbal Bean, and how he was ministering in an unprecedented way to the church. Uncle James continued; he was a powerful preacher, used in the gifts of the Spirit, and his sermons were never to be forgotten.

As a preface to this revival, my cousin, Jan Madden, later told me about her father, Uncle James, and his intense burden for the people of Life Tabernacle. It was a great church with many faithful saints, but he felt he was not seeing the revival and the influx of souls he desperately longed to see. One evening, Ronnie Wilhoite, one of the church leaders, came into what he thought was an empty church building. Standing in the sanctuary, he heard the moaning, groaning, and great outpourings of intercessory prayer. At first, he couldn't locate where these sounds were coming from, and it was disturbing to him. He thought there might be an emergency or great need, so he searched the building.

Finally, he found the source. It was his pastor on his face in an attic storage room. The room was hot and dusty, and Uncle James was lying on the floor, interceding in the Spirit. He was soaked with sweat and covered with dust. He never realized Ronnie had been there.

Jan went on to explain that Uncle James had told Imogene that he would stay at the church and fast and pray, returning home only to sleep at night until he was assured that God would send a harvest of souls. Soon after that, Bro. Bean visited Life Tabernacle on a Sunday night, and Uncle James asked him to preach. On the first night of revival, one of the faithful men of the church who had been seeking the Holy Ghost for twelve years was gloriously filled. The church was coming to a place of worship and freedom they had never experienced.

Uncle James began to relate many more wonderful details about the revival. Bro. Bean could sing and play the guitar. He was full of personality and fun, although this wasn't revealed until after the revival had broken. When he prayed, Heaven listened. He was single and highly available, although he had never been known to date anyone. Immediately, I became very interested. Uncle James closed this exciting conversation by repeating, "You're going to love my evangelist!" Little did I know that Uncle James's words would truly prove to be prophetic.

I rode to Houston with Uncle James to spend a few days with him and Aunt Imogene, whom I lovingly called Aunt Ima. I was happy to be with them and their darling girls, Jan and Jean. Most of all, I was excited because I would get to be in this incredible revival with such an exceptional evangelist.

When we arrived in Houston, Aunt Ima met us with more dramatic information about this evangelist, Bro. Bean. She had privately nicknamed him "The Pope" because of his single lifestyle and his authority in the pulpit. When she finished her stories, I was filled with excitement and anticipation about the coming service and the opportunity to meet this extraordinary evangelist.

Even though I was dating a young preacher, I must confess I dressed with extra care that evening. Aunt Ima had to put the finishing touches to my hairdo because of the wretched Houston humidity, which would wreak havoc on any hairstyle. My dress was chosen with thoughts of holiness and modesty uppermost. I had been made to understand that Bro. Bean was a 'Holiness Preacher Personified.' My father, Elder F. V. Shoemake, was also very holiness-minded, so nothing in my wardrobe was considered worldly, but you can't be too careful in these matters. If Bro. Bean was all everyone was saying he was, then I felt sure he would be someone I would want to impress favorably, boyfriend or no boyfriend.

The Kilgores lived next door to the church, and there was hustle and bustle as we all got ready in their small parsonage, which only had one bathroom. I hurriedly went through my suitcase, found the right dress, pressed out the creases from the packing folds, sprayed on perfume and hair spray, and made sure the seams in my nylons were straight. Before we left the house, I put breath mints in my purse along with tissues, being sure I would probably cry, expecting a powerful service. Finally, we were on our way.

I have never believed in love at first sight. I must confess, however, that when I walked into the church and saw Bro. Bean standing on the platform, I promptly, irrevocably, and devastatingly fell in love. And that was even before I heard him sing or preach. The intensity of that moment has never left me. I feared in my heart he would never be interested in me because Aunt Ima had already told me that he could have the pick of any young lady he wanted. These young ladies, I imagined, had talent, ability, beauty, and poise that I could never possess. There would be young ladies far more mature and spiritual than I in his future. It seemed to me a relationship with this wonderful man was only a pipe dream and a lost cause. The heart seldom follows reason; my heart was captured, never to be completely liberated. From that time onward, my heart belonged to Bro. Bean, and he didn't even know I existed. Truly, the heart is a careless thing, bounding recklessly into uncharted regions with no concern for the possibility of being injured or even broken.

If I was bowled over by just the sight of Bro. Bean standing on the platform, I was utterly unprepared for the impact of his ministry. I come from a family of preachers. My daddy was an excellent preacher, as is my brother, Jimmy Shoemake. My grandfather is a legend in the Hall of Fame of Pentecostal Pioneers, and my Uncle James always brought me to my knees with his ministry. I have uncles, cousins, and other family members in the ministry. Preaching is in our family's blood. We love preachers, and we love preaching, but this ministry was something new to me.

When Bro. Bean took the pulpit, the authority of his presence brought us to humble silence. As he began to speak, all minds were united in reverence. He began slowly, deliberately, considering each word carefully. I seem to remember the message he preached that night was *The Jewish Junker*. He started the sermon by describing a car that had seen better days. It had been wrecked, neglected, broken down, and was useless to the owner. Bro. Bean told us how it was loaded onto a tow truck to be taken to the junkyard. The car was then transported to the wrecking yard and placed into a compressor, which crushed every part of it into a cube of metal. Next, it was dropped into a burning incinerator to be melted into molten steel. Now, the car was unrecognizable. The hot metal was poured into molds, shaped, and put back together. Finally, a day arrived, and a brand-new car was driven off the lot, beautifully and perfectly restored.

Never had I heard the weight of sin portrayed in such a way. The heartbreak of the alienated soul was revealed in clear detail. The despair of the doomed was depicted in all its misery; then, Bro. Bean introduced us to the Jewish Junker. The ministry of Jesus Christ was offered as the last and best hope for the disenfranchised and broken-hearted. Hope was given to the hopeless. We were made to understand that in the ministry of Jesus, we could all be remade in His image.

As the sermon built, Bro. Bean described the love of a Savior who would seek out the lost and lowly, offer help to the helpless, and show a way of escape to the doomed soul. The beauty of a transformed life was displayed with anointing and power. What a message! At the close of his sermon, Bro. Bean began to sing, "There's Room at the Cross for You."

If I had felt drawn to Bro. Bean before the service, that seemed insignificant compared to how I was feeling now. I was simply overwhelmed.

The Kilgores invited Bro. Bean to the parsonage after church to have fellowship and get acquainted with us all. To be in the same room, breathing the same air, and hearing his voice was an absolute pleasure. And then, the hopelessness of my situation would wash over me, and reality would gain control of my emotions. I must give credit to Aunt Ima, though. She was in there doing all she could to bring me to Bro. Bean's attention. She had decided early in the revival that we would be a perfect match, and she never doubted for one minute that it could be achieved. He told me later he was very aware of what Aunt Ima was doing, which was funny to him. He could hardly keep from laughing out loud. He was twenty-six years old, a seasoned evangelist, and here I was, a naïve seventeen-year-old high school senior.

Bro. Bean had often been introduced to eligible young ladies, and arrangements had been made to bring him and these potential brides together. He confessed later that although he appreciated these attentions, they often made him uncomfortable.

Though shy at heart, Bro. Bean overcame this tendency through the demands of his ministry; it was often with difficulty that he entered the social scene. He also had a fear of arrangements. Although done with the best intentions, he felt pressured at these

The Seasoned Evangelist   ***The High School Senior***

times. In my case, though, he didn't. He just felt the entire thing was laughable. I'm glad I didn't know what was going through his mind that night. I was intimidated enough by my insecurities; it would have been devastating to realize just how ineligible he felt I was.

That night created a kaleidoscope of mental images that I carefully stored in my heart. I see Jan and Jean seated on the floor, listening intently to every story recounted. Aunt Ima was there, serving us all her delicious food and making sure we were offered more than we could possibly eat. My most treasured memory is a mental picture of Bro. Bean when he played the guitar and sang for us.

The conversation that night was exciting to me, but I was shy and reluctant to say a single word. I enjoyed just being there and hearing about the marvelous experiences Bro. Bean and the Kilgores shared. I felt his gaze on my face a few times and could only respond with a smile. All too soon, the evening ended, and he rose to leave to go to his mother's house. Whenever he preached in Houston, he resided with his mother, Sis. Bernice Bean, and that is where he would stay for the duration of the revival. She pastored a congregation in Greens Bayou that she had started several years previously.

After Bro. Bean left, we stayed up until the wee hours of the morning discussing him, the revival, and the service we had attended. Mother and Daddy were coming to Houston the next day and would join us in the revival service that night. I was eager for them to meet Bro. Bean and to know how they felt about him. Daddy was always a good judge of character and very keen in spiritual discernment, and it would be interesting to hear what he would have to say about the man who effortlessly and unwittingly captivated my heart.

When Mother and Daddy drove in from San Antonio, Mother expressed how sad she was to leave when Granddad was in such poor health. He had been released from the hospital and put into the care of her sister, Aunt Odetta, and her husband, Uncle Horace Wilburn, who pastored a church in San Antonio. Granddad had only a few more months to live from that time. We weren't aware of just how quickly he would be taken from us.

When Mother and I talked privately, I told her about my impressions of Bro. Bean. She was deeply interested in the details of my life, and nothing was too trivial for her to want to hear. We would talk about my dates, romances, and crushes–the ups and downs of a typical teenager. Daddy got into these discussions whenever he could, which was most of the time, and this occasion was no exception. They were both keen to hear about the revival service and what I thought about Bro. Bean. I admitted my attraction for him but didn't share the depth of my feelings with anyone. I didn't understand them myself and could hardly describe something so complicated that I hadn't yet sorted it out in my mind. We were eagerly waiting for the evening service to begin, and I was very interested to know Mother and Daddy's reaction to Bro. Bean's ministry.

The service that night only reinforced my impressions. I was raised in a Pentecostal home and had attended many outstanding services, but this level of worship and the depth of conviction were new to me. We all felt the same way. This was a unique revival, and this was certainly a unique evangelist.

The service for Mother and Daddy was probably as earth-shaking for them as it had been for me. Something in my parents' spiritual DNA connected them to Bro. Bean and his ministry. His anointing and the powerful outpouring of the Houston revival touched them. They had always believed in the operation of the Gifts of the Spirit, and Daddy was used in them many times in his ministry. Mother, too, was a great woman of faith. She was an intercessor, a gifted Bible teacher, and a precious example of the virtuous woman in her daily life.

Both Bro. Bean and his mother trusted God to heal them from any sickness they experienced; they neither used doctors nor took medicine. This was not an unusual conviction at that time. Daddy, too, had received strong teachings on divine healing and didn't go to doctors for many years. Bro. Bean carried this testimony of divine healing all his life. The only time he had any medical procedure done was when he was preparing to fly to Brazil to minister, and he had to be vaccinated to enter the country.

Once again, we fellowshipped together after service, and I could tell Mother and Daddy were just as impressed with Bro. Bean as I was. I had never doubted they would be, but I was pleased to know they shared my opinion of this extraordinary man. When Bro. Bean left to go home that night, I didn't know if I would ever see or hear from him again. I knew I would return home to San Jose and continue my life as though nothing had changed, but I would never be the same carefree young girl I had been. I looked at the world through different eyes. My spiritual expectations had been lifted, and I would always look back to that time as a spiritual awakening in my life. What I had seen and experienced in those two services would never be erased from my heart.

Years later, Uncle James stated that the Verbal Bean revival proved to be pivotal in the spiritual renewal of Life Tabernacle. It continued for eight weeks, and fifty-one people received the Holy Ghost. Lives were transformed, and it was not unusual at the end of services for cigarette packages to be left on the altars. From that time, Life Tabernacle became a revival church. The church grew, and there was rarely a night that someone did not receive the Holy Ghost; baptisms were a regular part of the services.

It had been an exhilarating experience, but the time came when we had to say goodbye to the Kilgores and drive back to San Jose. It was a long, sad journey for me. I was leaving with more questions than answers and unsure of my very future. But life went on, and I graduated from Campbell High School in June 1960. During this time, I broke up with the young evangelist I had been seeing and tried to be happy.

I did not see Bro. Bean again until the General Conference, which was held in Dallas, Texas, that fall. When we arrived, Aunt Ima told me he was there. That was a happy day! By this time, the Kilgores had become very close friends with him, and Aunt Ima was more than willing to tell me all she knew about the comings and goings of this wonderful evangelist. I hoped I would catch a glimpse of Bro. Bean or get to say a word to him during the conference. The crowd numbered about three thousand people, and I didn't stop searching at every service until I had located him in the crowd. You could say my mind was not truly on the services I attended, and that would be true because I was mesmerized and infatuated by this fabulous preacher.

One night after service, our family met in Mother and Daddy's hotel room for a prayer meeting. This was a common occurrence for us. Bro. Bean was there as well. By this time, Daddy was sincerely praying he would preach a revival for us in San Jose. We understood clearly that he didn't go anywhere for revival until he was satisfied it was the will of God. He knew his revivals were intense, and if the pastor was not ready for all that entailed, it could be a hindrance and not a blessing for everyone concerned. After the prayer meeting ended, Daddy invited Bro. Bean to come to San Jose for a revival. He did not commit to come at that time but assured Daddy he would pray about it. After the conference, I went home and took a job as a stenographer at a fruit packing plant and went on with my life.

Chapter 2

Bean Family History

Verbal Winston Bean was born April 15, 1933, in a rural community called Duetts Eddy, near the Sabine River in the Beauregard Parish of Louisiana. Verbal was the fourth and last child born to Bernice and Alexander Bean. Nylotis Virginia was the oldest, followed by Hobert Laroy and then Onyx Novelle. Bernice chose unusual names for her children, to say the least. The name of her oldest, Nylotis, was taken from the label on a box of face powder. No one knew where Verbal's name originated, but he often wished for a more conventional one. When Hobert was a toddler and first saw his baby sister, Onyx Novelle, he pointed to her and said, "Doll." And in the Southern tradition, the nickname stuck.

Verbal became deathly ill at three months old. Bernice had no pastor nor church family, and facing this crisis alone seemed overwhelming. Because of his high fever, cough, and difficulty breathing, she concluded he had pneumonia. She had grown into a remarkable woman of faith and began to pray fervently. However, Verbal's condition continued to deteriorate, leaving him listless and pale. Eventually, he stopped moving and breathing altogether and lay motionless for several minutes. Recognizing that he had passed away, Bernice, in her desperation, began to pray with unwavering faith, believing for a supernatural touch for her precious baby. God, in His infinite care, answered this mother's prayer, and Verbal began breathing again as life returned to his body. He was completely healed! She shared this story countless times, praising the Lord for His mighty healing power.

Verbal's father, Alec, older than Bernice by seventeen years, was hard-working and devoted. The siblings had loving memories of their daddy. He worked in the woods, felling timber, to provide for his family. Still, it was a meager living, and the family lived in relative poverty. However, they always seemed to have enough to eat and lived in much the same manner as their neighbors.

Alec was a homesteader of forty acres of land filled primarily with tall pines, chinquapin, mayhaw, sweetgum, walnut, oak, and hickory trees near the Sabine River. On hot summer days, one of the children's favorite things to do was to walk the mile or so between their house and the Sabine River with their daddy for a swim and come home to the blackberry cobbler their mother often had waiting for them. When they all returned home from their swim, Bernice was usually pacing the floor, afraid one of them had drowned, but they were all good swimmers and enjoyed the day.

Alec built the house where the Bean family lived, along with some of the furniture as well. It was a wooden, unpainted structure with a long hall separating the living room, dining room, and kitchen from the bedrooms. There was a water well adjoining the hall in the rear of the house and a porch across the entire front of the house. Alec built a fireplace from mud, moss, and water in the living room. Due to the lack of proper insulation, the wall between the chimney and the house caught fire once or twice, but the help of neighbors passing buckets of water from hand-to- hand saved the house without too much damage.

Like most of their neighbors, the Beans always had a vegetable garden. They canned fresh vegetables and fruit to enjoy in the winter. The chicken coop and smokehouse were located in the back of the main house. The family usually fattened a Poland China pig in the summer and slaughtered it as winter approached. They made sausages, smoked ham, and bacon from the pork, saving the lard in big crocks for cooking. The smell of ham and bacon in the smokehouse wafted through the metal chimney and windows on those cold days.

It was always a traumatic event when the pig was slaughtered. He had been the pet all summer, and the children were heartbroken when he was put down. This event was also upsetting for Alec–not so much for the loss of the pig but for having to hear his children cry and carry on about losing their pet. He often said, "I have to go through this every year with these children; I don't know how much longer I can take it."

It was the same sad story when they butchered a calf. Except in this case, Alec wouldn't or couldn't be around when the calf was shot. He would pace back and forth on the front porch until the shot was fired by his brother, who lived nearby. After the shot was heard, Alec would call out, "Is it over?" Then, he would join his brother in dressing the calf and dividing the beef between them. The Bean family grew up with animals and made pets of them all. When one died or was killed in an accident, he was given a fine funeral.

Doll was the self-appointed guardian of Verbal. He was seldom disciplined because he seldom needed to be. Now and then, when he didn't do what was asked of him by his mother, she would tell him if he did the 'thing' again, she would have to spank him. The spankings often resulted in long and loud cries from Doll. At times, this type of behavior worked. If not, Bernice would put Verbal in the smokehouse for what modern mothers now call 'time out.' When this happened once again, Doll would continue crying until Bernice couldn't take the noise any longer, and she would just laugh and tell Doll to get him. Verbal would be sitting atop a stack of peanuts drying in the smokehouse, not upset in the least. He was always able to achieve a state of calm that shuts out external forces.

Summer fun

As the depression worsened, the Beans had a very difficult time keeping food on the table. Alec would walk to the gravel highway to hitchhike to the nearest town, Starks, Louisiana, to ask for groceries on credit, and then hitchhike back, walking from the highway through a cow trail to their house. The family never knew when their father would return, as it would depend on how long it took to get a ride. They would watch for him throughout the day, and when they saw him coming through the trail with a box on his shoulders, they ran to meet him to find out what he had brought home. This made a happy ending to a long day.

Verbal's favorite snack was peanut butter. One day, Bernice found him sitting against the back of the house with a peanut butter jar and a spoon in his hand. He was trying to get the last dab of peanut butter stuck in the bottom curve of the jar. He had broken glass fragments from around the rim while trying to dig the peanut butter out of the glass. Small pieces of broken glass glistened in the jar, and they didn't know whether or not he had eaten any of it. Since

Bernice believed in trusting God for healing, seeing a doctor was not an option. Bernice prayed for the ills of all her children. Even if she had relied on medical care, the nearest doctor was thirty miles away, and they had no vehicle to drive to the doctor's office. The family was panic-stricken. Bernice began to pray, and the siblings began to cry. Verbal, as usual, showed no emotion and remained calm. They watched him closely all day and night for any signs of distress, but there were none. Bernice concluded the Lord had touched him, and he would be all right.

In the winter, when the children were small, Bernice made warm nightgowns for the girls and long nightshirts for the boys. Verbal stood too close to the fireplace one night, and his nightshirt caught fire. His back was horribly burned. He didn't cry after the initial burn except when his bandages were changed. The flesh on his back was covered with blisters. Doll was sitting on the floor beside his bed one night, crying and praying for his pain to go away. He reached down, patted her arm, and said, "Doll, don't cry. I'll be all right." He then, as he did throughout his life, cared more about the pain of others than he did about his own. As it happened, his burns were completely healed with no trace of a scar.

Verbal shared not only his father's good looks but also his personality; they both preferred listening to talking. Neither was shy nor timid but rather quiet and thoughtful.

Nylotis kept her siblings on their toes about cleaning the house. Once a month, she had them scour the wooden floors with hot lye water. She was also a source of great pleasure as she read to them at night from books that she had checked out from the school library: *Ichabod Crane, Little Women, Anne of Green Gables,* and *Daddy Long Legs,* to name a few.

Hobert was all arms and legs, fun-loving with a temper like his maternal grandfather, quick to get angry and just as quick to get over it. He would lock his long, skinny arms around Verbal's neck and hold him down on the front lawn while Verbal made no attempt to free himself. Alec watched this one time and said, "He's going to kill that boy one of these days." No one knew why he didn't intervene, except he was not the disciplinarian. Bernice handled that chore. Hobert and Doll always had their antennas up should anyone pick a fight with Verbal at school or on the bus. Not that he needed protection; he could defend himself, but they thought he did.

The Beans had kin folk living in the area, so they spent a lot of time with their uncles, aunts, and cousins. Best of all, Bernice's parents were also nearby. Poppa, as Bernice and the family called her father, was a very colorful character. He was a small man with a large wife and three large daughters, Althia, Bernice, and Elsie. However, his size never prevented him from operating as head of the family. Poppa was known not only for his short size but also for his short temper. He was easily offended and responded loudly, passing out corrections to all and sundry. However, his punishments seemed as short as his temper, and his anger passed quickly. The family all doted on him. He was clever and quick-witted and would tell fascinating stories about his family. The Carter family had moved from back East to join the Sooner Land Rush as land for the taking was opened in the Oklahoma Territory. The family eventually left Oklahoma in the late 1800s and moved to Louisiana, making their home there.

There wasn't a church in Duetts Eddy, but preachers came to visit from time to time. Families would come whenever they could and enjoy the preached Word. These times were especially cherished because it was rare for them to worship God with other believers.

As a young mother, Bernice was filled with the Holy Ghost when an itinerant preacher came through their community to preach about a 'New Birth' experience. She was hungry to know the Lord and opened her heart to the Word. After being filled with the Holy Ghost, she was baptized in Jesus' name and served the Lord to the best of her ability. She felt called to preach, and this calling stayed with her for the rest of her life. She was also a mighty woman of faith and could testify of the many times God answered her prayers.

At a very young age, Verbal became aware of spiritual things; at that time, his mother taught him to pray. Later, he testified, "As a child, I spent hours in prayer. Because I prayed so much, my daddy worried I would lose my mind."

A neighboring family, who weren't even churchgoers, became so fascinated by young Verbal and his dedication to God they wanted to spend time with him. They asked his parents if he could spend the night with them. In recounting this event, Verbal said, "They were probably sorry they had brought me home with them because I kept them up all night praying."

Once, Bro. Sam Mitchell was visiting with the Bean family; when they were ready to eat dinner, Verbal was nowhere to be found. Bro. Sam volunteered to go to the woods and try to locate him. He finally heard Verbal praying and approached to tell him dinner was ready. As he advanced closer, he heard Verbal praying aloud, "I know the devil would love for me to stop praying, but I'm not gonna listen to the devil!" Verbal later expressed what it meant to him when the old preachers would come by.

The preacher was understandably reluctant to interrupt this prayer meeting because he was afraid Verbal would associate the interruption with the voice of the devil. Bro. Sam returned to the house and told the family, "I found him praying, but I wouldn't stop him; he would think I was being used by the devil!" Verbal finally returned home on his own, and the family all had a good laugh about it.

> *"The richest day of my life as a boy was when those old preachers would come to our house and talk about when God would speak to them to go pray for someone. They got there and prayed, and the sick were healed. Then they would say, 'Well, I better go,' and I'd want to say, 'Tell me one more time about His healing power.'"*

Occasionally, a preacher would come to minister in their community; these services were mainly held under a brush arbor, and the Spirit of the Lord would fall with conviction. Verbal carried a heavy burden, even as a child, for the salvation of his father, and with tears streaming down his face, he would go to his father and beg, "Daddy, please, please, go to the altar with me!" Despite his son's tears, Alec was never persuaded to seek God. This was heartbreaking to Verbal, and he carried that concern for his father's salvation as long as he lived.

Verbal and his siblings were taught in the local county school. Their grandfather, Tom Carter, was the school bus driver. If the family thought they would get preferential treatment because their grandfather was driving the bus, they were sadly mistaken. He was often a cantankerous man and didn't weaken with age. The Bean siblings were expected to obey on the bus, along with all the other children.

Verbal was very good in his scholastic endeavors. He made excellent grades and was especially proficient in English and mathematics. With his reading and study habits, he also educated himself in other subjects throughout his life, even though he never pursued higher education.

SCHOOL DAYS 1945 -'46
Hyatt Elementary

One of the routines Bernice, Nylotis, and Verbal shared was reading and memorizing Bible passages. They would have scripture quoting contests, each one quoting, in turn, to see who could last the longest. They would be eliminated when one of them failed to quote another verse.

As a young child, Verbal had many spiritual experiences. He spent hours in the fields and woods around his house praying and developing sensitivity to the importance of being right with God. There were times when his childish uncertainties would give way to fear that he might not be saved. He felt guilty most of the time for no reason.

Verbal would often go to his mother and tearfully ask, "Mother, would you please pray for me? I'm afraid that I'll be lost." She would carefully explain to him the love of God and how repentance made everything right with God, but that concept was difficult for young Verbal to receive. Repeatedly, Sis. Bean would patiently and lovingly pray with him and assure him he was not lost.

Years later, as Verbal was recounting his early childhood, he said:

> *"Because we were poor, it seemed to me I should be last in EVERYTHING, even in the soup line. These feelings made me feel unworthy, even of the love of Jesus Christ. I spent my time in prayer, repenting or rebuking the devil. I thought the Holy Ghost should make me perfect, but I lived with constant condemnation until I understood the ways of God more perfectly, and I was helped by others. I learned there was a difference between thoughts and intentions. God understands that because He separates thoughts and desires from intentions. After I learned this, my faith began to grow."*
>
> *"One day, an old preacher, Bro. Sam Mitchell, shared wisdom with me that forever changed my relationship with Jesus Christ. Bro. Sam said to me, 'Son, you can't stop the birds from*

flying over your head, but you can stop them from making a nest in your hair.' When I understood that a random thought might come through my mind, but God knew I had no intention of acting on that thought, it was liberating for me. My spiritual life became joyous and fruitful because I was delivered from overpowering condemnation."

As Verbal grew older, he experienced a period of time in his life when he could not feel the presence of the Lord. This was devastating to him, and he would spend long sessions in prayer seeking God. Years later, as he recounted those days, he told the story of that dreadful time in his life. One lonely evening, Verbal said:

"I was walking in the woods seeking after God. This was during a long absence of feeling God's presence; I was desperate to feel the touch of Jesus Christ. I looked up into the dark, starless night and said, 'Lord, if I never feel Your presence again, I want You to know I will still serve You every day of my life.' As soon as I prayed those words, the Spirit of the Lord fell on me, and as I raised my hands to the heavens, I began to cry and speak with tongues. I will never forget the glory of that sacred encounter with Jesus Christ."

Throughout Verbal's ministry, this memory never left him. He cherished and valued the presence of God every day of his life. His preaching and teaching declared our need, and certainly our dependence on the Holy Ghost, to be made evident in every service, every time of worship, every sermon, every song, and every altar call. Some were frustrated when he would stop a service or refuse to begin a message until he felt the unction of Jesus Christ moving and giving direction. Many services were interrupted by long spaces of time 'Waiting on the Lord,' but when he did speak, preach, or sing after these times, it was clear to all the listeners that Jesus was in the house.

Young Verbal

Chapter 3

Life Changes

When Verbal was fourteen years old, his father died suddenly of a massive heart attack, leaving the family heartbroken and destitute. By this time, Hobert, Nylotis, and Doll had moved to Orange, Texas, so Sis. Bean and Verbal joined them there.

The move to Orange opened a brand-new chapter in Verbal's life. For the first time, he had a church home and, more importantly, a pastor, Rev. J. H. Stanton, a true man of God. This relocation provided an ideal place for the family to be together, a town to live in, good neighbors, and new opportunities for them all.

Verbal did well in school, and the older siblings had jobs that provided income for the family. They all enjoyed the fellowship of neighbors, friends, and the saints at church. Sis. Bean, Nylotis, and Verbal were given a warm welcome into the congregation. He and his family would later recount what these years meant. Bro. Stanton was an anointed man of God, a faithful and caring shepherd, and he recognized, in this family, a devotion and commitment to the things of God. Verbal was now part of a youth group for the first time, and they were kind and accepting of this handsome young man as a part of their fellowship.

Nylotis and Verbal

Later, Verbal would talk about this time in his life. It was a completely new experience for him in various ways. He said,

"For three years, I got to attend a church, and I wanted to be there every time the doors were opened. When I was young, we were seldom able to go to church. We had no car to get there, and there wasn't a church close enough for us to attend. So, when I moved to Orange, I considered it a privilege to be in service. Sometimes, I had to ride a rickety old bus to get there, but I always wanted to be in God's house, where I spent every Sunday fasting and praying. In the evening, the men would come an hour early for prayer, and

just to be in the room praying with them was a joy to me. They sought God so diligently that there would always be a mighty outpouring of the Holy Ghost in the service. It was unbearable for me to miss; I wanted to be there."

Verbal enjoyed the companionship with the youth group but felt shy and awkward around them. His friends never seemed aware of his discomfort and always included him in their gatherings. Once, they gave him a surprise birthday party. He was very happy but still struggled, reluctant to be the center of attention.

Birthday party

While Verbal was at church on Sundays, he endeavored to learn to play the piano. With no teacher to help him, he earnestly prayed for God to give him the ability to play. The Lord graciously granted his request, and Verbal was able to play not only the piano skillfully but also the guitar, bass, and mandolin. During this time, Verbal was included in a musical group that performed gospel bluegrass in local churches and at Station KOGT in Orange. They were called The Sunshine Melody Four. He played the mandolin; the other instruments were a guitar, steel guitar, and accordion. The group made a record, and there is a picture of the cover, but unfortunately, the recording has been lost.

After living in Orange for three years, the Lord put a burden for Houston in the hearts of Verbal and his mother. Although Verbal was only seventeen years old at this time, he was older than his years spiritually. He had sought the Lord all his life and had become very perceptive to the voice of God.

Sis. Bean and Verbal loaded up their few belongings and moved to Houston, feeling they were each led by God to start a church. Whether they had friends and relatives there or if they were given any promises of support is not clear, but they arrived in Houston and found a place to live. Verbal began his work in South Houston, and Sis. Bean started hers in Greens Bayou.

Verbal took various jobs to support them both. He worked in a department store and also sold vacuum cleaners door-to-door to keep food on the table and to support this unlikely home mission's endeavor. The faith of this mother and son was heart-touching. They truly trusted God for the next meal, for a place to hold services, for money to put gas into their vehicle, and to simply live.

Home missionaries

Verbal and his mother worked together, prayed together, and believed God for revival together. Gradually, their respective congregations began to grow. The two groups worked side-by-side, visiting the other's church services as often as possible. They began to see people receive the Holy Ghost, and backsliders pray through as God blessed their efforts. The two churches were established miraculously during this time. Verbal could finally quit his job and give his full time to ministry. He also began preaching in neighboring churches.

It seemed Verbal became somewhat of a sensation in the Houston area. This young man, who knew how to pray and trust God, was blessed with anointing and talent beyond his years. He was singing, playing his guitar, and preaching powerful sermons.

The altars began filling with seekers, which undoubtedly brought him to the attention of many people in the area. This proved to be a great asset and was helpful in the building of his church. He spent five years pouring his heart and ministry into his Home Missions effort.

Although Verbal was blessed with a growing congregation, he began to feel the call to evangelize. This decision was heartbreaking for Sis. Bean. She would cry and beg Verbal to reconsider. She felt she would be helpless if Verbal were not there to support her. It was very difficult for Verbal to see his mother in such sorrow, but he felt strongly it was the will of God for him to resign from his church and begin the evangelistic ministry, a calling too compelling to be disregarded. The weight of the calling of God seemed to supersede every other consideration.

Service in the home

Sis. Bean became so desperate she called Doll and told her Verbal wanted to resign from his church and evangelize. By then, Sis. Bean started crying and tearfully asked Doll to persuade Verbal to stay in Houston. She even put Verbal on the phone with Doll, hoping she could convince him to reconsider his decision. His response to Doll was calm and sympathetic, but he said it was time to do what God had called him to do. Doll quickly realized nothing she had to say would cause Verbal to change his mind.

Verbal describes this time in his life in a lesson he was teaching on finding the will of God in your ministry.

"I never had success scheduling revivals. The last revival I scheduled was not in the will of God. I endured many hardships and had to pray four hours a day to achieve any victory in the services. God had warned me in a dream before going to this revival that it was not in His will. In the dream, I was fishing on a riverbank. I looked across the water and saw a large sign with words clearly written, 'Out of Season.' Because of pressure from the pastor, I agreed to start a revival for him against my better judgment and struggled the whole time I was there.

God began to talk to my heart while I was pastoring in South Houston about starting to evangelize. This was a very difficult decision. My mother was sickly. She didn't have a driver's license because she couldn't drive. She begged me for days, often with tears, not to leave her. The family was against my leaving to evangelize, and my church certainly was against it.

To prove God's will, I accepted an invitation to preach a revival. During that revival, I felt the greatest power of God I had ever experienced, before that time or since. I knew I was in the perfect will of God."

Sis. Bean learned to drive, got a vehicle, and continued with her pastorate at the Greens Bayou Apostolic Church. At the age of twenty-one, Verbal returned home from his first revival, resigned from his church, and left on his evangelistic journey to begin the ministry God had been preparing him for since he was a child.

Combined South Houston and Greens Bayou congregations

Sectional meeting

Chapter 4

Revival Essentials

Verbal had always felt God's hand on his life, but he began to experience an intense transformation and a divine anointing as he evangelized. Guided by the Holy Ghost, he walked into new avenues of ministry and was used mightily in the gifts of the Spirit. As his faith deepened, he led those bound by unbelief to experience the delivering power of the Holy Ghost. Other spiritual doors opened in his life as he was led into prophetic ministry and laying on of hands for healing and miracles.

Evangelizing

As Verbal ventured further into the supernatural realm, he found himself leaning on the Holy Ghost's anointing in unprecedented ways. His prayer life intensified, enhancing his recognition of spiritual matters. Along with the profound anointing and inspiration he experienced, there arose a heightened awareness of his dependence on divine direction. Intercession was a way of life for him, and he learned to wait on the Lord for guidance in every service.

This path was not without its challenges. Verbal faced misunderstandings and criticism along the way, which were painful to him. But he persevered. He had glimpsed an intense connection to the supernatural in his ministry and never lost his love for that divine touch.

Verbal wasn't alone in being used by the Spirit during this period. He actively sought the companionship of ministers who could relate to his spiritual journey and discern the work of God in his life. These individuals served as his mentors and trusted confidants. They prayed with him, for him, and most importantly of all, they believed in him and his ministry.

Another facet of Verbal's ministry played a vital role in every revival: his staunch belief in Holy Ghost demonstration, but always with a solid Biblical foundation. During this time, another movement was making its way through churches known as Latter

Rain. Initially, its followers earnestly sought a genuine move of God as spoken by the prophet Joel:

> **"… and he will cause to come for you the rain, the former rain, and the latter rain in the first month." (Joel 2:23)**

However, over time, the true meaning became misinterpreted and sometimes misused for personal reasons.

The Latter Rain movement quickly spiraled into chaos without spiritual leadership or accountability, and soon, it was truly unmanageable. Numerous churches experienced division as previously devoted members became caught up with what they perceived as the operation of the gifts of the Spirit. It branched out into many controversial areas, as the leaders did not follow Biblical directives regarding the use of Spiritual gifts.

Because of Latter Rain's detrimental impact, many churches and pastors withdrew from any manifestation of spiritual gifts or demonstrative worship. The repercussions of this movement would reverberate for years to come.

Verbal was certainly not the only evangelist challenging collective thinking about the possible scope of revival. Still, he was one of the pioneers among several other like-minded men and women who opened their minds to the incredible possibilities of the power of Jesus Christ. It was a new way of thinking about revival. Until this time, many revivals were considered successful if just a few people received the Holy Ghost. Organized outreach and freedom of worship were rare. Some critics and doubters spoke their opinions freely. Despite this, God continued to bless, and numbers of people were receiving the Holy Ghost in churches across the nation. It was a supernatural outpouring of renewed Pentecostal harvest.

There were also those who had questions about the use of Spiritual gifts, and some weren't sure they could accept the exuberant worship that seemed to go hand in hand with revival. This brought about criticism and doubt about the authenticity of these "so-called" revivals. But this never stopped the move of God. Many pastors and churches had tasted the liberty and blessings true supernatural outpouring brings, and they never wanted to turn back.

A prophecy given by Verbal during this time:

> *"I prophecy, write it down, that Verbal Winston Bean prophesied, didn't predict, but prophesied, that the greatest dimension of latter rain you have ever seen in your life is now on the horizon. I tell you that I see a greater DIMENSION BECAUSE it's educated, has money, and everything it needs. It's coming from a far different area of the country but is still a dimension of Latter Rain. Beware when your gifts do nothing but*

> *bless you. If every interpretation of tongues says, 'I love thee, and thou art mine.' You better watch. You better watch when every prophet says 'more...bigger...better...' leaving the principles of doctrine unguarded and unprotected."*

Because of the success of his revivals, word spread, and Verbal began to have more invitations than he could fill. His ministry broadened and matured, and the number of people receiving the Holy Ghost was, in many cases, unprecedented. Churches that previously had seen only a few people pray through to the Holy Ghost in any given revival were now seeing the altars full and experiencing Holy Ghost outpourings all over the congregation. It seemed to open the doors of faith to what God could do in this present time. Verbal never believed "The days of revival were over," and he preached that God would save souls until the day of the rapture when Jesus Christ would return for His Bride.

When Verbal began a revival, he usually started teaching on prayer. He would announce 10:00 a.m. prayer meetings Monday through Friday. In these morning prayer services, Verbal often exhorted after prayer or began singing and worshipping the Lord.

Many women at that time were stay-at-home mothers and homemakers, and they made up the most significant number of attendees at these prayer meetings. They would bring their babies and toddlers, sometimes in their pajamas; it was a sweet time for everyone. There would also be elderly people in attendance, as well as anyone else who was available during these morning sessions. These meetings became very important and strengthened the revival immeasurably. Faith was high after the intercessory prayer, and freedom of worship would soon be manifested. It would be hard to overstate the importance of these prayer meetings to the success of the revival.

In addition to the prayer meetings, many members arrived early for prayer before church. In nearly every revival, Verbal would also ask people to volunteer an hour to institute a twenty-four-hour prayer chain that could last two or three weeks. These revivals were saturated with prayer.

Services started at 7:30 p.m., and the revivals were from Sunday to Sunday with no nights off. When Verbal felt the church was strong and revived, he would take Monday nights off. The accumulative effect of continual prayer and services brought this about. Feeling this intensive immersion in revival was an incredible and miraculous blessing. Because of this, it was fulfilling to see the people's response to this regimen. They did not want to miss a service because most seemed to feel this was a Spirit-chosen time for the church. Even when the services were heavy or intense, people remained faithful. A few saints in some of the revivals quit coming and even backslid, but these occasions were rare.

After so much prayer, faith was high. Verbal was preaching God-anointed messages, and the Holy Ghost would fall. He believed the saints needed to pray through early in the revival, and once that happened, Holy Ghost worship followed.

This liberty of worship brought mighty deliverance and was miraculous. Along with exuberant praise, inhibitions were removed, and people were free to yield to the move of the Holy Ghost. Inspiration would often fall on the song leader and musicians. They would put down their microphones, leave their instruments, and joyfully dance across the platform and down the aisle.

When a congregation gained this level of worship and praise, some who had been used in administering gifts of the Spirit in the past found fresh confidence to allow the gifts to operate in their lives again. Others discovered newfound faith to pray for the sick or lead someone to the altar. Some encountered heavy conviction in their hearts and began to dig out old wells neglected by months of complacency. They could now again experience living water springing forth in their lives. These services were, in effect, "perfecting the saints."

Verbal was also a firm believer in the ministry of angels. He taught that believers could receive angelic assistance by asking Jesus Christ to send and assign angels on special missions to benefit the church and aid in the salvation of souls. He would share many testimonies of angelic visitation with the saints to increase their faith and encourage them to pray and believe for their own miracles. Verbal told the following testimony about an angelic visitation.

"In revival in Texarkana, we were shipping out all kinds of angels. One lady stood up and said, 'Bro Bean, I've got a boy in Kansas City. Can you send one over to him?'

I said, 'Certainly, it doesn't cost a thing, and he doesn't have to ride a plane or a bus.' So, we shipped one out there. Later, I came back through Texarkana, and that young man was there.

He approached me after the service and said, 'Do you remember sending an angel to Kansas City?' Now, he didn't know we were doing that at the time. He said, 'I'm the boy that you sent the angel to. I was lying in bed one night, and a man clothed in white came and stood by my bedside. It nearly scared me to death. I dropped to my knees and screamed, Oh God, save me, and He filled me with the Holy Ghost. Later, his mother told him that she had dispatched an angel to him that night."

Frequently, when Verbal took the pulpit, he would quietly speak of the glory of Heaven and how he longed to be there with the Lord. People would feel a yearning for heavenly things as they prayed, "Come, Lord Jesus!"

Sometimes, these longings for Jesus Christ's return for His bride would remind the congregation about lost friends and loved ones. A burden would fall, and travail could be heard throughout the sanctuary as intercession was made before the throne of God.

Many times, after a convicting message was preached, Verbal would begin singing,

> *"Somewhere, a voice is calling.*
> *To the lost who have wandered astray.*
> *It's the Master who is calling,*
> *Sinner, come home today.*
>
> *He wants you back in the fold.*
> *He wants to account for them all.*
> *Somewhere, a voice is calling,*
> *Won't you heed the Master's call?"*

Altars would fill with sinners seeking repentance and salvation. Those who had been cold or lukewarm wept for reconciliation with their Savior. It was many years ago, and methods are often different now. However, may God's people never forget the power of a genuinely convicting message, anointed singing, and spirit-filled saints praying hungry people through to the Holy Ghost.

There was customarily a portion of time devoted to removing any impediment to the revival in the congregation. From time to time, the Lord would reveal unrepented sin to Verbal. He never used this occasion to browbeat or embarrass people but would deal with it as the Lord led. Verbal would discuss the matter with the pastor and then talk with the congregation. For instance, he might say something like this, "The Lord has revealed to me someone in this congregation is involved in adultery. You need to get right with God and with your pastor." It could be painfully shocking to the pastor when these sins were revealed.

This was a time of great conviction, and the fear of God would fill the house. Many people examined their hearts and lives to ensure they were right with God; it was a wondrous yet fearful time. The Shekinah presence of the Lord was so powerfully manifested that the congregation was almost afraid to move, recognizing the mighty hand of God at work among them. Some of these services were so quiet that you could almost hear a pin drop. Often, gifts of the Spirit would come into operation: tongues, interpretation of tongues, prophecy, or the word of knowledge would be revealed. People did not want to miss these meetings. Even those who were not right with God were drawn in ways they had never experienced.

Along with these glorious services, there were times that could be difficult for everyone, especially for the pastor and his wife. Often, they had been praying, fasting, and believing for a Holy Ghost outpouring. They had saved and sacrificed financially to support the revival effort. Many times, the pastor and his family had carried a heavy burden on behalf of the congregation for months or years. They would be grief-stricken to learn of church members who had shown a façade of righteousness. Their sins may have been hidden and covered for months or even years, and the unmasking was painful.

Occasionally, Verbal would feel the judgment of God lingering in the church house. This process was deep and heart-wrenching, but sincere people were driven to the altar by the conviction falling in the service. Heart-wrenching led to heart-searching as divine intervention drew the people of God into His presence. Verbal described a supernatural event he had experienced.

"I was in California back in the summer. I went to a church I had never been to before. I arranged my schedule so I could be there. I had such a sense of desperation, feeling burdened, feeling that I simply might die if something didn't move. I was physically sick the night I spoke in California; I feared whoever God was talking to knew it.

I couldn't sleep that night; I was so sick from the results of the service. In the service, there was a man standing to my right. He kept holding onto the pew, standing there, and would not let go. There was nothing to do. I went back to Texas, and two weeks later, the pastor called, saying that man had died."

Thankfully, a godly relief was felt after the outpouring of remorse, repentance, and confession to the Lord and the pastor. The people involved and the congregation would soon feel the glory that follows true repentance. It was a sobering time, but eternity will witness the miraculous salvation wrought by the workings of the Holy Ghost and by men and women who knew how to intercede before the throne of God.

"And Joshua said unto the people, sanctify yourselves: for tomorrow the Lord will do wonders among you." (Josh. 3:5)

An analogy of this season would be like deep cleaning a home. Curtains would be removed, rugs pulled up, trash gathered and thrown out, and walls, baseboards, and windows cleaned. It would appear to be a hopeless endeavor until everything started to be put back in order. It seemed these difficult times just had to be endured, all the while believing and holding onto faith until things started to come together.

It was true; things came back together much more meaningfully than most had foreseen. As saints made things right with their spouse, pastor, or brothers and sisters in the Lord, the oil of the Holy Ghost would flow and help erase the sorrow of past mistakes or sins. It would seem like a fresh new church, full of victory and glory. During these victorious days, the relief to the pastor and family was embraced as a gift from God. Like the celebration of a newborn baby, the labor pains were forgotten in the joy of new life in the family. God had seen every tear, every day of fasting, and heard every intercessory prayer.

> **"For God is not unrighteous to forget your work and labor of love, which ye have shewed toward his name, in that ye have ministered to the saints, and do minister." (Heb. 6:10)**

This pattern was certainly not repeated in every revival. Each revival was unique. The pastor, the church, the saints, and even the locations differed in many respects. However, it does seem that before the revival ended, the distinct features of a well-rounded ministry would be brought to the forefront for the edification of the body.

Spiritual maturity played a significant role in each revival. Many churches had already consecrated their hearts and lives to a high standard of holiness. Others may not have been taught, or the timing was not right, and these issues were not yet settled. It seems clear the Holy Ghost would lead the churches into the places they had faith and maturity enough to receive. Whatever their level of readiness, God would "Lead His dear children along," as the songwriter so eloquently expressed.

God Leads Us Along

*"In shady, green pastures, so rich and so
sweet,*

God leads His dear children along;

*Where the water's cool flow bathes the
weary one's feet,*

God leads His dear children along.

*Some thro' the waters, some thro' the
flood,*

Some thro' the fire, but all thro' the blood;

*Some thro' great sorrow, but God gives a
song;*

In the night season and all the day long."

Frequently, Verbal used music to bring the church together and
lead the congregation into deeper worship. He would ask the pastor
to order the new songbook *Great Gospel Hymns*, published by
Rev. O. C. Thompson. These songbooks had many new songs
written by Bro. Thompson, one of our Oneness preachers, along
with other composers. They also included many of the traditional
classics we enjoyed through the years. These were a few of
Verbal's favorite songs:

"He Wrote My Name"
"I'll Be Singing There"
"At Calvary"
"Heaven's Jubilee"
"It's All in Him"

When Verbal felt the saints were ready, he would invite them to come early for service the next night. After practicing with the musicians or playing an instrument, he would teach these songs to the congregation and lead them during the song service. This seemed a very simple thing to do, but it had profound results. After everyone was familiar with the songs, the song leader stepped back into the pulpit and led the people to a new level of Holy Ghost praise. Because Bro. Thompson was Holy Ghost-filled; this brought great anointing to his music. The songs were simple but beautifully written, and while singing these and other songs, the Spirit would fall on the singers, and godly worship would begin. It was wonderful to see the impact this music had on the revival.

As Verbal began to minister, he often sang a chorus, bringing the congregation together in mind and spirit. The sounds of "Amazing Grace" or "I Need Thee, Oh I Need Thee" would fill the auditorium, and God would enter the room. The value of these songs to the unity that covered the people was immeasurable; the message could then be freely delivered. Other times, he would start strumming his guitar and singing, "Ain't No Grave Gonna Hold My Body Down."

The crowd responded with worship, often running the aisles and dancing under holy anointing. Time after time during these meetings, those hungry for the Lord would come to the front, raise their hands, and begin speaking in tongues as they were filled with the Holy Ghost. Even many who remained in their pews responded to the Spirit of God, as the Holy Ghost would permeate the sanctuary and fall on them, too.

People would come from miles around to be in these revivals, and usually, they expected Verbal to preach a sermon. Occasionally, he would feel the pressure to preach, but God gave him the wisdom to follow the Spirit when this happened. Consequently, many services were conducted without a sermon. Still, regardless of the situation, Verbal would always minister to the congregation, though it might be in various ways, such as exhortation, teaching, or recounting miraculous experiences he had seen. Though it was not a titled sermon, the Word went forth and did Its work in the hearts of the listeners. Verbal shared an event he faced during the Texas Camp Meeting one year.

"Once, a preacher friend and I prayed all night during Texas Camp Meeting. About eight o'clock the next morning, the Spirit lifted from me, and I ceased to pray. The Holy Ghost spoke a message, 'You will be used to break through for my people.'

I said to my friend, 'You better get ready; one of us is going to preach.'

When I walked onto the campground that morning, one of the preachers on the Pulpit Committee came up to me and said, 'We want you to preach this afternoon.'

When I got up there to preach, I wanted to preach my best sermon. You don't get to preach at camp meeting every year. Well, I latched onto some thoughts, and they would leave me. And then, of all things, God began to deal with me about tongues and interpretation. The pressure was on from all sides. You could almost hear them scream, 'Preach!' I knew where I was, and I knew the pressure was on. Sis. Nona Freeman was there, and I called her up to pray. I knew she wasn't afraid to follow the Spirit, and she never prayed a drier prayer in her existence. I could almost hear God say, 'Next time I call you up to do something, don't put it off on somebody else.'

Finally, I said, 'Yes, God, I'll do it.'

I led the folks into worship, those that would. Sure enough, the Spirit began to speak and told them what He wanted to do, which was to heal and bless them. And without me saying a word, folks came up for prayer in their body. Before it was over, there was a double line across that entire auditorium. In that service, there were many miraculously healed. I'll never forget the very last one. I remember praying for a lady who brought a handkerchief for me to anoint. She said, 'There is a woman in my community who is dying of cancer. She only has a few days to live. She cannot speak above a whisper and does not have the Holy Ghost. She is so weak she can't lift her head from her pillow.'

Under the anointing of the Holy Ghost, you'll do things that will nearly scare you to death when you come back down to earth and think about what you said. I remember pouring oil on the handkerchief. I said, 'Alright when you put this on her body, she is going to receive the Holy Ghost and be healed.' Well, either she does, or I'm a false prophet, and it only takes about two or three cases like that, and you're ruined.

I received a letter from the lady a while later. She wrote, 'When I laid the handkerchief on her, she jumped out of bed, speaking in tongues, healed by the power of God.' The next week, she was in the yard mowing her lawn."

Seeing people pray through to the Holy Ghost is a wonderful event, and watching these new converts become rooted and grounded in the Word was always gratifying. When Verbal felt that the revival was drawing to a close, he began teaching the whole church, but especially the new converts, what could be called "Christian living as required by God." These were practical lessons clearly taught and included godly standards of living, tithing, faithfulness, and understanding their relationship and responsibilities toward their pastor.

Sometime during the closing nights of revival, Verbal would turn to the pastor and ask him to stand. He would say, "You see this man standing here? He is your pastor chosen by God, and it's a biblical requirement that you accept his preaching, teaching, and admonitions. On the Day of Judgment, he will be called on to give an account of your spiritual condition while you were under his care. You will want him to give a good report, and he, too, will want to witness to God you were a good and faithful saint." These were moving services. Often, Verbal would ask the pastor and his family to stand in front of the pulpit and call the saints to come by and express their love and appreciation to them. These were the times when people bonded with their pastoral leadership, and the spirit of unity would overshadow the church. Verbal loved this scripture.

> **"Remember them which have the rule over you, who have spoken unto you the word of God: whose faith follow, considering the end of their conversation." (Heb. 13:7)**

Once, Verbal was asked to preach in the Friday night service at a conference in Silsbee, Texas. Some had come from hundreds of miles to hear him minister. When he went to the pulpit, the congregation stood as he read his text. Then, he began to pray. It was not a casual prayer, but he began interceding as a burden for the lost fell on him. Some folks became restless because they had come from so far to hear him preach, but Verbal believed in "Waiting on the Lord." After a few more minutes, he spoke softly into the microphone. "God doesn't want me to preach tonight, saints. We need to pray. Someone's life is hanging in the balance."

Feeling the burden, the congregation fell to their knees, and everyone started praying earnestly. During this time, people gathered around two backslidden young men where they stood and started praying with them. Before the service was over, they were gloriously refilled with the Holy Ghost, along with many others. The following day, the heartbreaking news came that the two young men had been tragically killed in a car accident on their way home Friday night. Because of Verbal's sensitivity to the Holy Ghost, those young men's life stories had a different ending.

Chapter 5

Shoemake Family History

Mother grew up under her father's ministry, Rev. C. P. Kilgore. As a young couple, Grandad and Grandmother lived in a small community between Social Hill and Malvern, Arkansas. Granddad worked as a crane operator for the Saginaw Lumber Company. He was a staunch Mormon. The summer before, an evangelist, Roxie Hughes, came to their village, put up a tent, and began a brush-arbor revival. Grandmother visited the revival and was filled with the Holy Ghost. She tried as hard as she could, but Grandad was not to be persuaded to attend the revival with her.

Grandmother had prayed for Grandad's salvation all year following the revival. The next summer, Roxie Hughes returned to their community for another revival. It took firm persuasion for Grandmother to convince Grandad to go to the brush arbor meeting with her, but finally, she succeeded. They walked with their small family and found a place to sit. As soon as the meeting started, the Lord touched his heart.

When the preacher began her message, Grandad instantly felt the need to get right with God. As soon as the altar call was given, he went to the front, lifted his hands, and repented with all his heart. The Holy Ghost fell on him, and he walked back and forth across the front of the altar, speaking in tongues for an hour. Several months after that, Grandmother and Grandad heard a message, and the preacher powerfully quoted:

> **"Then Peter said unto them, Repent, and be baptized every one of you in the name of Jesus Christ for the remission of sins, and ye shall receive the gift of the Holy Ghost." (Acts 2:38)**

Like the early saints, when they heard this, they both gladly received the Word and were baptized in Jesus' name.

From that time forward, he and Grandmother lived righteous lives of sacrifice and dedication to the Kingdom of God. Just a few months later, Grandfather felt the call of God on his life and left his job; he and Grandmother put their three small children and few belongings into a wagon, pulled by a mule named Toby, and started their journey to carry the Gospel to a lost world.

He became a true Pentecostal pioneer and preached the Acts 2:38 message in countless towns and communities where it had never been preached. They raised eight children on the evangelistic field and rarely lived in a home of their own. Mother's life story was sacrificial yet beautiful, filled with the miraculous and wondrous works of God.

Daddy's story is different. He was born in Morris, Oklahoma, and was raised in a godless home; there was never a Bible in the house, and no one ever prayed or discussed the things of God. When he was fourteen, his father died of kidney disease. Daddy had ten siblings, and at this time, most were married and gone from home. Daddy, his mother, and his younger brother, Freeman, were left penniless and homeless. They lived with the older siblings, going from one place to another as need demanded. Daddy became rebellious at the age of fourteen, and from then until he was twenty-one, he lived a life of drinking, fighting, riding freight cars from town to town, and consequently, became an alcoholic.

Early one winter, while Daddy was staying with his mother in Morris, Grandad happened to be preaching a revival there. The townspeople were talking about the holy rollers and that preacher who could quote page after page of scripture, so he decided to see for himself what was creating such a stir. During the service, as he looked around the congregation and observed the people, they appeared happy and blessed. His life seemed hopeless, and he couldn't see a way out of his dilemma. A longing was born in his heart to be delivered from the sorrow and guilt he was suffering. At the close of Grandad's message, he went to the altar, repented with all his heart, and immediately felt the presence of the Lord. Later, Daddy often said that when he felt the forgiveness of God that night, it was the most incredible experience he had ever known. After his repentance, he was taken to a pond on the outskirts of town, where friends broke the ice so he could be baptized in Jesus' name. It was a life-changing event for him, and he willingly left his sinful lifestyle behind him, covered by the blood of Jesus.

Mother and Daddy soon became acquainted, had a short courtship, and were married in the Morris Pentecostal Church before Grandmother and Granddad left for another revival. In later years, Daddy marveled that their marriage had survived; they had come from different backgrounds and had such a short time to become acquainted before the wedding. But God had His hand on this young couple and had a plan for their lives.

Daddy sought earnestly to be filled with the Holy Ghost during every service, but it was three months before that happened. One night, he and Mother were in a cottage prayer meeting with a few faithful saints. Daddy was desperate to receive the Holy Ghost; he kept praying, hour after hour. The loving saints continued praying with him, and at midnight, he was gloriously filled with the Holy Ghost. After that night, the rest of his life was gladly given over to the service of the Lord.

Their marriage began during the Depression, and they lived a hand-to-mouth existence for some time. They found a deserted hen house, cleaned it up as best they could, and glued newspaper to cover the walls. Daddy took his responsibilities as a husband very seriously and did his best to provide for his new bride.

Within a year of receiving the Holy Ghost, Daddy felt the call of God on his heart to preach. He had a very natural speaking ability, loved people, and was friendly and outgoing. People were drawn to him because of his charisma but were drawn to Mother because of her kind, loving nature. Before long, he was invited to speak in his home church and some of the neighboring churches as well. In a few years, he became pastor of the Morris Church, where he had received the Holy Ghost.

Mother, Daddy, Dayna, and me

While living in Morris, Mother and Daddy had their first child, Jimmy Lee. Regina Ruth was born three years later, and I was born five years after that. In another five years, my younger sister, Dayna Joan, completed our family.

Morris was a wonderful place to raise a family, and we children were given the run of our small town. We walked to school and could ride our bicycles wherever we wanted. Main Street was a block from our house, and we loved to walk there and enjoy a milkshake in the local drugstore. We lived next door to the church house and spent many hours there 'playing church.' It was an excellent place to play on rainy days. I've always been grateful for the freedom we enjoyed during childhood.

Daddy pastored in Oklahoma for several years until he felt a call to take a small church in Modesto, California, where they experienced significant growth and revival. Bro. Clark, who was a young boy at the time, tells the story he heard about two men discussing that revival. Neither had the Holy Ghost, but they knew people in the church. One told his friend, "That pastor went fourteen days without eating any food, and after that, the church filled up with people." It was true; they were blessed to see a harvest of souls. Daddy pastored there for two years, and they became so

My school picture

homesick for Oklahoma that they moved back home. They were only briefly in Oklahoma when Daddy felt the call to move to San Jose, California, and pioneer a work there.

It was overwhelming for us all when we drove into Santa Clara County. It was the Garden of Eden to me. Although I was not yet ten, I was captivated by the beauty of the area. Fruit orchards and strawberry fields surrounded us. Although our arrival was in November, and the fruit-gathering season was past, it was still stunningly idyllic. San Jose, like Morris, was a wonderful place to grow up. The schools were amazing, and we were delighted to discover many delicious new things to eat, like avocados, halibut steaks, tacos, and pistachio nuts. I still feel blessed when I remember those outstanding ten years I was privileged to live there before getting married and moving away.

Mother and Daddy dedicated their lives and talents to establishing a congregation called the First Pentecostal Church. We all poured our hearts into this endeavor and were thrilled to be part of the amazing story being written day by day. During his tenure there, Daddy built two church buildings and established a very successful witness of the Gospel of Jesus Christ for the city of San Jose. This was to be their home for many years until they were both taken to be with the Lord.

Chapter 6

San Jose Revival

After anxiously waiting for several months following the General Conference, where Verbal assured Daddy that he would pray about preaching a revival in San Jose, Daddy received the long-awaited call from Verbal. They decided the revival would begin in three weeks. He arrived in San Jose during the summer of 1961. It would be difficult to express how excited my parents, the church, and I were to have Verbal come. He stayed in our home, and I gave up my bedroom for his use. I shared a room with Dayna, my younger sister. My brother Jimmy and his wife Bobbie came from Oklahoma to be in the revival.

This revival was a new experience for all of us. Verbal first instituted a 10:00 a.m. prayer meeting, Monday through Friday. Many who had never experienced intercessory prayer or praying in the Holy Ghost learned to participate in this intensive type of prayer during the revival. The meetings were not conducted the same way each time. We would usually begin with prayer, then often Verbal would teach or share encouraging stories of events and answered prayers that had occurred in previous revivals. During these prayer times, I learned to pray in ways I had not known before. It was thrilling to pray in the Holy Ghost and feel my prayers were reaching the throne of God. I still cherish those lessons and times of supplication.

Sometimes Verbal would sing, and if Jimmy and Bobbie were there– and they usually were– they would sing together, and the Spirit of God would move into the meetings. These gatherings could last from an hour to two or more hours of worship, praise, and prayer. We would leave the prayer meeting fired up in the Holy Ghost and could hardly wait for service to begin that night. He also instituted a twenty-four-hour prayer chain that lasted four weeks.

Jimmy and Bobbie had come to California to be in the revival but needed an income while they were there. Our Uncle Freeman was in the construction business building homes, and he hired Jimmy to work for him. He would go to work as early as possible, but when it was time for the prayer meeting, he would go home and clean himself up to be there on time. After that, he would return to work and come home just in time for service that night. Jimmy and Bobbie were a great blessing to us all during the revival.

In addition to the prayer meetings, all who could came early to pray before church. The morning prayer meetings and before-church prayer flooded the saints with faith and Holy Ghost anointing. This time with God brought the church together in unity, worship, faith, and hunger for a move of the Holy Ghost. Some were slower to get into the spirit of revival, but before long, practically the whole church was seeking God and renewing their dedication to the cause of Jesus Christ.

After this intensive groundwork, people had prepared their hearts, and they were ready for a move of the Holy Ghost. Sermons that may have been difficult to hear before were now received with open hearts, creating fertile fields for a revival harvest. And the harvest came. Forty people received the Holy Ghost, backsliders returned home, and we experienced a new level of worship and praise. Gifts of the Spirit were in operation, and God showed himself mighty to save and deliver.

It was a time to remember. Verbal did not preach a sermon every night. This was hard for some to understand because we were all programmed to believe a sermon must always be preached. The sermons he did preach were masterpieces: *The Last Mite, Israelite Women Are Not as Egyptian Women, The Unjust Judge, The Friend of the Bridegroom,* and many more. Visitors from nearby churches attended and were blessed as well. A man who had been seeking for many years was gloriously filled with the Holy Ghost and became a pillar in the church. A young couple both prayed through; they became foundational members of the San Jose church and are still a part of that church today. The revival produced a tremendous harvest of souls.

It was also disclosed to Daddy and Verbal that a couple in the church who had been together several years and who had seriously rededicated their lives to God during the revival were not married. They were discreetly advised to travel to Las Vegas, get married, return home, and be faithful to the Lord.

We enjoyed beautiful music during the revival. The Rutherfords, one of the church's founding families, were all gifted musically. Woodrow, the father, sang bass. His wife Hazel had a lyric soprano voice, and their daughter, Ruth Ann, added the harmony. She was also a gifted pianist, and they made up a beautifully anointed trio. Verbal had asked Daddy to buy the O. C. Thompson songbooks, and he did. Verbal taught many of those God-inspired songs to the congregation, and they brought a fresh glow of worship into our song services. Bro. and Sis. Murrell moved from Tulsa, Oklahoma, to San Jose, and he became our song leader. He always led the song service with great power, but there was a fresh anointing on him as he led the congregation in these new songs. These memories bring back the holy feeling of the glory of God we experienced during those services.

Verbal's burden was reflected in his powerful and convicting altar calls. Nearly every evangelistic service ended during that time with a call for sinners to come to God. As Verbal led us in song, we would join singing, "Come Home."

Come Home

"Softly and tenderly, Jesus is calling,
Calling for you and for me.
See on the portals He's waiting and
watching, Watching for you and for me.

Come home, come home,
Ye, who are weary, come home,
Earnestly tenderly, Jesus is calling,
Calling, O sinner, come home."

After the drawing of the Holy Ghost and the anointed singing of the congregation, many a rough, hardened sinner would tearfully find his way to the altar. Couples would join hands and go together to pray, and children would bravely leave their parents to kneel at the altar. No wonder there was such a Holy Ghost outpouring.

During the revival, Verbal was sick part of the time, and Mother cared for him as if he were one of her own children. She cooked the things she thought would be helpful and treated him as the treasured guest he was. One day, Mother was trying to think of something to prepare for Verbal to help with his illness, and she asked, "Bro. Bean, do you think you could enjoy some oyster stew?"

Verbal smiled and said, "Sis. Shoemake, maybe I better try to think of something to eat myself."

Mother and Daddy had poured their hearts into every service and were deeply grateful to Jesus Christ and Verbal for the revival. Not only was the church rejuvenated, but many also received the Holy Ghost, which placed the church on a new trajectory of victory. It was a glorious time.

Chapter 7

Friendship

The Verbal Bean revival in our church was a wondrous time for me. In addition to seeing the marvelous meeting unfold before my eyes, I also got to spend quality time with Verbal and get acquainted with him personally. He was a great conversationalist and very knowledgeable about many things. He was usually serious, so his sense of humor could be surprising, but it was always welcome to me. Many people were never privileged to see that side of him. Verbal had progressed from being an insecure young man to becoming a seasoned evangelist, enjoying the companionship of the ministry. We had many long conversations about life, family, dreams, and always the things of God. Before long, we were comfortable talking, laughing, and sometimes praying together. My family was also thankful for this time and the opportunity to build a closer friendship with him.

Verbal stayed on in our home for several days after the revival closed. During this time, we would take rides around San Jose, drive through the Santa Cruz Mountains to the coast, and visit other scenic places in our area. We also spent time with Jimmy and Bobbie, as well as David and Regina. It was such fun going out to eat together, laughing, and sharing thoughts of ministry and life. It was a lovely time for me and Verbal as well, I suspect.

Verbal and Dayna had become fast friends and could always make each other laugh. I'll never forget when Verbal would sit down at our piano with Dayna standing beside him, and he would start banging out 'their' song. Then they would begin singing at the top of their lungs in the flattest, most hillbilly style imaginable, "Where could I go? Oh! where could I go…" This unlikely duo kept it up until we were all laughing non-stop.

When Verbal finally left to start a revival in Fresno with Bro. and Sis. Murray Layne, our house seemed very lonely. But since Fresno wasn't that far from San Jose, we would visit those services when we could. A description of the Fresno revival can be found in the Revival Testimonials.

After the Fresno revival, I didn't see Verbal again until the United Pentecostal Church (UPC) General Conference. By this time in our relationship, Verbal would call me frequently. These calls were precious to me, and the familiar sound of his voice was positively entrancing.

Mother and Daddy weren't going to the General Conference that year, but David and Regina attended, and I rode with them. We shared a hotel room when we got to Kansas City, Missouri. They planned to visit his family in Indiana after the conference, and I would accompany them on that part of the trip. It was fun to be with them and their flaxen-haired toddler, Pam.

I knew I would see Verbal soon, and I could hardly wait. He had called me at home to make sure I would be at the conference with David and Regina and assured me he was looking forward to our time together. After we had checked in at the hotel, it wasn't long before I received a call from Verbal, and he asked me to sit with him at service that night.

Verbal acknowledged me publicly for the first time in our friendship, and we sat together during almost all the services. This was big news to our friends and acquaintances, and it was an exceptional time for us, too. The understanding was we would also be together after each service, and I was happier than I could have imagined. Verbal and I also spent time with the Kilgores. Aunt Ima was interested in every aspect of this romance as if she had planned it from the start.

One day, I left the hotel to do some shopping. When I returned to our room, Verbal was there with David and Regina. He told me that a young evangelist who seemed to like me had come and left a box of chocolates. I exclaimed, "Well, wasn't that sweet! I'll be sure to thank him tonight." Of course, I knew Verbal had brought the chocolates, and I just couldn't resist a little good-natured teasing.

Once, during the conference, Sis. Vestal Mangun spoke to me and told me she and Bro. Mangun were staying in the hotel room next to ours. Verbal walked me back to my room each night, and we would talk together in the hall before I went inside. Later, Sis. Mangun told me that when she learned Verbal and I were seeing each other, she would listen for us, her ear against the door, trying to hear what we were saying. We had a good laugh, and she expressed how happy she was that Verbal was interested in me. The memory of that conference is etched in my mind, cherished and treasured.

Before I left San Jose, Daddy had carefully instructed me that I was to go on to Indiana with David and Regina after the conference and that I would not by any means go back to Houston with the Kilgores. He sternly told me it would look like I was pursuing Verbal if I did.

These instructions became difficult to obey since Uncle James and Aunt Ima insisted that I go home with them. Aunt Ima stated flatly, "Nita, you don't know David's family; you won't enjoy being with them. Come on home with us."

Verbal was also very insistent that I go back to Houston. He said he would be there for some time before starting his next revival. They were preaching to the choir. I certainly wanted with all my heart to go back to Houston, where I knew I would spend time with them all, especially Verbal.

Finally, Uncle James said, "Nita, come home with us, and I'll explain to your dad how we changed your mind." I knew this would be a little 'iffy,' to say the least, but I allowed my heart to rule my head.

When we arrived in Houston, I called Mother and Daddy to tell them what was happening. When Daddy asked where I was, and I told him I was in Houston, he got very quiet and said, "Nita, I told you not to go to Houston." I felt sure I was in serious trouble. I had not disobeyed my father since I was a child. Uncle James came to the rescue when he took the phone from me.

"Now Voar," he said, "don't be upset with Nita. We made her come home with us; we knew she didn't want to go to Indiana." Then he added, "Verbal also asked her to come back home with us." Daddy was quiet a moment longer but finally agreed it was a better plan for me. Mother and Daddy had already arranged to visit the Kilgores after the conference so I would have a ride home. It all worked out beautifully, I thought.

Chapter 8

Questions

During my time with Verbal in Houston, I felt our relationship deepened. We had long conversations expressing our thoughts and feelings, speculating about the future together. We also talked about the things of God, and he shared with me his deep commitment to ministry. He had sometimes been misunderstood and criticized; however, these things never lessened his deep belief in his calling. His love for the evangelistic ministry was clearly conveyed in all he said.

The Houston trip was exciting for me in many ways. Verbal took me to meet his mother and also introduced me to his sister, Nylotis, her husband Eugene, and their three adorable daughters, Susie, Genia, and Velda. I found out later that this was the first time Verbal had brought a young lady to meet his family.

One day, we rode out of town to a place Verbal said would make a beautiful homestead. The house was set on a small incline toward the back of the property. There was a barn, and cattle were in a fenced field beside the house. I knew from his expression that he would always long for the farming lifestyle. I wasn't sure how this would fit into ministry, but I was thankful he felt comfortable enough with me to share his dreams.

Being a great storyteller and having a splendid sense of humor, Verbal often left me laughing with his many tales. I never tired of hearing the stories about Buck, their renegade ram, and about his cantankerous grandfather, Poppa. Our times together were unforgettable, but his feelings toward me, while kind and warm, were impossible to decipher. I didn't know if we would be a 'couple' or not.

Sadly, it was also during this time that Verbal began to doubt whether it was God's will for us to be together. It was frightening for me to think that maybe our marriage wasn't in God's perfect plan. Our future together was in doubt, and the uncertainty weighed heavily on us both. We were grieving to think maybe it was not meant to be, and it filled our hearts with a profound sense of loss.

It was heartbreaking to say goodbye to Verbal, especially since I didn't know when I would see him again or if our romance would continue. Verbal's uncertainty unnerved me and left me feeling that maybe I wasn't qualified to be married to such an anointed man of God. In many ways, that was true. I was almost nine years younger than he; I certainly had not shared the spiritual connection he felt since he was a young boy. He was used mightily in ministry and was experienced in walking with the Lord. I had led a blessed life with no personal knowledge of Verbal's sacrificial lifestyle. Daddy had taken good care of us; we lived in a beautiful home. I had a lovely wardrobe and was always given the money to attend youth camps and conferences. When I considered all these things logically, it seemed clear to me I might not be qualified enough to be Verbal's wife. But that didn't change the love I felt for him. I believed I would be willing to share his life on the evangelistic field and all that entailed, but I had not walked that road. I had loved the Lord all my life and served Him to the best of my ability, but my spiritual background and his were miles apart.

I returned home after experiencing these exhilarating, though at times, uncertain days with Verbal. I remembered and cherished the hours we had spent together at the conference. He seemed to enjoy being with me publicly and allowing friends and relatives to see we were a couple. Then, there were the golden hours in Houston when I was introduced to his mother and family. I was heading home more seriously in love with Verbal than before, but also deeply perplexed. I had no idea where this relationship was heading or how it would end.

When I arrived in San Jose, there was a huge comedown from the previous weeks, which was very depressing. I really couldn't imagine my life without Verbal. I was undoubtedly in love with him but didn't clearly understand where it would all end. I returned to my everyday life, which was just too ordinary for words. Plus, I was hundreds of miles away from Verbal, and there would be no occasion for us to see each other. These were painful days.

Verbal, too, was experiencing some lonely times after I left. He had never spent much time alone with a young lady before, and he found the companionship very rewarding. This was a new experience for him, and I don't think he realized what he had been missing until now. When I left, I'm sure he also felt empty and alone. Although his ministry was always crucial and fulfilling in his life, he now struggled with loneliness. This had not been a problem previously. All in all, we were both suffering.

It was a frustrating time for my parents as well. Daddy felt Verbal should know his mind by now, and he could see the toll all this uncertainty was taking on me. Being the protective father he was, he began saying some negative things about how Verbal was approaching our friendship, or romance, with me. Daddy believed Verbal should declare his love for me and move forward with our relationship or break up with me permanently. He told me later that he was just about ready to call Verbal and insist he leave me alone if he felt we should not marry.

By now, Verbal and I were both living in this uncertain situation. He would call, and we would talk. I could hear the sorrow in his voice when he told me how he missed me, and I was certainly longing to be with him. He would say, "Nita, I shouldn't be calling. I still don't know the will of God for us. Maybe this is wrong, and I'll probably have to repent later, but I felt I just had to talk with you for a while." Or he might end the conversation like this, "Nita, I can't feel like moving forward in our relationship, so we should stop having these conversations. It's too painful for us both; I'm going to tell you goodbye."

I would sadly but composedly reply, "All right, Verbal. If that's how you feel, then that's what we'll do. Goodbye."

I wouldn't beg, but I couldn't stop the tears.

Then another call would come again in a day or two, and he would say, "Nita, I know I shouldn't be calling you, but I just want to hear your voice. How are you?" Then we would talk and talk. After we hung up, Verbal would feel troubled and puzzled about all this, but we were deeply in love by now, and it seemed impossible for us both.

Chapter 9

Oh, Happy Day!

One day, Daddy came into the kitchen where I was cooking with Mother. "Nita," he said, "There's a call for you; it's person to person." Since Verbal was the only one who ever called me person to person, I knew this call was from him. I went into my parents' bedroom to take the call privately. While I was usually thrilled to talk with him, I felt uneasy. Our last conversations had been painful, and I wasn't sure whether what he had to say would break my heart or not. As he began the conversation, I listened quietly but was very anxious. This is the story Verbal related to me after we had each said our hellos.

"Nita, I know our friendship has sometimes been troubling for us both, but especially for you. I'm so sorry for the hurt it has caused. As you know, I haven't felt free to move forward to an engagement because I wasn't sure about the will of God in our relationship. Still, I haven't been able to forget you or stop loving you."

"I know, Verbal," I replied, "The past few weeks have been incredibly heartbreaking. I miss you more and more every day."

He continued, "In desperation, I called Bro. Dees and asked if I could get counsel and advice from him and Sis. Dees about our situation."

Bro. and Sis. Dees were neighboring pastors in Houston and were very close friends of Verbal and his mother. They held similar convictions as the Beans and trusted God for their healing. These families held each other up in prayer when any of them were sick and shared a deep bond of faith. Bro. and Sis. Dees were both anointed speakers, and I admired them very much.

As it happened, Bro. and Sis. Dees were free that day and invited Verbal to come and meet with them at their home. When he arrived, they exchanged greetings, and he was taken into the living room, where they sat down together. Verbal began to explain his dilemma and why he had sought their help and counsel. He told them, "I've been seeing Nita Kay Shoemake, and I believe I'm in love with her; she says she loves me, too. However, I haven't been able to feel in the Spirit that she is the right one for me to marry. I don't understand why, but it troubles me. I can't see anything in Nita's life that would cause me to feel this way; she seems to love the Lord with all her heart."

Bro. and Sis. Dees were well acquainted with Mother and Daddy and had met me briefly. Verbal went on to explain that nothing had happened to cause him to feel that way, but he still felt hesitant to move forward. "But," he said, "I can't stop thinking about Nita."

At this point in his narrative, Sis. Dees stood up and began to speak to Verbal with some indignation and Holy Ghost authority. She said, "Verbal Bean, you've lived a life of sacrifice to Jesus Christ and His Kingdom. You've been used mightily by God, and His hand of anointing has been on your life. But you have also felt that when anything special or beautiful was offered to you, it must be placed on the altar. You did this in order to maintain the anointing of God. Now, you've fallen in love with this young lady, and you feel your love for her must also be put on the altar. It seems you believe God wouldn't want you to have these feelings for Nita. I'm telling you, Bro. Bean, this isn't the right way to understand what God wants for you, and it's clearly His perfect will for you to marry her. Never believe God doesn't want your happiness and joy in marriage. Marriage is ordained and blessed by God. You need to go to California and marry Nita."

Verbal told me he was astonished to hear these emphatic words from her. "Then," Verbal said, "Sis. Dees did an amazing thing. Still, under the anointing, she went to the piano, sat down, and began to play and sing a song God had just given her that moment; this is the message as Verbal remembered it:

> *"My son, everything I have put in your hands,*
> *You have placed on My altar and set it apart.*
> *My perfect will for you, please understand,*
> *Is for Me to give you the desire of your heart.*

I will bless you in marriage to the one you hold dear.
I will cover your pathway and guide from above.
You have honored Me deeply throughout every year.
I will bless you, my son, and the one your heart loves."

It's heartbreaking to think that this anointed song sung by Sis. Dees has been lost in the passage of time. It was not recorded or ever sung again. These words and the anointing of the song resonated with Verbal. His life had been filled with the voice of God guiding him, and he recognized His voice that day. All the doubts and uncertainties disappeared, and he was grateful that God had graciously chosen to speak directly to him.

Verbal and Bro. and Sis. Dees began weeping and thanking the Lord as the holy afterglow of His presence lingered in the room. Finally, Verbal expressed his thanks and appreciation to Bro. and Sis. Dees and quietly said, "I'm sorry to rush off, but I'm going home to call my Nita."

As Verbal related these incredible events to me on the phone, I was very moved. It was humbling to know Jesus Christ would come to reassure him during this emotional turmoil. I'm sure Jesus saw the desire in Verbal's heart to please Him in every area of his life, both spiritually and personally. Maybe it was a test, I don't know, but we were both overjoyed to see the hand of God on our lives in such a particular way. Finally, I heard the words I had longed to hear, "Nita, I love you so much. Will you marry me?"

After all the months of uncertainty, I felt overwhelming relief and joy. Through my tears, I whispered, "Yes, Verbal. Yes! Yes! Yes!"

Verbal couldn't stop expressing his happiness, feeling the weight of indecision lifted from him. And now, for the first time, we could freely express our love for each other. My heart was overflowing; the constraints were gone, and we shared the pent-up words we had held for many months. It was unusual, a proposal by phone, but it was beyond price to me. My heart was overflowing with love for our Lord, but also my love for this wonderful evangelist, my Verbal. My dreams were coming true.

Oh, happy day!

We didn't make all our wedding plans that day, but we began discussing how this wonderful event would occur. The proposal was made in the middle of November. Verbal wouldn't be able to come to California until just before the wedding, so we wouldn't see each other until then. We had to be satisfied with holding long, tender conversations and exchanging romantic love letters for the rest of our engagement.

I found out months later, after Verbal proposed to me, he called Bro. Layne, one of his close friends, and said, "Bro. Layne, the Lord told me I could marry Nita."

Planning a wedding by telephone was a little difficult, but not impossible. While discussing our wedding date, I asked Verbal if he would be willing to have the wedding in January, a week after my twentieth birthday. I felt this would make me seem a little more mature, to no longer be a teenager. This was fine with him, so we began planning our wedding and life together.

Chapter 10

Engagement and Wedding

After my conversation with Verbal, I returned to the living room where the family had gathered to hear 'the rest of the story.' Many people had concluded Verbal would probably never marry. Daddy reminded me later of my words when I entered the room. I looked around, smiled at everyone, and said, "They said it couldn't be done."

This broke the tension in the room, and we all laughed happily together. I'm sure my family was glad to see me smiling again, filled with joy to be engaged to my handsome evangelist.

While I was busy in San Jose with wedding plans, Verbal was also busy in Houston. He had contacted a real estate agent and talked with her about buying a small house. Verbal had always lived with his mother; even when he began evangelizing, this didn't change. Understandably, he wanted our marriage to begin in a place of our own.

Our real estate agent found us a small two-bedroom brick home on a quiet street in a nice neighborhood. I don't remember the cost, but it was inexpensive, with a small down payment and monthly payments of $79.00. This was to be the first home for either of us, and we were thrilled to have our own place. We could only stay there when we were between revivals, but we were still grateful to be homeowners.

Verbal did his best to prepare the house for us. He moved his bedroom furniture from his mother's house and set it up in our front bedroom. For a wedding gift, the saints from Sis. Bean's church raised money and bought a dinette set for our kitchen. This was as far as Verbal could go in furnishing the house before I arrived.

Verbal had discussed the type of wedding he felt we should have. We wouldn't be exchanging rings because Verbal preached against them, and Mother and Daddy had never worn rings either, so that seemed natural to me.

Verbal continued, "Since so much of my ministry concerns sacrifice and modest living, I wouldn't be comfortable with a lavish wedding. I don't think that would be consistent with my teaching. Is that all right with you, Nita?" I was in total agreement with his feelings and explained this to Mother. She later confessed she was very stressed during all the preparations to ensure our wedding didn't become too extravagant for Verbal's comfort.

Meanwhile, back in San Jose, my life was filled with the delightful responsibility of planning a wedding to the man I adored. Daddy was a very generous father to us all, but he didn't like to spend large sums of money on our weddings. He felt the money could be put to better use furnishing our homes. Daddy gave me $500.00 to spend on the wedding, and I was happy to have what seemed to be such a large sum of money. Looking back, I realize that was very little money to have for a wedding, but it seemed sufficient to me at the time.

The first order of business was to find a wedding gown. Mother and Daddy went shopping with me the next day, and we first visited Macy's Department Store. Macy's had come to our community, and we considered it the epitome of fine shopping. Our first stop was in their bridal salon. We all looked around at the beautiful gowns displayed there, and to our surprise, we found a sale rack. There, I discovered the wedding gown of my dreams. It was white crepe with a collar and a row of tiny buttons down the front, and it had long sleeves that came to the wrist. The skirt was gathered closely at the waist. I hurriedly carried it to the dressing room to try on, and it fit me perfectly. Looking back on that golden day, I believe God had this dress in store just for me. The only possible immodest element of it was see-through lace covering the shoulders. That was no problem since my mother was an excellent seamstress, and lining the lace would be a simple task. The most exciting thing of all was the price. It was marked down to $50.00 and was the first and last wedding gown I tried on that day. I joyfully left the store with the dress carefully placed on a padded hanger and covered with a zippered plastic bag.

The rest of the wedding plans were very simple also. I chose four bridesmaids, and Verbal chose four groomsmen. The flower girl and candlelighters completed our wedding party. Early in Daddy's ministry, he married a couple, and they divorced very soon after the wedding. I don't know why, but Daddy felt this was a blight on his ministry, so he stopped performing weddings. After he had refused to marry a few couples, it seemed to him it wouldn't be fair to marry any others. However, he was willing to dress up, stand on the platform with the wedding party, and pray a blessing on the newlywed couple. That was his responsibility at our wedding. Uncle James flew from Houston to perform the ceremony.

We rented a room for the reception from a nearby school, ordered a lovely, tiered wedding cake, and bought decorations. Mother arranged for ladies from the church to make the punch and help with the serving and clean-up.

Verbal and his mother traveled from Houston to California a week before the wedding. They first went to San Francisco, where Doll lived, and Verbal left his mother to stay with Doll until the wedding. Then, he continued his drive to San Jose.

Verbal finally arrived at our home. I met him at the door, and we just gazed at each other, sharing smiles. He stepped into the room and took me in his arms. This was the first embrace; it was another cherished moment, doubly treasured because it was so long in coming. My heart could hardly handle the joy of that day and the days that followed.

We were together at every possible moment because most of the wedding preparations had already been made. Verbal and the groomsmen had to rent their clothes, white dinner jackets with black tuxedo pants. A few more errands were carried out, but most of the time, we just enjoyed the hours spent together. Verbal stayed with my sister and brother-in-law, Regina and David.

One morning, Verbal went to San Francisco, picked up Doll, and they drove to Carmel to select a hotel for our honeymoon. It is a charming coastal town renowned for its stunning beaches and ocean views. Doll had been told the Highland Inn was a favorite location chosen by engaged couples for their honeymoon. When she and Verbal went to the hotel, they were told it was full and would not accept any more reservations. They drove around the area, found a smaller but still very beautiful hotel, the Tickle Pink Inn, and reserved a room for us.

Finally, the longed-for wedding day arrived. It was January in San Jose, but the day dawned clear with beautiful blue skies. Our house was filled with out-of-town friends and relatives. I didn't see Verbal that day, but we talked on the telephone. I could tell he was a little nervous, but so was I. It was comforting to hear his voice, and that carried me through the day.

Soon, it was time to prepare for the wedding. I carefully combed my hair, and it cooperated on this important day, which was not always the case. Then Mother came to help me get into my wedding dress. I stood with raised arms as she carefully lifted the dress over my head and lowered it slowly until I could slip my arms into the sleeves. She pulled it down gently, and the dress fell into place over my hoop. After pulling up the side zipper, she fluffed the skirt of the dress to her liking. I glanced up into the mirror, looking seriously into my image, and trusted I was prepared and equipped for the future that was before me.

A few minutes before 7:00 p.m., when the wedding was scheduled to begin, Daddy helped me carefully into the car. Mother and Dayna climbed in, and soon, we were at the church. When we arrived, Daddy escorted me into the vestibule, and I was careful to stay out of sight until the wedding began.

Verbal, Uncle James, and the groomsmen were waiting in the church office. They walked onto the platform and stood under the decorated archway when the music began.

We had many out-of-town guests and relatives attending our wedding, and of course, saints from our church and the neighboring churches. It was sad to me that very few of Verbal's close friends and relatives were able to make the long trip to San Jose. Knowing he was dearly loved by all who knew him in California helped.

The organist began playing "I Love You Truly" while Mother and Sis. Bean were ushered in. My sister Dayna lit the candles as the soft music continued. My bridesmaids walked down the aisle and

took their places while Daddy and I stood quietly at the back of the church.

Soon, I heard the "Wedding March," and holding Daddy's arm, we walked down the aisle. When we arrived at the

altar, Daddy gave me away, and Verbal joined me. I took his arm, and we walked onto the platform together.

Bobbie Shoemake sang "Whither Thou Goest," and the beauty of the song and the solemnity of the occasion swept over me. The picture of Verbal and me standing before Uncle James as he performed the ceremony showed us both very seriously listening to every word. Uncle James spoke about the sacredness of marriage and then asked us to repeat our vows.

David Theobald sang "The Wedding Prayer," and when the song ended, Daddy placed his hands on our heads and prayed for us. Uncle James said, "I now introduce to you Rev. and Mrs. Verbal Bean." We were finally

married! We turned to face the audience and could hardly stop smiling as we left the platform. Verbal and I stood in the vestibule and greeted our guests as they left for the reception. It was a joyous day for everyone but marvelous for Verbal and me.

When we left the church, we got into the back seat of the car to be driven to the reception, and Verbal gathered me closely in his arms. As he leaned in and our lips met, it was our first kiss, a tender and unforgettable moment.

At the reception, we had cake, punch, and mints, posed for more pictures, and then opened our wedding gifts. We were blessed with many practical and beautiful things to use in our new home in Houston. After the formalities were over, we drove back to the house.

Verbal and I went inside and changed from our wedding finery into our going-away clothes. Our suitcases were packed; we said our

goodbyes, got into Verbal's beautiful white Pontiac and started on our drive to Carmel. As we left on our honeymoon, it began to snow, an almost unheard-of event in San Jose. Aunt Ima couldn't attend the wedding, but when Uncle James called to tell her about it and announced that it was snowing, she exclaimed, "The heavens are shaken because Verbal Bean got married!"

It was about seventy-five miles to Carmel, so we enjoyed some quality time all to ourselves. We slowly relaxed, and the joy of the day filled our hearts. We talked together the whole way. We discussed the wedding and expressed how wonderful it was to have so many friends and relatives with us to celebrate our nuptials.

Verbal told me how thoughtful his mother had been on the road trip they shared on the way to the wedding. She was very happy he was getting married, but she was struggling with the thought he was moving into another more important relationship than the one they had shared for twenty-eight years. One night, after they settled into their motel room for the night, she had an emotional episode. She became acutely aware things would never be the same for them after this trip. Soon, she began to cry. Verbal was kind and patient with her and assured her she would always be his mother, and that would never change. Finally, she found comfort in his words and was careful to make him understand she was really pleased that he was getting married. She ended the conversation by telling him she knew he would be a wonderful husband.

Soon, we arrived at our destination, the Tickle Pink Inn. Verbal unloaded our luggage, and we were shown into our charming hotel room, which overlooked the beautiful Pacific Ocean. In January, whales migrated off the Mexican coast to Alaska from the Sea of Cortez. During the day, the whales were visible from our room as they made their way north to the food-dense hunting grounds of the Arctic.

We had looked forward to this time for so long and cherished every moment. We talked and laughed and enjoyed getting to know each other better. Although I knew Verbal could be very entertaining, I was delighted to find he had a playful side that I had not seen before. He sang silly songs to me, mimicked some funny preacher mistakes, and thoroughly charmed me with these new revelations. He had seemed perfect to me before but was now more wonderful than ever, if that were possible.

Carmel was a remarkable place for our honeymoon. Even in January, the sun shone brightly, and we held hands as we walked the quaint streets admiring all the sights. The waves splashing on the beach could be heard whenever we stepped outside our room, and the fragrant salt air surrounded us. One day, we took the Seventeen Mile Drive. This is still considered one of the most magnificent drives on the California coast.

 We stopped along the way and walked close to the cliffs to watch the seals and sea lions diving into the waves and sunning themselves on the rocks. The seals barked incessantly, and the sea lions, especially, were loudly proclaiming their predominance and dominion over this coast. Some of the rocks were covered with sea birds, and hearing their calls and watching them dive-bomb into the ocean to capture their lunch was delightful. It was a cacophony of noise, and we loved every minute. We took our time to soak up the loveliness all around us, sharing smiles of gratitude because we were together now, husband and wife.

Chapter 11

Houston Bound

After our fabulous wedding and honeymoon, we returned to San Jose to enjoy several days with the family before driving to Houston. Daddy took us to a few excellent restaurants, and Mother prepared some delicious meals. It was fun to be with Jimmy and Bobbie, as well as David and Regina and their children. Of course, my younger sister, Dayna, was always a delight. She was full of life and laughter and was the star of our get-togethers. Finally, the bittersweet day arrived. We carefully loaded the car with our wedding gifts and clothes and began the next chapter of our lives.

Mother and Daddy ensured I had a nice wardrobe as an evangelist's wife. They were very kind and affectionate to me during my last days at home. They loved Verbal, too. Daddy always said the San Jose church was forever changed and blessed by Verbal's revival. Tearfully, I hugged and kissed my family goodbye, got into the car with the love of my life, and headed to Houston.

Bro. Terry invited Verbal to preach when he learned we would pass through Bakersfield. During that telephone conversation, Bro. Terry gave an update on his church, following the revival Verbal had preached there the previous year. "We have to put out folding chairs to hold the crowd. The victory we reached during the revival continues. Two to three people pray through every service. The other night, conviction fell so powerfully that fifteen people received the Holy Ghost while sitting in their pews. None of them even came to the altar." Then he continued, saying, "We'll be so glad to see you and Sis. Nita, again."

We drove south on Highway 99 and stopped in Bakersfield to be with Bro. and Sis. Terry. We were warmly welcomed, and they graciously provided us with a hotel room. After a powerful service that night, Bro. Terry asked to see my Bible. I handed it to him, and he turned to Proverbs 31:29 and underlined the verse, "*Many daughters have done virtuously, but thou excellest them all.*" We said our goodbyes to our friends and returned to the hotel. The following day, we continued the drive to Houston.

When we arrived in Houston after an uneventful, although enjoyable trip, Verbal brought me to our new home. We were both thrilled to have this small, modest house where we would begin our lives together. Though the furnishings were sparse, it didn't discourage us; we were excited to have a home to share.

The thing I enjoyed most was organizing the kitchen. We unpacked our wedding gifts, put shelf paper in the cabinets, and arranged the space as best we could. Fortunately, we had been given the necessary items to furnish our kitchen. After a trip to the grocery store, I was happy to cook for my bridegroom in our own home.

One of the first dinners I prepared for Verbal was vegetable beef soup. Sis. Bean had cooked this for us, and I asked her how she prepared it; she kindly explained how it was made. On my first attempt, I was pleasantly surprised by how tasty it was. Verbal seemed to think it was delicious, and it became one of his favorite meals.

In the defense of that young bride, I knew how to cook a few things, and I could also read and decipher a cookbook. I could make breakfast and put a sandwich together, but most importantly, I knew my mother's phone number. When I would call her for help, she would always patiently walk me through the intricacies of whatever I was trying to prepare.

While in Houston, we spent time with Hobert and Ruth, Verbal's older brother and his wife. They were very kind and welcoming. Although Hobert was tall and handsome, he didn't look like Verbal, and he was personable and funny. Even though the time these brothers spent together was limited because of the differences in lifestyle, they were devoted to each other. I thoroughly enjoyed getting acquainted with Hobert and Ruth; our friendship lasted through the years. The family was delighted Verbal had married; they felt he had needed a wife for some time, so I was warmly welcomed into the family circle.

This time in Houston was special to me as I had my first opportunity to be in service with Sis. Bean at the Greens Bayou

Church. She pioneered the church and, through the years, prayed many people through to the Holy Ghost. I felt blessed to become acquainted with the precious saints there. These families who stayed with Sis. Bean and worked with her in the church were foundational members. They were strong in faith and holiness and committed to the work of God. It wasn't a large group, but they certainly seemed to be of one mind in their loyalty to Sis. Bean and shared her burden for the lost. This church had powerful worship and had been built on intercessory prayer. Verbal would preach there most of the time when we were in Houston, and the congregation loved these occasions.

Verbal always respected his mother and honored her ministry and walk with God. Her godly example and dedicated prayer life had tremendously influenced his early years. She was totally committed to Jesus Christ and His service. It wasn't until she started the church in Houston that she took on the call of God to preach in such an extensive way. Most of her ministry was confined to the church she pastored, but she was highly regarded by those who knew her because of her life-long dedication to the Lord. She was a remarkable example of the virtuous woman.

In early February, Verbal was scheduled to preach for Bro. Irvin Baxter, Sr., who, along with his wife, Ruth, pastored in Richmond, Indiana. Although we were sad to leave our home, we loaded up and started the journey to our first revival as husband and wife.

Chapter 12

Richmond Revival

The trip to Richmond was unremarkable. I was eager to be going to my first revival with Verbal. He, too, was very happy to be making this trip. Verbal had preached a revival for Bro. and Sis. Baxter when they pastored in Joplin, Missouri. He certainly admired them, counted them as close friends, and assured me I would love them as soon as I got to know them. It had been several weeks since Verbal's last revival and he was filled with anticipation to be back in the pulpit again.

Verbal told me a lot about the Baxter family during our trip to Indiana. He said they were a unique couple; both were very anointed and invested in ministry. Sis. Baxter had been called to preach as a young lady and pastored a small work near her home church. Irvin Baxter started attending the services there and was soon under conviction. After he received the Holy Ghost, she baptized him, and it wasn't long until God called him to preach. They married soon and continued in ministry together.

As we were getting close to Richmond, reality began to set in. While looking forward to meeting this amazing couple, I wasn't sure how they would feel about me. I was younger than Verbal and a virtual novice in the evangelistic world. I thought people might feel Verbal could have chosen a more prepared lady than I was, someone who was better equipped for his ministry. These thoughts crowded my mind, and I was very close to tears as the miles passed. This episode itself reveals my immaturity and insecurity. Bravely, I kept my feelings inside and reminded myself that Holy Ghost people are filled with love and kindness.

As we grew close to the Baxter residence, I could see they lived in a beautiful home on an acreage outside of Richmond. I was impressed by the fenced fields behind the house and could see the cattle contentedly having their supper. In addition to raising cattle, Bro. Baxter also grew crops of hay and grain. Sis. Baxter planted a vegetable garden each year, and we were blessed to enjoy some of the fruits of her labor during our stay. Verbal loved everything about cattle and farming and was overjoyed to be in this rural environment. He was eagerly waiting for the opportunity to drive a tractor.

 When we pulled into their driveway, Bro. and Sis. Baxter came out to welcome us with glowing smiles. They invited us into their home and their lives. The Baxters were gracious, friendly, and charming. I was relieved, realizing my foolish fears were just that– foolish.

As we entered the house, we could smell the tantalizing aroma of supper. Verbal and I were very grateful we could be in the company of these wonderful people. We were shown into the guest bedroom where we would stay; the luggage was brought in from the car, and we carefully unpacked, putting everything into place.

Sis. Baxter had prepared a delicious roast dinner, and sitting down with them and their family was pure happiness. Bro. and Sis. Baxter had three children: Marian, who was married and lived in a nearby city; Irvin Jr., a senior in high school; and Roseanne, who was ten years old and still in grammar school.

That evening, after dinner, the Baxters and Verbal got caught up on their news. It was enlightening to hear their conversation as they shared stories and testimonies of their lives since they were last together. I was thankful to be in this home with these delightful people and see the friendship they shared with Verbal.

Bro. and Sis. Baxter were very interested to learn about our courtship and marriage, and Verbal was pleased to recount our love story of how God brought us together. I was always overjoyed by the opportunity to describe our wedding. These people were very dear friends of Verbal and remained so until his death. I, too, was taken into the warm embrace of their friendship, and I still cherish the memories of those priceless times together. An unknown author penned, "There are friends, there is family, and then there are friends that become family."

The Richmond church was strong and solid in doctrine and holiness, with around two hundred people in attendance, but the Baxters longed for a Holy Ghost revival. They had pastored the congregation for five years at that time. On the first night of revival, Verbal expressed his burden and desire for a Holy Ghost outpouring and his determination to follow the will of God in every service. He also announced we would have ten o'clock morning prayer meetings Monday through Friday.

Verbal preached a highly anointed message that night and closed out the sermon with the chorus,

> *"Oh, Lord, didn't You promise to hear us pray?*
> *Oh, Lord, didn't You promise to hear us pray?*
> *Bow down Thine ear, Lord,*
> *And hear us, we pray."*

As he sang, people began to come to the altar. Soon, the sound of weeping and prayer filled the auditorium. When hungry people fall on their faces before God and pour out their longing in prayer, something happens in the Spirit. God met with us as we implored Him to move in the hearts and minds of the congregation and in the city of Richmond. We were filled with gratitude for the prayer anointing we experienced as we met together in unity of spirit for revival.

Verbal established the morning prayer meetings as an essential element of every revival. He usually closed these prayer meetings by encouraging the saints to come early to church that night and fill the prayer rooms.

It was an education for me to be around the Baxter family. The Shoemake family had much to share, and we engaged in many lively conversations about church matters, politics, and current events. The Baxter family had a lot to say, and they said it vehemently and with enough volume to be heard above the rest. They were good-natured about it all, but often, I was simply amazed at the quality and quantity, not to mention the volume of these family discussions and friendly squabbling.

"Now Irvin, remember I baptized you," Sis. Baxter would laughingly say. Bro. Baxter would sternly reply, "Ruth, I'm the pastor, and you are instructed to be under submission to me." This was all done in fun, and it was clear to anyone who knew them they were a matched pair.

Sis. Baxter was an outstanding cook, and her meals were, without fail, delicious but not particularly low in calories. All the family, except Irvin Jr., had concerns about their weight. Despite this, much time was spent discussing food and what we would have for our next meal. Roseanne, especially, loved food. She would read the weekly menus sent home by her school, licking her lips as she described how delicious tomorrow's lunch would be. Sis. Baxter encouraged Roseanne to control her weight but served tempting dinners every night, which included pie and ice cream. As young and inexperienced as I was, I could discern the problem with this food regimen.

One evening, Bro and Sis. Baxter had obligations, and we offered to babysit Roseanne so she could stay home. She was really a delightful young girl, very friendly and talkative. Verbal and I were charmed by her company, and we spent the evening talking and laughing with her. Sis. Baxter explained to us before they left that evening, "Roseanne won't need to eat again after supper tonight because I've put her on a diet."

Just before bedtime, Roseanne came to us and said, "I know I'm on a diet, but Mother always says that when we're watching our calories, we can take a break now and then and have a treat. Could I please have some ice cream?" We certainly weren't going to go against Sis. Baxter's wisdom regarding diets, so we got the ice cream and enjoyed a bedtime snack.

As the revival continued, I saw the dedication and love that Bro. and Sis. Baxter poured on their congregation. They were absolutely sold out to the Kingdom and worked untiringly for their church and revival. One memory is still clear in my mind. I had gone to the grocery store with Sis. Baxter, and while we were there, she saw a young man who had once visited the church. She approached him warmly, smiling. "Oh, I'm so glad to see you. Did you know we are in revival with a wonderful evangelist, Bro. Bean from Houston, Texas? Would you please come to church with us one night? I know you will enjoy it. Won't you please come? Everyone would love to see you." She entreated him with such love and kindness I didn't see how he could refuse. I'm unsure if he visited the revival services, but Sis. Baxter certainly did her utmost to persuade him to come to church.

There were many young couples in Richmond church when we were there. One of these couples, Bob and Dot Arthur, captured our attention because of their fervor and faithfulness. They were a beautiful couple with a gorgeous baby boy, Kevin. It became my delight to carry Kevin around after church whenever I had the opportunity. Bro. Baxter explained to us that he believed Bro. Arthur was called to preach, and he was sure they would go into the ministry after they had more experience. Bro. Baxter was certainly correct about this couple.

A few years later, Sis. Dot Arthur expressed to me how she and Bro. Arthur had been spiritually grounded and gripped by a desire to pray in that revival. He had received the Holy Ghost about eighteen months before the revival and was still a new convert. He had already committed his life to the Lord and was hungry for more of God. Bro. Arthur developed a dedication to the Kingdom of God during that time, which lasted throughout his life and ministry. Both Bro. and Sis. Arthur were used by the Holy Ghost and led into the ministry of intercessory prayer.

Bob and Dot Arthur later spent years on the mission field, having great success, and raised their family to follow their steps into ministry. Bro. and Sis. Arthur's oldest son, Kevin, now pastors the church in Richmond, and their children are all involved in the work of God.

Verbal understood the Richmond church was strong in many ways, but some issues needed to be addressed as usual. He preached challenging messages, pleading and persuading the saints to take on the burden of prayer and intercession, exhorting them to reconsecrate and rededicate their lives to Kingdom matters. Some of the services were very solemn and heavy with the burden he was carrying for the revival, and occasionally, he would give a message in tongues and interpretation. One night, the Spirit spoke through him,

"Who have I but you to reach this city? How will the lost be saved except you testify of my goodness?"

During this time, the Lord revealed to Verbal there was sin in the congregation. He confided this to Bro. Baxter, and they discussed how this issue should be addressed. In the next service, Verbal called no one out personally but told the people what God had shown him. Soon after this service, it came to light that a lady in the congregation was guilty of adultery, but she would not repent. This was a difficult time for the church, but it seemed an increased fervor for God and his righteousness gripped the people as they sought the face of God.

It was a good revival, with many receiving the Holy Ghost and backsliders being restored. We had healing services and times of great rejoicing as people ran around the church or shouted down the aisles. There was a lady in that church who would start a beautiful, graceful dance when the Spirit of the Lord fell on her, and we all loved to watch her worship.

When Verbal felt the revival had finally attained the desired level of victory, we could take Monday nights off. The Baxters, who were always kind and thoughtful, would sometimes take us to a nearby city during those Mondays. It was such fun to spend this time with them. They took us to Chicago once, and we had an excellent time seeing the sights; then, we capped the day by eating in a nice restaurant. Verbal and Bro. Baxter enjoyed a deep, genuine friendship and, on these occasions, shared wonderful stories. Bro. Baxter had many fish tales to tell; most were about the northern pike they caught in the lakes of Wisconsin. Sis. Baxter and I were an attentive audience to these stories and were pleased to see our preacher husbands relax and enjoy the day.

One Monday morning, I walked into the kitchen, and Sis. Baxter was sitting on the floor, defrosting her freezer. Verbal and I had talked together earlier and decided we would take a little trip of our own that day. As I told her to tell her about our plans, Sis. Baxter misunderstood me, or else I didn't express myself clearly enough. She assumed I was suggesting the Baxters take us out for the day. She slowly replied, "Yes, we can do that." Then she proceeded to get up off the floor, put away her cleaning supplies, and headed for the bedroom to get ready for the trip. I was mortified and couldn't find the words to explain that we were not asking them to entertain us that day. We would look after ourselves. I was embarrassed, knowing I must have sounded like a spoiled child to her.

When I returned to our bedroom to tell Verbal about this turn of events, we were both very perplexed but didn't know how to change the situation. We just joined them as if this were the original plan. I felt guilty for the longest time for interrupting her cleaning day. Finally, years later, I confessed to her we would never have expected her to change her plans on her one day off just to entertain us. We laughed about the misunderstanding, but honestly, I still get a little embarrassed when I think about that day.

We had some cold winter weather at that time. Even though there were many snowy days, this caused very little hindrance to revival. I soon discovered that Northern people were hardy, and church attendance was better than expected. Of course, the weather couldn't hinder a red-hot Holy Ghost service, so we continued to enjoy the outpouring of anointing and power despite the weather.

After we had been in Richmond for a month, I discovered I was expecting our first child. Verbal and I were ecstatic about this pregnancy. We shared our good news with the Baxters, and they both expressed their joy concerning this wonderful event.

I have always been grateful that my first experience in a revival with my wonderful bridegroom was in such a caring environment. I'm sure I fell short in many ways, but I was never shown anything but love and kindness from this remarkable family and my very understanding husband. Verbal was mature enough to realize I hadn't shared the experiences he had been through, and he also was wise enough to be tolerant of his young bride. It is impressive to me as I look back on those years to grasp the extent of Verbal's forbearance. He was a mighty man of God used in the gifts of the Spirit, but he also manifested a gentle nature that made me love him even more, if that were possible.

We had mixed feelings about leaving Richmond and the Baxter family. After thirteen weeks of revival, we looked forward to returning to Houston and enjoying our home for a few days, but it was hard to say goodbye.

Chapter 13

Texarkana Revival

After the close of revival, we loaded our car, said our goodbyes, and headed south. We were excited to return to our modest home and spend time there. We finally purchased a couch and a rocking chair, which added much to our comfort. Verbal hung some curtains in our living room, and I bought a few more things for the house. We decorated in a very modest way.

Verbal and I were both excited about the coming birth of our first child. Before our marriage, Verbal asked me if I would trust the Lord with him for our healing. I agreed I would do my best. Verbal's conviction about trusting God for our healing was very strong. So, while trusting God for healing was not unknown, only a few of our acquaintances held this conviction.

Thankfully, Verbal didn't expect me to have our baby at home. He felt it would be wise to have the baby delivered in a clean environment with experienced doctors to care for me. He insisted that I find a female obstetrician for the delivery. Imogene Kilgore had recently given birth to her third child, James Kilgore II, and she gave me the name of her doctor, who was a woman. Verbal also felt I should use as little medication as possible for the birth. I set up an appointment to meet with the doctor, and during our first visit, I explained how we would like the delivery of our baby to be managed. She was a little skeptical but willing to go along with our wishes.

I was blessed with a worry-free pregnancy, just the common morning nausea to deal with. I read all the books I could find on natural childbirth and trusted my sweet husband and God to see me through this brand-new experience.

We were also happy to be with Sis. Bean and her church family. Verbal's ministry there was a blessing to her and her congregation. These people loved Verbal and were delighted when he could be with them. Verbal also preached in several of the local churches, and it was helpful to me to become acquainted with more of Verbal's friends, whom he had known for years.

Mother and Daddy made a trip to Houston during this time to be with the Kilgores and to spend time with Verbal and me. I was proud to show them our very modest home, and they were pleased we had a place to call our own.

After spending several days in Houston, it was time to leave for our next revival in Texarkana, Texas, to be with Bro. Huss Shearer and his wife and family. Bro. Shearer came from a background of solid belief in the gifts of the Spirit and freedom of worship, so he and Verbal were in close spiritual agreement regarding the moving of the Holy Ghost.

Bro. Shearer's aunt, Sis. Schrader, was recognized in her home state of Oklahoma as a great woman of God. People would meet with her to determine if she had a word from the Lord for them. It was commonly believed she was a Prophetess, and God used her in a mighty way. When Mother and Daddy were pastoring in Morris, Oklahoma, in the early fifties, Daddy felt a strong urge from the Holy Ghost to start a church in San Jose, California. This would be a huge move for them, and Daddy wanted to make sure he was in the perfect will of God before he made the final decision. He and Mother visited Sis. Schrader, along with some of their other friends. They had a prayer meeting, and after they stopped praying, Sis. Schrader had a word from the Lord for Daddy. She told him God would direct him to a place toward the setting of the sun, and he would establish a church there. Out of that church, five other churches would be born. This was the confirmation Daddy had been looking for, and they soon began preparing to move from Morris to San Jose, California.

The church in Texarkana was a good church, but Bro. Shearer felt it had never come to the place of deep commitment to the moving of the Holy Ghost and freedom of worship, which he felt was essential for revival. Verbal moved into this revival with a burden, longing for the outpouring of the Holy Ghost and to see the victory that Bro. and Sis. Shearer had been interceding with God for.

Verbal organized the ten o'clock morning prayer meetings as in all his revivals. We would also go early to church every night to pray before the service started. During the morning prayer meetings, Bro. and Sis. Shearer and faithful prayer warriors entered a time of intercession along with Verbal and me. These times of prayer were intense, and God always met with us there. While teaching on the power of intercession, Verbal recounted this story:

> *"One night in a revival, I knelt in desperation, asking God for someone to receive the Holy Ghost. I said, 'Lord, daylight won't catch me here in the morning if someone isn't filled with the Holy Ghost tonight. I refuse to stay in a place where I can't pray someone through to the Holy Ghost.' By the time I raised my head from praying, two men were receiving the Holy Ghost."*

Resistance to the moving of the Holy Ghost brought about tension in some of the services. This was troubling. Finally, after some nights had passed and after some fearful judgment messages were preached, we had a Holy Ghost overshadowing, and the Lord brought great victory and anointing to the revival.

Verbal and Bro. Shearer talked about taking the revival out of the sanctuary and into a tent, which would be set up in the church parking lot. It was late springtime; the weather would be accommodating, so they went forward with these plans. God smiled on these efforts, and many visitors were drawn to this unusual revival setting. The Holy Ghost fell in a mighty way, and soon, we were seeing the harvest of souls we had been longing to experience.

Early in his ministry, the Lord had spoken to Verbal and promised to give him a one-hundred-soul revival. This proved to be a blessing in his evangelistic meetings because he approached every revival with that promise in mind. He would pray and believe, trusting this would be the manifestation of the promise. This lifted his faith, and he could also inspire the congregation to believe with him for this mighty outpouring. Although he had many victorious meetings with numbers of people receiving the Holy Ghost, he had yet to experience the long-awaited revival. However, he never wavered in his belief that God would fulfill the promise He had made to him.

While we were in the tent revival, Mother and Daddy came to be with us for a few days. One night, after the close of service, Mother told me of an angelic visitation she had seen that evening. She said, "When Verbal took the service, as he was standing there waiting on the Lord, I saw an angel step to the pulpit and close his Bible." She understood that, by this angelic visitation, Verbal would not be preaching a message that night but would minister in another way.

Bro and Sis. Shearer had provided a room for us in a small motel near the church. In addition to our bedroom, we had a small kitchenette, supplied with the essential dishes and utensils needed to prepare a meal. I enjoyed this feature, although I was still not skilled in the culinary arts.

The Shearers lived in a house on the outskirts of Texarkana at the top of a sloping lot. It was a modest home but very comfortable, filled with their lovely family and kind hospitality.

Sis. Shearer prepared many meals for us, and it was a pleasure to be in their home with their children. Everything she cooked was delicious, but our favorite part of these dinners was her homemade yeast rolls. They were perfect, and from time to time, she would make cinnamon rolls, too, which were simply fabulous.

During the last week of the revival, after the altar service had ended, Sis. Shearer asked me to go with her to the dining room in the back of the sanctuary. There, they had prepared a baby shower for me. The women of the church donated money for this shower, and Sis. Shearer bought everything I would need for our newborn baby and carefully wrapped each package. I sat down to the joyful task of opening the gifts. They had provided blankets, gowns, diapers, undershirts, socks, shoes, and anything else I could have wished for. Afterward, we were served cake and punch, and I felt I was the most blessed, expectant mother in the world. When we returned to our room that night, I took everything out of their boxes and wrappings and examined them again. Verbal and I were both gratified to know our baby was supplied with every essential needed. It was still a few months before the baby would be born, and these beautiful gifts made it seem very real.

The closing of the revival was bittersweet. Since revivals usually lasted several weeks, we were blessed with the time and opportunity to become closely acquainted with the saints. Verbal won the hearts of the congregation with his preaching and his burden for them, their families, and their city.

There was also the faithful group committed to the ten o'clock morning prayer meetings. These people shared the burden for revival and loved the work of God. We truly learned to love them during this time, so saying goodbye after forming these close friendships was not always easy. Nevertheless, Verbal was always careful to ensure the whole congregation understood their loyalties belonged to their pastor, not to an evangelist who would soon be out of their lives.

Again, we loaded up the car, including the new baby clothes, expressed our love and appreciation to Bro. and Sis. Shearer and their family, and then headed back to Houston.

Chapter 14

Return Home

After leaving Texarkana, we returned to Houston, and it was good to be home. We continued preparing for the arrival of our newborn. Of course, we didn't know what the sex would be, but we were both hoping for a baby boy. The three grandchildren in Sis. Bean's family were girls, and all the grandchildren born into the Shoemake clan at this time were girls, too, so a baby boy would have been held in high regard.

Verbal and I talked about names for the baby; I was set on Verbal Winston Bean II if it was a boy, and we thought Laura Kay would be a beautiful name if it were a girl. Somehow, Laura Kay captured our imagination and often our conversations. I don't know what triggered our silly habit, but if we saw a disobedient or unattractive baby girl, we would say, "That's probably Laura Kay." This didn't happen frequently because most baby girls are delightful, but occasionally, we would notice one who didn't fit our perception of what we would expect, and we would laugh and say, "There goes Laura Kay again, screaming her head off." We did this so often and for such a long period of time that we utterly turned against the name Laura Kay.

We had another pretty unorthodox conversation about our upcoming parenthood. One day, Verbal looked steadily at me and said, "What if our baby is ugly?"

I calmly replied with the wisdom of the ages, "We'll never know." And it was true; our babies were all astoundingly beautiful.

While in Houston that fall, the Greens Bayou church also gave us a baby shower. They pooled their money and bought us a Porta-crib. We couldn't have imagined anything more exciting than this. We were both so entranced by this whole baby situation that we could hardly wait to get back to our house and set the crib up in our bedroom. The lovely layette the Texarkana church had given us was all carefully washed, folded, and placed in the drawer set aside for this very purpose.

It's touching to remember Verbal's involvement in this chapter of our lives. He came from a very loving family; as I've said before, his siblings doted on him. I, too, had been born into a very affectionate family, and to tell the truth, we were both just a little out of balance regarding the importance of babies in our lives. Verbal was totally committed to the importance of his ministry, but his devotion to me and his family was completely unconditional.

I was still reading about natural childbirth and calmly discussing with Verbal how all these things would impact my labor. I tried to show a brave, confident attitude, but I was secretly hoping and praying I would have the strength and courage to go through the labor and birth the way Verbal and I wanted it to be done. I suspected that some of the more challenging aspects of childbirth had not been clearly described. I remember thinking the Kilgores, when hearing about our plans, were a little skeptical and unconvinced it would be as easy as the author seemed to believe.

During this time, Verbal preached in various local churches. Sometimes, just for a night or the weekend. The holidays were coming up, and since Verbal's revivals usually lasted several weeks, he didn't schedule one. Consequently, these shorter meetings were a real blessing to us.

That fall, Verbal took me to Bay City to meet and spend time with Bro. and Sis. Marvin Cole. Verbal was scheduled to preach a few nights in the church they pastored. This allowed me to become acquainted with these very special friends of Verbal. He had expressed to me how important his friendship with Bro. Cole had been. Verbal and Bro. Cole had been raised close together and had been acquainted for several years. They greatly respected each other but could hardly have been more different in looks, demeanor, and personality.

Verbal had previously preached a revival for Bro. and Sis. Cole and their friendship became even closer than before. He believed Bro. Cole was a prophet of God used mightily in the Spirit; they were indeed kindred spirits. He also had a lot of appreciation for Sis. Cole. She was a committed intercessor and carried the burden of Bro. Cole's ministry close to her heart.

Verbal often talked about the trip he and Bro. Cole had taken to the South American nation of Brazil. It had been a life-changing experience for him. He had long been fascinated by the stories he had heard from missionary accounts. He loved to recount testimonies he had heard from Bro. Larsen, Bro. Drost, and the Thompsons. This had been a long-awaited dream for Verbal, and he was filled with anticipation to minister in a country that had long weighed heavily on his heart.

He then told me about their flight to Brazil. The night before they were to leave on their trip, Verbal and Bro. Cole felt called to deep intercessory prayer. For two and a half hours, they prayed and interceded. The following day, they left on their trip.

They were on a flight that would stop off for refueling on an island in the Caribbean, and the runway ran right down to the ocean. Verbal said there was a heavy, dense fog; the pilot could not see the runway and was relying on information he received from the tower for directions. Somehow, he was given the wrong information and undershot the runway about a mile. "It looked certain the plane would crash into the ocean," he said, "When

Passport picture

suddenly it seemed a hand lifted the aircraft one hundred feet into the air, and we landed safely. That was the reason for the hours of intercession we experienced."

Verbal continued his narrative, "After we landed, the pilot walked past everybody straight to us and said, "Gentlemen, come watch us fly." Bro. Cole wasn't interested, but I was thrilled to be invited to sit with the pilot and co-pilot. Being allowed to stay there for the rest of the flight, I was able to see where we were going before any of the rest of the passengers could. I got to see miles ahead of us, mountains and gorges, the green forests and lakes. It was a marvelous experience. Then, to top off this unforgettable day, the Lord spoke a scripture to my heart. 'Blessed is the man whom thou choosest, and causest to approach unto thee.' (Psa. 65:4) It is a blessing," he said, "when God calls you into the cockpit to see what lies ahead. He lets you know His plan before it happens and prepares you for things that have not yet occurred."

This evangelistic trip to Brazil was a highlight of Verbal's life. He was deeply touched by so many of the things he experienced, but the worship of the saints made a permanent impression on him. Later, he told the saints in our church, "In Brazil, while you're preaching, you never stop and ask the people to praise the Lord. If you do, you will never get to finish your message. They get lost in the Spirit and will continue as long as possible. I hope and pray we can reach that level of worship here in Greens Bayou."

While telling me about Bro. and Sis. Cole, he also described the revival he had held in Bay City. It was a wonderful revival, and the church was blessed with a prophetess. Verbal said she was a very quiet, reserved lady and was always conscious of the need to operate her gifts in the perfect will of God. She was a blessing in the revival and was extremely careful to stay under the leadership of Bro. Cole.

They had a victorious revival with many signs, wonders, and works of the Holy Ghost. They also had a great infilling of people receiving the gift of the Holy Ghost. Verbal said this was one of his most fruitful revivals.

Then, Verbal continued his Bay City stories. "While walking downtown one day, I passed a department store. In their window was a large box and a recliner. The sign in the window stated that anyone who could reveal the box's contents would receive the recliner as a prize. A hint was given about the contents of the box. It said, 'Many men use this, and a few women do.' I went back to the parsonage and told Bro. and Sis. Cole, 'I'm going to win that recliner for you.'

Verbal told me how he learned what was in the box. Soon after seeing the department store promotion, Verbal said he remembered a newspaper story about Bonnie and Clyde. The article described the unlawful exploits of these outlaws and included a picture of the couple, which showed Bonnie smoking a cigar. He immediately returned to the department store, told the manager a cigar was in the box, and claimed the recliner for the Coles.

We spent many hours fellowshipping with them and discussing the things of God. I was touched to hear of the wonderful works of Jesus Christ that they had seen and experienced.

Bro. Cole told us that after he received the Holy Ghost, he wanted to be involved in every aspect of the church, and it became his heart's desire to sing in the choir. He said, "The choir director discouraged me in this endeavor because she recognized I couldn't carry a tune, not at all, not even a little bit. This became a conflict between the choir leader and me because we were both convinced, we were right. I wanted to sing for the Lord, and she was hindering me. Some nights, I managed to slip into the choir before she could stop me, and I counted this a great victory. Our disagreement went on for some time until I was completely discouraged and upset."

"Finally, in desperation," he continued, "I went out to a chicken coop in my backyard. There, I had an intense conversation with Jesus. I explained my desire to sing in the choir and glorify God. I told the Lord, 'I don't need to sing solos or special songs; just ordinary songs or hymns will do.' I prayed intensely over this issue, burning in my heart until I finally felt victory. Miraculously, God gave me the ability to sing. It was amazing. I could carry a decent tune and finally was good enough to sing not only in the choir but also with a men's quartet in the church."

We laughed as he dramatically told us about this experience, especially at his ongoing disagreement with the choir leader. But despite the humor of this situation, it revealed the personal connection Bro. Cole felt with his Savior.

Verbal's ministry was somewhat controversial at this time. Consequently, it was important to Verbal to know he and the pastor were in agreement regarding his ministry, standards, the operation of the gifts of the Spirit, and freedom of worship.

Because he was a revivalist, Verbal never wavered in his conviction that it was the heartbeat of God. After the revival 'broke,' as he described it, he searched, sought, and reached for the sinner or backslider in every service. His sermons on hell were compelling and usually filled the altars with saints and sinners alike. He would describe the desolation and despair covering the lost on Judgment Day. His descriptions of hell were detailed and heartbreaking. But the greatest sorrow of all, he would explain, was to know that people who rejected the Lord would be cast from the presence of Jesus Christ for all eternity. These sermons filled the hearts of those who were away from God with conviction and soul-crushing grief and fear. They would fall on the altar, with tears streaming down their faces, seeking a place of repentance.

But there was another side of the coin, which Verbal also described with great conviction and power. He preached Jesus came to suffer and die on Calvary so no one would have to go to hell. After describing the agony and suffering of our precious Savior on the cross, he would go on to depict the glories of Heaven in word pictures. I can still hear the sound of his voice as he began to quote:

"And I John saw the holy city, new Jerusalem, coming down from God out of heaven, prepared as a bride adorned for her husband.

And he carried me away in the spirit to a great and high mountain, and shewed me

that great city, the holy Jerusalem, descending out of heaven from God.

Having the glory of God: and her light was like unto a stone most precious, even like a jasper stone, clear as crystal;

And had a wall great and high, and had twelve gates, and at the gates twelve angels, and names written thereon, which are the names of the twelve tribes of the children of Israel:

On the east three gates; on the north three gates; on the south three gates; and on the west three gates.

And the wall of the city had twelve foundations, and in them the names of the twelve apostles of the Lamb.

And he that talked with me had a golden reed to measure the city, and the gates thereof, and the wall thereof.

And the city lieth foursquare, and the length is as large as the breadth: and he measured the city with the reed, twelve thousand furlongs. The length and the breadth and the height of it are equal.

And he measured the wall thereof, an hundred and forty and four cubits, according to the measure of a man, that is, of the angel.

And the building of the wall of it was of
jasper: and the city was pure gold, like unto
clear glass.

And the foundations of the wall of the city
were garnished with all manner of precious
stones. The first foundation was jasper; the
second, sapphire; the third, a chalcedony;
the fourth, an emerald;

The fifth, sardonyx, the sixth, sardius; the
seventh, chrysolyte; the eighth, beryl; the
ninth, a topaz; the tenth, a chrysoprasus; the
eleventh, a jacinth; the twelfth, an
amethyst.

And the twelve gates were twelve pearls;
every several gate was of one pearl: and the
street of the city was pure gold, as it were
transparent glass.

And I saw no temple therein: for the Lord
God Almighty and the Lamb are the temple
of it.

And the city had no need of the sun, neither
of the moon, to shine in it: for the glory of
God did lighten it, and the Lamb is the light
thereof."
(Rev. 21:2, 10-23)

By the time Verbal had finished quoting this glittering description
of New Jerusalem, we were all longing and determined to reach
Heaven and attain eternal life no matter the cost. Saints and sinners
alike were drawn into the awareness of the place Jesus Christ had
prepared especially for us so we could be together with Him for all

eternity. Hands were raised all over the auditorium, and we would make our way to the altars as the Holy Ghost flowed like a river of oil over us all. The memory alone of these messages still moves me today, just as it did many years ago. I trust I will always treasure the touch of the divine in my life until the day I die.

Chapter 15

The Waiting Game

Nylotis and Eugene Goudeau, and Verbal

We spent Thanksgiving that year in Orange with Verbal's sister Nylotis and her family. Sis. Bean came, too; it was a houseful of hospitality and joy. Nylotis, being the excellent cook she was, had baked pies, made candy, and done all she could to make this time memorable. She was also very patient while explaining exactly how to make cornbread dressing. Mother had cooked cornbread dressing for years, but I was never curious enough to ask how it was prepared. Things were different now; I had a wonderful husband and wanted to be an excellent cook for him. Sis. Bean had many abilities, but cooking was not her strong point. I was in the enviable position of being able to cook meals for my husband, and he honestly thought they were delicious.

During this holiday season, Sis. Bean shared the story of a beautiful eight-year-old boy with brown eyes, dimples, and dark curly hair. His name was Michael Joseph. Upon learning about his terrible home life, she felt guided by the Lord to adopt him. It was a lengthy process, but she was successful after a year had passed. He was welcomed into the Bean family, and we were delighted to have this young boy join us.

After the holiday, we returned to Houston, and as my due date drew near, both Verbal and I longed to meet our new baby. December 17 passed, and still, we waited. Mother had flown out to Houston a week before to be with me when our baby was born, but, alas, my baby hadn't gotten the memo of her birth date, so she ignored it.

One evening, we were at the house with Mother and started talking about baby names. Since the name for a boy was settled, we discussed what name we would choose if I had a girl. I explained to Mother we had chosen the name Laura Kay but decided we didn't like it after all. We talked about names we would like if the baby were a girl, but none of them seemed an exact fit. Finally, Mother said, "Bro. and Sis. Wilson named their baby girl Jana.

How do you like that name?" It seemed perfect to Verbal and me, so we settled on Jana Kay. Several more days passed, and there was still no baby. Finally, exactly one week after my due date, my labor started.

When I was taken to the labor room and prepared for the birth, I tried to recall the information in the books I had read explaining that natural childbirth can be relatively pain-free. That all just seemed to me to be lies from hell when I started labor. Those were the days when the husband was sent to the waiting room–which was aptly named–until the baby was born. Thankfully, Mother was allowed to be with me through most of the labor, and she was a loving comfort. Finally, on December 24, 1962, Jana Kay Bean made her appearance. She weighed in at 9 lb. 6 oz. Verbal was soon called into the room, and we were absolutely mesmerized by her pink cheeks and headful of dark hair. We loved her that day and have loved her ever since.

The sad ending to this epistle was that since Mother was a week early for Jana's birth, and Christmas was the next day, she felt she had to fly home as soon as possible. Early the following morning, she gave me a beautiful dressing gown, hugged me tearfully, and left for the airport. My doctor kept Jana and me in the hospital for five days, which was common during that time. Those five days proved to be a great blessing to me. When we went home, I was feeling better and had become closely acquainted with my new baby girl, so my first few days at home were better than I expected.

Jana's Porta-crib was set up in our bedroom, under a window. One night, we had gone to sleep in a very warm house. Houston weather had been unseasonably hot, but a cold front blew in during the night. When Jana cried for her 2:00 a.m. feeding, we awoke to a freezing cold room. We quickly jumped out of bed and rushed to her crib, and horror of horrors, she felt chilled. We were devastated to think our precious baby girl had gotten very cold during this dreadful night. I climbed back into our bed with Jana to feed her, and we were all wrapped up together in our blankets. Verbal was still worried she might be too cold, so he moved her crib into the hallway next to our wall heater. Jana was no worse for the wear because of this adventure during the night, but Verbal and I suffered regret for some time.

When Jana was two weeks old, we couldn't wait any longer to introduce her to the world. The Rambo family was singing at Bro. O.W. Williams's church, so we dressed her in her finest, wrapped her up well, and went to church to enjoy the concert. Verbal and I were very impressed with the Rambos. Dottie was the picture of holiness, and their music was simply marvelous to us both. For years, whenever they released a new album, we rushed to buy it. Dottie's music was very distinctive, and she wrote many unforgettable songs. Verbal sang several of her compositions through the years as a solo or with a trio, as was his preference. These were some of his favorites:

"Is That the Lights of Home I See?"
"He Looked Beyond My Faults and Saw My Need"
"Sheltered in the Arms of God"

As I've already stated, Verbal loved gospel music. He never listened to any other kind. We always had the record player on when we could. It was a blessing to hear the Goodman Family, the Statesmen Quartet, and the Blackwood Brothers. When I hear those classic songs now, it takes me back to those days, and I remember once more what a large part gospel music played in our hearts and in our lives.

We stayed in the Houston area for the next month until it was time to get back into the harvest field. We loaded Jana's crib and her things, put our suitcases and boxes into the car, and headed to California for a revival.

After visiting for a few days with my family and introducing Jana to her relatives, we drove to Madera, where Verbal was scheduled to preach a revival for Bro. and Sis. Winfred Toole. We immediately fell in love with the Toole family. They had a precious daughter named Karen and were the epitome of gracious hospitality. Their modest home was spotless, and they arranged for us to stay in one of their bedrooms during the revival. They were all very witty, including Karen, and the hours spent with them were some of our most precious times.

Bro. Toole was an outstanding Bible teacher, and he taught most Sunday mornings. Verbal was always blessed when the pastor would preach or teach, and Bro. Toole was no exception. His sermon, "The Uncommitted Christ," remained a treasured memory for Verbal.

Sis. Toole was an extraordinary homemaker and cook. I'm a little embarrassed to remember how much she did and how little I did. I always helped wash the dishes but was not confident enough in my cooking ability to offer to cook a meal for them. They seemed to delight in having Jana there and gave her a lot of attention.

The Madera revival was remarkable in many ways. It lasted sixteen weeks, and we saw many demonstrations of the Holy Ghost during that time. Bro. Harvey and Sis. Cora Conner started coming to the revival; this is their testimony, as told by Bro. Harvey Connor: "We were afraid to come to the services, and we were afraid to stay home. But we could not stay away because of the power of God in each service. This power helped to establish us to live for God for the rest of our lives. We developed and maintained a deep love for the real Apostolic Power. We kept coming nightly and became rock-solid members of the church."

Bro. Toole witnessed this spiritual encounter, "The Connors were faithful pillars in the church until their deaths, many years later."

During this revival, while Verbal was praying one day, God revealed to him that a certain leader in the church was smoking. When Verbal told Bro. Toole about this, he could hardly believe it. He said, "This man is the best man in our congregation."

In humility, Verbal said, "I'll go pray about it again." After praying, he returned to Bro. Toole and told him, "Yes, it's him."

Bro. Toole and Verbal met with the man and told him what God had revealed to Verbal, and he confessed he had been smoking and committing some other sins as well.

During the revival, many visitors from neighboring congregations attended, and revival fires seemed to spread to many of those churches. Bro. and Sis. Toole had fasted, prayed, and believed God for a Holy Ghost breakthrough in Madera, and God answered this faithful couple with a mighty revival.

One night remains clear in my memory. After I got settled in the pew with Jana and all her paraphernalia, I looked down at my feet and saw I was wearing my house slippers. Those days, you always dressed up every night for church, and ladies always wore high heels. There I was, the evangelist's wife, in house slippers. The depth of that embarrassment is proven by this fact; I have forgotten many incidents of the revival, but I still remember the House Slipper Fiasco. More of the events of the Madera revival are in the Revival Testimonials.

Chapter 16

Laurel Revival

After Jana's birth, we continued evangelizing, staying in evangelistic quarters or in the pastor's home. When we went to Laurel, Mississippi, they had evangelistic quarters in the church's basement. We always took Jana's Porta-crib with us, so no matter where we were, she had her familiar bed to sleep in.

Both Bro. and Sis. Roy Lawrence were friendly and kind. I thought Sis. Lawrence was very beautiful, and she had a lovely soprano voice. At this time, they had three lively sons. It always amazed me to see her interaction with her boys. She never seemed to raise her voice, no matter how chaotic the situation. She would gently take one or two boys by the hand and talk quietly to them. It was amazing to see how effective this type of correction was. Sis. Lawrence was a wonderful cook and hostess, and we spent many hours visiting and fellowshipping with the family.

Bro. Lawrence was a very dignified and scholarly man; it was always a little surprising to see him under the anointing and worshipping freely and exuberantly.

The Laurel revival was challenging, to say the least. A deep-seated element in the church stood against Bro. Lawrence and Verbal's ministry. Hours were spent in intercessory prayer, and Verbal's ministry reflected the power brought to the pulpit by this intercession. It was spiritual warfare, and often, it seemed the future success of the church was threatened.

After many nights of powerful, stirring sermons, with gifts of the Spirit operating frequently, the opposition group became more open in their resistance to this revival. Some doctrinal issues were at stake, and certainly, the authority of the pastor was questioned. Tongues and interpretation by Verbal Bean from a recorded message.

"For indeed, it is not my desire to leave you, for I have loved you and desired that you be saved. How long have I dealt with you and spared you, when you cared for nothing for your soul and for your God? O careless soul, I have dealt, spared, and shown mercy, and all of my love has been turned in your direction.

But you have said, 'Away, for I do not want to serve the Lord.' But I say unto you, this is your hour; this is your moment. When I have hidden my face, whether it be from a man or a nation, who can find me? When I cover my throne with darkness, who can touch me? I say unto my people who walk before me: fear me, for the hour is late. Stay close to me, for I am coming to visit among you. I must awaken you with the visitation of judgment. If there is not an awakening, my hand shall come upon you, and the heart that has

> *resisted me will be the target of my divine judgment.*
>
> *I appeal to my children. If you care, draw near tonight. Come close, pray, search your hearts, and purge yourselves. I will not accept partial repentance; I will not take half-heartedness. I must have all of you."*

Conviction gripped the audience, and saints flooded the altars, pouring out their hearts to God. Sadly, some did not respond and were left in the hands of a righteous God. Thankfully, even with all the spiritual opposition, the Spirit of the Lord still moved powerfully. Finally, a few families left the church, but the revival continued. Victory and deliverance came in a mighty way, and the church was blessed to experience a wonderful harvest of souls. Verbal told of this experience:

> *"During one service, two backsliders were in the audience sitting in the next to last pew. While I was trying to reach them, in the middle of my message, I said suddenly, 'Don't tell me you don't know what I'm talking about.' They immediately started crying and came to the altar and prayed through to the Holy Ghost.*
>
> *Later, a saint who was sitting behind them told me that just as I was about to say those words, one of them leaned over to the other and said, 'I don't know what he's talking about.'"*

Chapter 17

The O'Briens

As newlyweds, Verbal and I enjoyed long conversations about friends and family. I loved these times because I felt I was learning to know Verbal more closely as he described his friends to me. He spent a long time talking about Bro. A. L. and Sis. Emalie O'Brien and describing the Starks, Louisiana, church. This was a powerful Holy Ghost church with a large congregation, probably numbering between 250 and 300 members. This was amazing because the population of Starks itself was very small, around 1,000 people.

Verbal had preached a very long and successful revival in Starks, and he told me of many manifestations of the Spirit they had experienced during that time. They had somber services when it seemed the judgment of God might be poured out any moment; some had squandered their lives to the rule of Satan, who had left them bereft and broken, and they would walk, weeping all the way, to the altar. Conviction was so strong that backsliders would fall on their faces, pleading for forgiveness. Then they would have power-packed services where people would be dancing and shouting all over the building; worship saturated the atmosphere. One night, Verbal told the church that he felt a mighty reaping was coming. The following Sunday night, there were thirty in the altar, and twelve received the Holy Ghost. It was a defining revival for the Starks Pentecostal Church; fifty people had received the Holy Ghost, and the impact of it lasted many years.

Before Verbal and I met, I had heard a lot about Bro. O'Brien, his powerful anointing and stern persona. Verbal confirmed this to me but went on to say that Bro. O'Brien was a powerfully anointed pastor and was certainly in charge of the congregation; however, he was also caring and protective of his saints. Though these two men were different in temperament and expression, they had become very close. Their friendship had deepened through the years, and they would spend hours discussing various Biblical principles, sharing their extensive views and insights into Scripture. After I had become more closely acquainted with the O'Brien's, I was privileged to hear some of these conversations, and I felt very honored to learn about the wonderful experiences they had shared.

Bro. O'Brien, like Verbal, took the calling of God on his life very seriously. It would only be after many months of friendship with Bro. and Sis. O'Brien that he felt comfortable enough around me to share his sense of humor. One night, we stayed up late visiting, and finally, Sis. O'Brien said, "Honey, I'm so tired I think you might have to carry me to bed tonight." Bro. O'Brien turned to Verbal and said, "Elder, I think we're going to have to go find my winch." We had a good laugh about this, and even Sis. O'Brien thought it was funny.

Sis. O'Brien was a unique individual and was deeply devoted to the work of God. She never preached but was highly anointed as she taught the young people and ladies in their church. She was also very involved in the music ministry. Sis. O'Brien could move the hearts of the congregation as she introduced the songs she would be directing. She often led the choir during general conferences and was used to direct choirs during camp meetings and youth camps in the Louisiana District. She was quick to smile, and I was truly drawn to her because of the loving force of her personality.

After visiting with the O'Briens, we returned to Houston and finished preparing for our next revival. We didn't hear from the O'Briens for several weeks, but as we were closing the revival in Sulphur for Bro. and Sis. Cranford, Verbal got a call from Bro. O'Brien. He explained he felt the need to take a three-month leave of absence from the church and asked us to come and care for the congregation while he and Sis. O'Brien were gone. We were pleased with this invitation because we wouldn't be under the load of a revival but would still be working for the Lord, and we always looked forward to being in Starks.

Before the O'Briens left on their trip, Sis. O'Brien carefully schooled me in all the ministries she carried for their congregation. She taught the Sunday school class for the young people and led them in prayer in the 'Upper Room' before the Sunday night service. This was a powerful time for them all, and she did her best to make sure they were prayed through and ready for the coming week.

Sis. O'Brien also led the Tuesday morning prayer meeting for her ladies. These ladies knew how to pray, and the Tuesday meetings were power-packed. After prayer, she would talk to the ladies and encourage them in their spiritual lives. Sis. O'Brien also led the Ladies Auxiliary, whose primary function was to raise money.

After the O'Briens left on their trip, my first responsibility was to lead the Tuesday morning ladies' prayer meeting. I got through the prayer part of the meeting, but when it came to encouraging the ladies and sharing the Word, I felt I was a novice. I had spent a lot of time just thinking of a subject to talk about, and then preparing to share this was very challenging. I would study the Bible and meditate to make sure I wasn't falling short in my ministry with these precious ladies.

I taught children in Sunday School as a teenager at home but had never taught a youth class before. When preparing for these lessons, I would visit Bro. O'Brien's office, pull out his concordances and Bible study books and write my pages of notes. Verbal thought this was very funny. He even went so far as to draw a cartoon of me teaching. He illustrated me standing behind a pulpit covered with a stack of books I could barely see over, and I held a Bible in my hands. In the balloon above my head, I said, "Now, class, some commentators disagree with other commentators, so we will have to go to the Bible for our conclusion."

Earlier, one evening, Verbal heard Sis. O'Brien as she was teaching her young people the importance of paying tithes. She told them they should be faithful tithers so that they would be blessed. Inspired by this, he also drew a cartoon of her. He depicted her leading a choir, and she was giving the 'repeat' sign to the song they were singing, "If you pay tithes, Heaven belongs to you!" We spent the rest of the evening laughing about his artwork.

While teaching the youth class, I had the recurring fear that I would run out of the lesson before I ran out of time; then what would I talk about? One Sunday morning will never be forgotten. Verbal taught the adult Bible class while I was teaching the young people. This Sunday, Verbal's teaching became preaching, and conviction fell on his class. The altar call took a while, and in my classroom, what I had dreaded came to pass. The lesson was finished, but I couldn't dismiss the class; Verbal was still preaching.

The lesson that Sunday was about leprosy. As the class time lengthened, I spent a long time describing the horrible repercussions of leprosy and how it is a type of sin. Frankly, I was trying to kill time. I found out later that two young men who were backslidden came to Sunday school hung over from a Saturday night of drinking. As my descriptions of leprosy became more graphic, the two boys became sicker and sicker until they had to leave the class. Finally, after what had seemed an eternity, the signal was given to dismiss my class.

Verbal later described our time in Starks this way: "Nita pastored the church while I babysat." It was true. Verbal took care of Jana while I tried my hardest to carry on Sis. O'Brien's ministry, but he was still the dynamic evangelist I had married. We had powerfully anointed services while we were there and were blessed to

Verbal, Jana, and me

introduce twenty new converts to the O'Briens when they returned home.

This was a truly enjoyable time in my life. It was rewarding to feel needed in Kingdom ministry. The Starks congregation was loving and patient with Bro. Bean's bride and kindly shared their love for him with me, too.

After the O'Briens returned home, and Sis. O'Brien heard of my struggles preparing for my various responsibilities. She said to me one day, "Nita, you didn't need to go to all that preparation for the ladies' prayer meetings; I just always talk about something from my heart." I didn't tell her, but the fact was, there wasn't a lot in my heart to teach about at that time, so I had to go to the Word for a word.

The O'Briens had been avid hunters for several years and had become very well-educated about the ins and outs of deer hunting. A few years later, we were in the company of several young preachers, and the subject of deer hunting came up. Sis. O'Brien stated she, too, loved to hunt deer. One of the young preachers proudly told us he had killed twenty-five deer during his hunting experiences. He turned to Sis. O'Brien and asked, "Sis. O'Brien, how many deer have you killed?"

She smiled, then replied, "I quit counting when I reached one hundred."

When the O'Briens returned from their leave of absence, we stayed on for a few days to fellowship and catch up on all the news. Bro. O'Brien asked Verbal if he liked to hunt deer, and Verbal told him he would love to try but never had the opportunity. At the next service, Bro. O'Brien proceeded to raise an offering to purchase a .30-06 rifle for Verbal. The church responded very generously, and Verbal could buy his beautiful rifle.

Soon afterward, Bro. and Sis. O'Brien arranged a hunting trip in the Texas Hill Country, where they had a deer lease, and invited us to join them. We gathered all the needed camping equipment, dropped Jana off in Houston to stay with Sis. Bean, and drove to Fredericksburg. Then we unloaded two tents, ice chests, a Coleman camping stove, warm clothes, bedding, and cots.

This area of Texas was ideal for camping and hunting. It's a land of many springs, rivers, stony hills, and steep canyons. There are trees of every description, from the Texas persimmon to chinaberry trees, and the air was clean and fragrant with the scent of nearby plants and bushes. Bro. O'Brien did most of the cooking, and soon after the camp was set up, we could smell the burning charcoal he was using to grill the steaks we would enjoy for dinner. Our senses were keen as we viewed the millions of stars covering the skies, smelled the sweet country air, and knew that the beauty of this experience would be forever engraved among our favorite memories.

Verbal killed his first deer there and was hooked for life; he loved deer hunting. Early one morning, he took me out to the deer stand to see if I, too, would enjoy hunting. He told me the first hunting requirement is to remain completely silent, which I didn't relish but was willing to try. After I had unwrapped my third piece of candy, he kindly informed me that maybe hunting wasn't my sport.

The Hunter and his Bride

Sis. Emalie O'Brien and me – Sharp Shooters!

During our stay, Verbal set up a target and encouraged me to try
out his new rifle. He carefully showed me how to hold the gun and
aim my shot. I tried to follow his instructions, but I wasn't a fan.
The rifle kicked too hard, no matter how closely I placed it into my

shoulder, and the sound of the rifle shot was deafening. I never did learn to enjoy shooting a gun.

However, I enjoyed camping with Verbal and the family whenever we had the opportunity. Verbal continued hunting when the occasion arose, which was an enjoyable part of his life. But now it was time to get back onto the road and into the evangelistic life we loved.

As we continued to travel, we had less time to enjoy our home. We relished the times we spent in Houston, resting and catching up with family and friends, but these occasions seemed to become fewer and farther apart.

It soon became apparent that we would be better served by selling our home and getting a travel trailer. Bro. and Sis. Ronnie Willhoite were good friends, and they had recently begun traveling full-time, conducting Sunday school promotions and revivals. While we were having dinner with them one evening, they told us about the travel trailer they had designed and ordered. The manufacturing company was willing to rearrange the floor plan to their specifications. We were very interested to know this was a possibility. We had looked at some travel trailers, but none seemed to have the arrangement we felt suited our small family.

After we met with the Willhoites, we put our home up for sale. The house payment had become a burden on an evangelist's income.

This was bittersweet for us; we had spent some wonderful times in our home and had many cherished memories, but it became increasingly difficult to travel from our car and stay in various places. Our house sold quickly, and we began to pack our household goods into barrels. We sold our few pieces of furniture and loaded up our car again to return to the evangelistic field.

When Verbal contacted the trailer manufacturing company, they were willing to work with us on the floor plan for our new residence. Although we only had one child at the time, we hoped to enlarge our family before long, so we ordered twin bunk beds to be installed in Jana's small room. Until our trailer was finished, we stayed in the evangelistic quarters or the parsonage with the pastor and his family.

By now, I was longing for a place of our own. Jana was a good toddler, but she was still very young. While we were staying in someone else's home, I worried constantly that she would break something or be an inconvenience. I was counting the weeks until our trailer would be finished. Also, I discovered I was expecting another baby, so having our place was essential to Verbal and me.

Chapter 18

Fort Worth Revival

I had heard many stories about Bro. C. W. Shew, and felt some anticipation to meet him, but I also felt a small amount of dread. It was said he was severe and could sometimes be judgmental. When we closed our latest revival, we went to Fort Worth, Texas, for the Fourth of July Conference Bro. Shew and his church hosted each year. Bro. and Sis. Shew invited us to stay in their home. Outstanding preachers from many different states came to preach and fellowship there.

In the morning service one day, I met Bro. and Sis. William Garrett, a remarkably attractive couple. They were pastoring in Joplin, Missouri. They had been new converts in the Orange, Texas, church when Verbal had attended there, and they all had remained friends throughout the years. Bro. and Sis. Garrett preached a revival for Verbal while he was pastoring in South Houston. Bro. Donald Haymon describes one of the services during that revival. He said, "Bro. Garrett preached his first revival there. Oh, how sweetly the presence of the Lord flowed. I'll never forget that I was caught without a handkerchief in that meeting. While on my knees weeping, I removed a sock to wipe my tears of praise!"

The Ballestero family and many other great preachers were at the conference. It was a preacher's conference, and we were all blessed with the rich Word of God.

Sis. Shew entertained in their home most nights after service. She was also a great Bible teacher. Bro. Shew used to say, "God didn't call my wife to teach. I did." Whoever was responsible for her calling had blessed all of us who were privileged to hear her minister.

Bro. and Sis. Shew had a beautiful German shepherd dog. Jana was just a toddler at this time and loved to be in the backyard of the parsonage. We noticed that one day, while Jana was playing outside, the dog came alongside her and seemed to push her back. Bro. Shew was getting ready to discipline his dog for aggressively pushing Jana aside when he saw the rooster, who had Jana in his sight and was on his way to jump on her. The dog had quietly intervened, and we all heaped loads of praise on this protective animal.

We stayed on after the conference, and Verbal preached a revival there for Bro. Shew. During that time, the longed-for news came that our travel trailer was ready to be picked up. Verbal took a few days off to drive to Indiana to pick up the trailer and drop it off in Ft. Worth. Verbal drove to Houston the following day, loaded our car with the household belongings, and returned.

The day Verbal arrived back in Fort Worth was a blissful day for us. I loved putting our things away, hanging our clothes in our very own closets, and unpacking cooking utensils so I could prepare a meal in our kitchen, minuscule as it was.

As usual, Verbal taught the necessity of prayer, and the revival in Fort Worth was no exception. He was convinced there could never be a successful, victorious revival until the saints were willing to take on the burden of prayer and intercession. These lessons on effective prayer were taught in most, if not all, of his revivals. It became very important, and most people who heard and received these lessons learned to pray as they had never prayed before. At the conclusion of the message, he would then read the following verses:

> **"And whiles I was speaking, and praying,
> and confessing my sin and the sin of my
> people Israel, and presenting my
> supplication before the Lord my God for the
> holy mountain of my God;**
>
> **Yea, whiles I was speaking in prayer, even
> the man Gabriel, whom I had seen in the
> vision at the beginning, being caused to fly
> swiftly, touched me about the time of the
> evening oblation."**
> **(Dan. 9:20- 21).**

The revival in Fort Worth was victorious, and there were many Holy Ghost infillings. Being with the Shew family had been an education for me, and I was happy I had the opportunity to get acquainted with them all.

Leaving Fort Worth was the first time we traveled with our new trailer. The preparations for moving the trailer were not complicated, mostly making sure nothing was left on the shelves or cabinets, and we were pleased to find this was much easier than packing up suitcases.

Chapter 19

Port Arthur Revival

Bro. Murray Burr had asked Verbal to come to Port Arthur for a revival, and after several months, Verbal finally felt the time was right for a meeting there. When we arrived, Bro. and Sis. Burr's kindness and hospitality put me at ease as they welcomed us into their home. Bro. Burr had arranged a place to park our trailer in the back of their church, which was exactly where we wanted to be. Verbal was always pleased when we stayed close to the church, and he could spend time there whenever he wanted.

Bro. and Sis. Burr had one daughter, Janet, who was the light of their lives. When we would fellowship in their home after service, and it was time for Jan, as her parents called her, to go to bed, she would stand at the door of the room and quietly beckon to her daddy. No matter who the guests were or how many of them were there, Bro. Burr would leave the room and take Jan to bed, tuck her in, pray with her, and kiss her goodnight.

Sis. Burr was a very lovely lady and a fabulous cook. Her scrumptious fried shrimp was my introduction to delicious Gulf seafood, and her gumbo was mouth-watering. She was also an excellent seamstress and made most of Jan's clothes, which looked as if they had come from an exclusive children's shop.

Bro. Burr continued teaching the Bible class on Sunday mornings during the revival, and Verbal was very pleased with this arrangement. He was blessed and encouraged to hear the Word from such an excellent teacher. Bro. Burr was a learned Bible scholar, and his lessons were a blessing not only to his church congregation but to Verbal and me as well.

One Sunday morning, Bro. Burr was teaching about Joseph and his brethren. Joseph had accused his brothers of being spies. The brothers were desperately trying to convince Joseph of their honesty, and Bro. Burr read this verse in Genesis:

"We are all one man's sons; we are true men, thy servants are no spies." (Gen. 42:11)

"True men," Bro. Burr thundered, "True men! These brothers plotted to kill Joseph," he continued, "sold him into slavery and lied to their father for years, saying Joseph had been killed. True men, they were not!" Then, he continued the lesson, warning of the danger of self-deception. It was a marvelous lesson which I've never forgotten.

As the revival continued, Verbal was dealing with rebellious spirits, unrepented sin, and carnality. One night, he brought a paper sack to the pulpit with a small green plant showing out of the top. He talked about the fact that the plant looked green and healthy; then, he pulled it out of the sack, revealing a long root, much larger than the plant itself. He said, "There is a root of sin in this church which has been here for many years. This is a root which must be removed." Most of the members were faithful, loyal, and obedient, but that was being overshadowed by the few in rebellion. Verbal told the church the problem must be dealt with, and revival would follow.

> *"I believe in preaching strong messages when led by God. I don't preach those messages because others are preaching them but because God laid them on my heart. I have been impressed to bring a hard message to a congregation, but before I preached, I would pray until I felt it was the Spirit leading me and not my own feelings. God told Ezekiel to 'Eat the roll.' It must be consumed, digested, and absorbed into my spirit before I deliver it to the people. One time, I prayed three hours before I got the message in me. Then, when it was time to deliver the Word, it was like when God took Ezekiel by the lock of his head, lifted him up, and told him to prophesy.*
>
> *Hard preaching must be anointed and usually preached with tears, or it will do more harm than good. It is important for the saints to know I love them and care for their souls. Then, they will hear me."*

Verbal's approach to false doctrine, spiritual warfare, or wolves in sheep's clothing was far different from his domestic persona. He was a peace-loving man and always hoped for an agreeable outcome. However, he would stand fearless and confident and tear down the gates of hell when he was defending and protecting the tenets of faith. His courage during these times was unstoppable. He would confidently approach a demon-possessed person with no doubt in his mind about who would be the victor in these battles. Over and over, Verbal saw monumental triumphs come about as he would boldly declare the deity of Jesus Christ, who was Lord of all and had never lost a battle. This was Verbal's mindset when defending righteous precepts in his revivals.

The Port Arthur revival was a turning point for that church. For many years, the church board had controlled the tithes, and this always seemed to be an unhealthy and unscriptural situation. One night, Verbal had a dream about the church, and in his dream, there was a long serpent lying in the center aisle of the sanctuary. He stepped out, measuring the length of the snake, and it came to seventeen feet. He felt the dream had come from God and shared it with Bro. Burr. Verbal preached powerfully on the Biblical authority of the pastor for several nights, and there was some opposition, as was expected. The revival continued with fervent prayer and God-anointed messages.

A church business meeting was announced, and during that time, the suggestion was brought forward that Bro. Burr should oversee the tithes, not the church board. This resolution was put to a vote, and all the attending members voted in the affirmative except for seventeen people. This, along with many other signs from the Lord, completely changed the administration of the church. Bro. Burr and Verbal, too, felt this would bring a great victory for the future of the church, which proved to be true. Revival continued; many people received the Holy Ghost, and the name of Jesus Christ was glorified.

This was the last revival before Jennifer's birth, and Sis. Burr arranged a baby shower for me. I felt so blessed to have all these beautiful new things for our soon-to-be newborn. One lady even brought a beautiful gown and robe set for me to wear after the birth of our baby. My cup of joy overflowed with gratitude for these precious people of God.

Late in the summer of 1965, we pulled into a trailer park in Greens Bayou. We would stay here until after the birth of our second child. During that waiting period, Verbal preached in several churches in the surrounding area. Bro. Olson invited Verbal to preach for them while we were in Houston, and I discovered they were a friendly, fun-loving family. Bro. Olson was the brother of Sis. Baxter, and Verbal had been acquainted with them for several years. The Olson family, much like the Baxters, were lively, loud, and entertaining. We had good church services and great fellowship there. One thing I have remembered all these years was the delicious black walnut cake that Sis. Olson served us.

As before, Mother came to stay with us for the birth of our baby. My younger sister, Dayna, was also there, bringing her infectious personality with her. Laughter was always in the room when Dayna was there. Mother cooked some fabulous meals and helped in countless ways. But, again, our baby missed her due date, and this time, she was three weeks late before my labor began. After she was born, Verbal, Mother, and Sis. Bean were called into the room to meet this new arrival to our family. Jesus had again blessed us with a perfectly beautiful baby girl. Our Jennifer Ellen was chubby with lots of bright golden hair and made her entrance, weighing in at 9 lbs. and 6 oz. on August 30, 1965. Sadly, Mother had to return home a day after I came home from the hospital. Dayna stayed on a few days later, but too soon, she also left to return to Texas Bible College.

Jennifer proved to be a happy baby and soon was smiling at everyone. Verbal nicknamed her "Bubbles" because of all the pleasure she brought. There was almost a three-year difference between Jana and Jennifer, and they were the joy of our lives. The bunk beds in Jana's room were against the wall on one side. We had a carpenter come and build a fold-down side with slats for Jennifer's bed. We put Jennifer in the top bunk, which proved very convenient and worked well for us since our trailer had no room for a proper baby bed. We were a perfectly happy little family in our thirty-six feet by eight feet home. It was crowded at times, but we didn't mind since we were so thankful to have our own place.

While preaching in a revival one night, Verbal congratulated the pastor on moving into a new house they had just built. He expressed how thankful he was to see the parsonage finished and the pastoral family enjoying their new home, which was greatly needed. Then he added, "But I'm not sure he loves his new parsonage as much as I love our house trailer."

Verbal was captivated by children and always connected with them in his revivals. Many people have told me they received the Holy Ghost as a child in one of his revivals. He also loved to tease them and make them laugh. This side of him was surprising to many,

Verbal and me with "Bubbles"

but the fact was that he spent time getting acquainted with the children because he loved their company.

Jennifer started walking at nine months and toddled happily from one end of the trailer to the other. Now that Verbal had his own children, they were an endless joy to him. He was affectionate and generous to them. He never objected whenever I felt our Jana or Jennifer needed clothes, toys, or books. During this time, he felt his girls would enjoy a record player. For one whole afternoon, he searched for one small enough to fit in their room. He finally purchased one he thought would be suitable and bought several records for them. Verbal only listened to Gospel music himself but didn't object to our girls enjoying children's records of stories, songs, and funny tales. This was a small thing but a good indicator of Verbal's balance in life and love for his family.

Looking back at our marriage and homelife, I realize Verbal was a very balanced preacher, husband, and father. His spiritual life was well known, but his personal life was also as dedicated in its way as his spiritual life. The outcome was that his family life never detracted from his spiritual life; his spiritual life never detracted from his family life. This amazing quality left our family with a treasure trove of memories that are recounted and valued still today.

Chapter 20

Evangelistic Travels

The revival Verbal preached in Bakersfield was before we were married, but I was privileged to attend some of the services with my parents. The Bakersfield church was known as a strong, growing congregation. Verbal often talked about Bro. Terry and the impression he had left on his life, and he told me he considered Bro. Terry to be one of his close friends. This friendship was strange and complicated in some ways. Bro. Terry loved Verbal deeply and counted his ministry to be unparalleled. Verbal loved Bro. Terry, too, and admired his strong Bible preaching and teaching. Although they held many identical Biblical beliefs, Bro. Terry was not a demonstrative worshipper. Freedom of worship was one of the cornerstones of Verbal's ministry, but he told me he was not sure that Bro. Terry was ever truly converted to his way of thinking about the necessity of praise and worship. As contradictory as it seems, Bro. Terry's church was very demonstrative in their praise in worship.

Verbal described one night in the Terry household while fellowshipping with them after church. Bro. Terry began complaining to his beloved wife, Maggie, about her worship. He said, "Maggie, when people get up to sing, I want to hear the song and understand the words. But there you are (at this point in his complaint, Bro. Terry stood to imitate Maggie and her worship). You're spinning around with your hands in the air," Bro. Terry then turned in circles for emphasis, "Saying 'oooh, oooh,' and I can hardly hear a word they're singing!" Sis. Terry was unperturbed and not at all upset at this display. She just smiled at him, and everyone in the room understood that Maggie would continue to worship in the Spirit the way she always had. Verbal felt her godly praise was a sterling example of true worship to their congregation, and they happily followed her lead.

Bro. Terry carried this concern about his worship to the service one night. Standing behind the pulpit, he said to his congregation, "Bro. Bean has told me he would love to see me worship more. So, I will." He had gathered up some of the musical instruments the Sunday School children used in their classes and placed them on the pulpit. He rang a small bell for a while, then picked up a tambourine and shook it vigorously; staying in the spirit of this worship, he beat a small drum a few times, then turned to Verbal and said, "Is this better, Bro. Bean?" Verbal couldn't stop laughing by this time, and I think he and Bro. Terry considered the worship contest to be a draw.

A few months after this revival ended, Verbal visited Bro. and Sis. Terry, one day, as he was passing through Bakersfield. When invited into the living room, he was surprised to see Bro. Terry and one of his preacher friends sitting on the floor. Bro. Terry was clapping his hands together like a child. Considering there should be some explanation for this strange behavior, Bro. Terry explained to Verbal, "Bro. Bean, I need the Holy Ghost."

His friend vigorously objected to this astounding statement and said, "Now, Bro. Terry, you know you have the Holy Ghost; you've had it for years."

Not to be deterred from his confession, Bro. Terry said, "Yes, I do need the Holy Ghost, and you need it too." Verbal's perception of this meant that Bro. Terry longed for a fresh touch of the Holy Ghost and began praying with them. As they prayed, Bro. Terry received the refilling of the Holy Spirit for which he had hungered.

Bro. Terry called Verbal one day and asked if he would come and pray for him. He explained he had been very ill for days and was suffering agonizing pain. Verbal, of course, got there as soon as possible, and Bro. Terry explained what the problem was. He said, "I've been terribly sick with pain and nausea for days, so I finally went to my doctor. After an examination and tests were taken, the doctor returned to the room to give the diagnosis and treatment he strongly recommended."

"Rev. Terry," the doctor flatly stated, "you have a diseased and infected gall bladder, and you must have surgery to remove it."

Bro. Terry replied, "Doctor, I'll go home and diet."

To this, the doctor replied, "You'll go home and die."

Bro. Terry returned home, and Maggie and the church continued to pray. It was during this interval that Verbal arrived at the parsonage. Bro. Terry was terribly ill and not sure he would survive this sickness without the operation, but he was determined to trust God for his healing. They earnestly prayed together for Bro. Terry's healing. After a while, Bro. Terry turned to Verbal, saying, "The Lord has given me this scripture, and I want you to read it to me. It's Jer. 15:20."

Then he handed his Bible to Verbal, who turned to the scripture and read aloud:

> **"And I will make thee unto this people a**
> **fenced brazen wall: and they shall fight against**
> **thee, but they shall not prevail against thee: for**
> **I am with thee to save thee and to deliver thee,**
> **saith the Lord." (Jer.15:20)**

As Verbal spoke these words, he began to worship the Lord and said, "Bro. Terry, you're healed! The Lord said He would make you a brazen wall, strong and unbreakable. We need to thank the Lord, Bro. Terry, God has healed you!"

Bro. Terry was indeed healed from that day. However, soon after this event, Bro. Terry contacted Verbal again and wanted to see him. When they were together, Bro. Terry explained, "Bro. Bean, if I had agreed to have the surgery the doctor recommended, it would have cost me $500.00. I feel the Lord would want me to give the $500.00 to you."

"Bro. Terry, I would never feel free to be paid for something the Lord has done," Verbal replied. "I'm very grateful for your kindness, but I don't feel free to accept the money." This argument didn't sway Bro. Terry; he felt the Lord wanted him to give the money to Verbal. He urged Verbal to take the check, but Verbal refused to accept it from Bro. Terry that day. Through the months, when Bro. Terry saw Verbal, he would slip him some money. We didn't keep track of those offerings, but I'm sure they would have amounted to $500.00 if we had.

In all the revivals we experienced, there were many common elements. The ten o'clock morning prayer meetings, prayer before service, a shared burden for the lost, and determination to worship and praise freely. Also, never to be forgotten or overlooked was the desire for the Holy Ghost to move, the operation of the Gifts of the Spirit, and conviction in altar calls. When these elements were present, we would witness the church come together in unity with a burden for the lost. Many congregations were more developed in some of these areas than others, but it seemed every church went through this process. For some, it happened quickly, but for others, it was a belabored course of action. In every case, where the congregation was humble and willing to submit to the will of God, there was Holy Ghost revival.

Another precious element in our evangelistic travels was the love we experienced from the pastor and his family. I never recall hearing an unkind word or criticism. These wonderful friends cared for, fed, and supported us. Without fail, a close, loving friendship was developed with the pastors and their wives by the conclusion of the revival, which was an added blessing to the evangelistic life.

My favorite chauffeur

Every revival had its own unique essence, but some stand out for various reasons. The revival in South Bend, Indiana, was one of those. In late January 1967, Verbal drove our car up to Indiana to start the revival, but I was to remain in Houston for two weeks with the girls because Jennifer had been very sick. After that time, we would fly to Indianapolis, and Verbal and Bro. Ballestero would pick us up.

After Verbal arrived for this revival, he called me to describe where we would stay. "Nita," he told me, "the Ballesteros have provided a wonderful one-bedroom apartment with a fully equipped kitchen. The place is completely furnished, and you'll have everything you need to cook our meals here." He was thrilled to tell me how comfortable our living arrangements would be during the revival, and I was just as happy to hear this wonderful news.

Verbal had already formed a deep bond with Bro. and Sis. Ballestero, although we had met briefly, I was not as well acquainted with them. This proved to be one of the most joyous connections we were privileged to be a part of for years to come. The Ballesteros were totally sold out to the ministry and had lived a life of great sacrifice for many years. Bro. Ballestero was a preacher's preacher, and I remember hearing young ministers describe the glory of his sermons when he reached his 'high notes.'

Sis. Ballestero was an incredible woman of God and an awesome mother and homemaker. Her meals were simply delicious, and being with them and their three daughters, Carlene, Ramona, and Nila Rose, was an absolute joy. Martyn, the oldest child and only son, was already married to the lovely Marcia Starr Ballestero, and they attended many of the revival services when they could. They both stepped up to share the burden of the revival, and their presence blessed us. A description of the South Bend revival is in Revival Testimonials.

Another revival has also remained a cherished memory for me. We held that one in Lafayette, Louisiana, pastored by Rev. Benoit. Being in the heart of Cajun country was a brand-new experience for me. Sis. Benoit was a fabulous cook, and we were always overjoyed when invited to the parsonage to share a meal with them. Our travel trailer was parked next to the church, which was convenient for us. Verbal could spend as much time as he wanted in the church in prayer and study. We had powerful services, and many received the Holy Ghost at this time.

The saints in this congregation seemed to fall in love with Verbal, his ministry, and our family. They shared their delicious Cajun food and showered Jana and Jennifer with gifts and clothes. We were there for seven weeks, took a week off, then went on for another two weeks. Bro. Benoit and the saints wanted the revival to continue, but Verbal felt it was time to move on. Two sisters of the church told me later that when we pulled out of the parking lot with our trailer, several saints stood on the church grounds and wept as we left. Evangelistic work had its challenges, but it also had lasting benefits, and bonding with the loving people of God was one of those.

Verbal talked to me extensively about his love for the brethren. He was careful not to be critical or speak unkind words against anyone in ministry. In all the years of our marriage, I don't remember Verbal ever speaking disparagingly about any fellow minister. He cherished the fellowship of the brotherhood and loved the times he could get together with his ministerial friends. They would discuss sermons they had heard or preached, debate points of agreement or even disagreement about certain aspects of ministry, and he firmly believed "Iron sharpeneth iron."

It was Verbal's conviction that brothers in Christ had a divine obligation to lift, encourage, and help one another. He loved to sit under the anointed ministry of his fellow ministers as they preached or taught. There were times when Verbal felt estranged from certain brethren, but he was careful to repair the breach as he was able. Usually, this happened, but it was a source of sorrow for him when the separation was permanent. "To love one another as Jesus loved us is a challenge," he taught, "but it must be done."

Often, Verbal taught about Calvary and the death Christ suffered on the cross; he explained it was because Jesus loved us, and as difficult as that might be to understand, He truly loved us. Often the Lord would use Verbal in tongues and interpretation to bless His people.

> *"My people, when you receive me, you receive not weakness but strength. When you receive me, you receive not sickness but healing. I am in your midst now with my strength and power. Will you rise in Faith and make your claims that are yours by choice? Doubt not in your heart my power. I will move in your midst for I do love you and care for you. I carried your sins. I bore your iniquities. I suffered for your healing. Will you make your claim?"*

One of Verbal's favorite songs was "My Thanks to Him," and he often closed a message by singing it.

By the time Verbal had sung all the verses, he would become lost in worship and praise. The anointing oil would permeate this Holy place, and we would pour out our love to Christ Jesus. This high praise would allow us to approach the throne of God, and the process of changing us into His image as we beheld Him would take place. Some may have underrated this part of Verbal's ministry; it was not as dramatic as other aspects of his calling. To bring a congregation into unity of love for Jesus Christ and for all to recognize the Kingship of our Lord and Savior was beyond price. As our love for Jesus made us willing to become clay in the Potter's hands, He could carefully and meticulously, as a skilled surgeon, remove our carnality and self-will and replace it with His likeness.

We called these consecration services. We were urged to set ourselves apart for the ministry of Jesus Christ. We would spend long intervals bowing over the altar, weeping, dying out to self, and asking the Lord to fill us with His righteousness. Many of the holiness issues were settled in these altar services. Selfishness and carnality would melt away as we humbled ourselves before the Lord. Often, the altar was where the voice of God was heard in our hearts, calling us to ministry, missions, or a life of service.

In his gentle voice, Verbal would speak words of encouragement to the people in the holy hush that would come after pouring out ourselves to God. He assured us it was the voice of the Savior who was speaking to our hearts. Jesus would be with us. He loved us despite our shortcomings and wanted to guide us as a loving shepherd guides His flock into green pastures. I loved every aspect of Verbal's ministry, but sometimes I felt these services were designed just for me.

During revivals, when Verbal felt the leading of the Holy Ghost, he would announce a healing service. Because he had strong faith in divine healing, his faith was not only for himself and his family but also for the church. He didn't preach against using medical assistance from doctors, but he did strongly feel we should all seek the touch of Jesus Christ before we went to the medical field for help.

Many saints would come from surrounding areas when they learned there would be a healing service during the revival. Verbal would exhort and preach a message on God's power. He would recount many of the miracles he had witnessed or experienced. This is one of the stories he shared.

> "I was sick for several months with stomach issues and had everyone near to me praying for my healing. Nothing happened. I said, 'All right, God, I won't ask You to heal this affliction again. Instead, I'll thank You for healing it.' Every time I sat down to eat, I said, 'Thank you, Lord, for healing me.' This went on for a few months, and one day, I woke up, and I was completely healed."

When the saints came together in unity of praise, and faith was high, he called for the healing line to begin. Verbal, the pastor and church leaders would begin anointing with oil and laying hands on the sick. The musicians and singers would often begin with the song "Reach Out and Touch the Lord." After a while, Verbal would love to sing, "God is God, and God don't ever change. God is God, and Jesus is His name."

This was a glorious time. Often, people would be slain in the Spirit, and others would begin shouting and dancing, praising God for the healing touch they had felt.

After Verbal's passing, I found the following note from Deborah Grant in his papers.

> "In 1971, my father, Rev. Lynn Varnado, went to hear Bro. Bean preach. I was born blind, and when I was two years old, Dad took me and asked Bro. Bean to lay his hands on me and pray for me. The Lord healed me instantly, and I received my sight. Bro. Bean was an awesome man of God."

Chapter 21

The Crisis

When we were near Houston and had a few nights between revivals, we would leave the trailer where it was parked and visit Sis. Bean for two or three days. This was one of those occasions. Jennifer was twenty-one months old and was recovering from a bad case of measles. Her little body was covered with angry red whelps, and she was suffering from a high fever. Finally, the fever broke, and she seemed to be on the road to recovery. She was eating and wanted to be on the floor to play with Jana. We were so relieved to know she was feeling better. We didn't take our children to the doctor because Verbal firmly believed in trusting God for our healing. God had been good to us; this was the sickest Jana or Jennifer had ever been.

This respite didn't last long. Soon, Jennifer's fever was very high again, and she was developing a tight, nagging cough. She lost her appetite, and we tried desperately to entice her to drink fluids; we were concerned about her becoming dehydrated. We felt the agony of seeing our innocent baby suffer, feeling utterly powerless to ease her pain. Her condition continued for three days, and by then, we were desperate, praying for a healing touch.

Since we were staying at Sis. Bean's house throughout Jennifer's illness, it was helpful for me to be with her then because she was such a woman of faith. Jennifer's illness worsened hourly. We called neighboring friends and pastors, asking them, along with their congregations, to join us in intercessory prayer for Jennifer. It was very reassuring for us to have these men and women of God to help carry this burden we were living under.

One day, there was a knock at the door, and Verbal was surprised to see Bro. Joe Duke and Bro. William Cranford standing on the doorstep. We brought them right into the house, thankful that these great men of faith were there to help us pray for Jennifer's healing. They prayed earnestly and sincerely for our baby girl, and when they finished, Bro. Duke turned to me and said, "Sis. Bean, I would rather be horsewhipped than to say what I feel the Lord wants me to tell you." He continued, "I feel in the Spirit you have not reached the level of worship God desires from you. He uses Bro. Bean in this ministry, and you should be an example of his calling."

I'm sure there was more conversation after that, but I don't remember another word being spoken. I was stricken to my heart and overcome with condemnation. I felt I had not been a good example of what Verbal was teaching the people of God. I could have made allowances for my lack of worship. I felt all eyes were on me, being the wife of the evangelist. I didn't want to be in the limelight because I felt self-conscious, but the truth of the matter is I had not known that I had fallen short in this area. I did worship and praise the Lord, but not with the freedom of worship God desired from me.

When the enormity of my shortcomings dawned on me, I felt I would die from grief. Was it possible I was preventing the healing of my baby, Jennifer? Was I the cause of this terrible, heart-rending illness? I quickly ran to the back bedroom of Sis. Bean's house where I could be alone. I fell on the bed and began to pour out my anguish and sorrow in repentance. I'm sure people up and down the block could hear my agonizing cries of heartbreak. I'm not sure how long I was there, but when my weeping finally subsided, I felt wrung out, but also, I felt a sense of relief. I knew I had emptied my heart to our loving Savior, Jesus Christ, and I felt He still loved me despite my failures.

Verbal told me later that Nylotis had come to him while I was pouring my heart out to God and said, "Verbal, you've got to stop her. She will be broken under the grief of condemnation."

Verbal, too, was stricken to understand the Gethsemane I was experiencing, but he replied, "I can't, Nylotis. This is between her and God."

I was hopeful that after this outpouring of prayer and intercession, Jennifer would be healed, but it was not to be. She continued to burn with a fever, and it was becoming even more difficult to persuade her to drink her fluids.

When Mother and Daddy learned how sick Jennifer was, they flew out to Houston as quickly as they could get there. It was a relief to have them with us; both were a tremendous source of comfort and support. They understood the enormity of what we were facing. I couldn't bear to think that Jennifer wouldn't be healed. In addition to the grief of losing our beautiful baby, Jennifer, I knew there would be great reproach because we didn't seek medical attention for her. So many frightening, faith-killing thoughts were coming to me, but I continued to try to hold onto hope even when the path seemed obscured by darkness. I knew Jesus was by our side; we felt His presence continually, and I knew whatever the future held, He would not leave us to carry this grief alone.

Verbal was praying almost continually, and we would take turns staying with Jennifer in prayer while others of the household rested. One evening, I was so exhausted that I lay on the bed and drifted off to sleep while Verbal and Daddy were sitting up and praying for Jennifer. This is Verbal's description of those days:

"Last year, around Christmas time, my two children became sick with the big red measles. Jennifer's case was far worse; she was a solid mass of measles. She began to improve, and we let her up to play for a little

while. But soon after, she relapsed and came down with pneumonia. Later that night, she woke us up, making a strange noise. When I got to her, her eyes rolled back in her head. I felt she was dying, and it seemed death filled the room. I was so scared at the moment that I could not pray. My mother was strong in faith, but she lost every ounce of it that night. Death was that strong.

It seemed Jennifer was in the last moments of her life. There I stood, as helpless as a baby myself. We called preachers and our families, desperately asking them to pray. This went on for several days. She had a high fever, and it seemed to be burning her up. My wife and I would look at each other and I would hold her in my arms, trying to bring what comfort and encouragement I could.

Finally, I had all I could take. I went off to an empty room and closed the door. I said, 'God, my bones will bleach in this room, but I'm not coming out until You answer me. Either tell me my baby's going to die, and if You want to take her, I won't say no. I love her, and I want to keep her if I can, but You're going to have to do one or the other. Tell me she's leaving us and give me the grace to face it or tell me she's going to be well. I won't come out of this room until You have answered me. I will not move until Heaven has spoken to me.' I've never gotten so desperate with the Lord in my life that He did not answer me. Standing in that dark room, God spoke to me and said, 'I'm going to heal your baby.'

> *I came out of that room praising God.
> Everyone was heartbroken, and there I was,
> speaking in tongues with my baby lying at
> the point of death. She seemed to get worse,
> but I held onto the word I had received. A
> bolt of Heaven's glory came into the room,
> and my wife and I both were knocked to the
> floor under the power of God. We began to
> rejoice, and God spoke these prophetic words
> through me, 'Now, I know that you will not
> withhold anything from me, and I'm going to
> answer and confirm what I said I would do.'"*

When we heard those words, we all began to worship and praise the Lord. I couldn't stop the tears of joy, and the relief from the fear I had been experiencing was almost overwhelming. Jennifer's fever fell, and she broke into a sweat right then. She drank some water and went into a deep, restful sleep. When she awoke the next morning, she said, "I want eggs." It was a miracle; it was an outpouring of God's grace.

Mother and Daddy stayed for another day to enjoy this great victory. Sis. Bean had suffered along with us during this testing time, and she, too, was grateful that baby Jennifer was well and whole. This was a life-changing experience for us all, especially for me. I had never faced such a situation in my life before, and to see this miracle unfold right before my eyes was truly joy unspeakable. I couldn't stop thanking God for His goodness and hugging our precious Jennifer.

Chapter 22

Port Allen Revival

We continued traveling the evangelistic field three more years after we purchased the travel trailer. We held revivals in many different cities, and without fail, God always moved in a mighty, miraculous way. Bro. Spell invited us to preach for him in Port Allen, Louisiana, and we were very happy to be going to such a growing revival church. We loved Bro. and Sis. Spell and their family from the start. Verbal was especially fascinated by Bro. Spell and his high energy. We had never seen such a busy pastor. Sis. Spell was right by his side, trying to keep up with him while caring for her six children, entertaining the evangelist and his family, and being ready to respond every time Bro. Spell cried, "Dorothy!"

Verbal would later describe him, saying, "Bro. Spell is so busy he doesn't like to stop and take time to counsel the newcomer. He thinks it would be easier to just pray someone else through to the Holy Ghost."

Bro. Spell provided a space for our trailer in a very nice RV park near the church. Three families from the church also lived there and were very good neighbors to us. We had a little yard beside our trailer, and Jana loved playing outside during our stay there. One day, she came into the trailer with a handful of rocks. I said,

"Jana, don't bring rocks into our house; this isn't the place for rocks."

She looked at me solemnly and said, "This is not a house; it's a trailer. Can you say that? Trailer." Verbal loved all the funny things she would say and couldn't wait to share his latest toddler tale with our friends. We often shared Bible stories with Jana, and one of her favorites was the story of Jonah and the whale when God insisted that Jonah was to go to Nineveh and preach.

We had sliding doors in the trailer, and Jana was prone to banging them back and forth. I kept reprimanding her, "Jana, if you keep doing that, you're going to break the doors. Now stop it."

One day, I walked into the living room, where she was carefully looking at the sliding door she had just pulled off its track. She glanced up at me and then prayed, "Lord, if you'll fix this door, I'll go to Nineveh and preach."

The revival in Port Allen lasted over twelve weeks, and one hundred and seven people were filled with the Holy Ghost. Finally, Verbal rejoiced as he was able to see the promise God had given him of the one-hundred-soul revival fulfilled before his very eyes. On the last night, Bro. Spell called all those who had received the Holy Ghost during the revival to stand at the front of the church. It was very touching to see the crowd fill the whole area. Though we didn't know it at the time, this would be the last revival Verbal would preach while on the evangelistic field.

Verbal was usually spent physically and mentally after the close of a revival, which might last from six to sixteen weeks. We would take time off between revivals for rest and recreation. Verbal loved to fish and hunt. Since we lived in a travel trailer most of the evangelistic years after we were married, we would pull into a campsite near a river or lake, and he could spend time fishing. These are precious memories to me for many reasons. I learned to fish at this time, and I loved it. Granted, I could not bait a hook by myself, but Verbal was kind enough to do it. If lucky, we would have a good catch to bring home and have fried fish for supper. Even now, when I am near a lake or river and smell the scent of the water and fish, memories of those wonderful days return like a flood and fill my heart. Bittersweet, some might say, but mainly sweet to me.

Between revivals, Verbal would frequently be invited to minister in churches for a night or two or a weekend. These meetings were a blessing to us financially since he might still feel he was not ready to start another long revival. During these intervals, we would also spend time with friends and family, which was helpful to us. Being surrounded by those who loved and cared for us while we cooked, laughed, and talked together nourished us in many ways.

We were abundantly blessed with many like-minded friends and relatives, and sooner or later, the conversation would turn to the work of God. We recalled hard-won victories and described and celebrated miraculous healings. And if at least one preacher was in the room, he would always share a new message he had been working on or preached lately. Scriptures would be quoted, and anointing would fall on that roomful of Holy Ghost friends and relatives. What a treasure those days and hours were. Confidences and burdens would be shared, advice given; then love and concern for one another would fill our hearts. We would pray together and, indeed, were strengthened and edified.

However, not every gathering was always this spiritual. After being together, some would tell funny or embarrassing incidents. Usually, these were things that had happened during church services. Many stories were so entertaining they would have to be told repeatedly; they were still funny to us, and we would wind up laughing until we were out of breath. Verbal was a great storyteller, and he loved to recount the many funny events of his childhood. This story, though often told, would be repeated.

When Verbal was young, the Bean family had a renegade ram named Buck with a formidable set of horns. Verbal often repeated the stories about this ram who refused to be civilized or taught proper behavior. If an interesting object entered his range of vision, it was the challenge of his life to butt 'said' object. Often, this object would be a neighbor, a stranger, or even one in the family. The victim would be knocked off his feet, and the unrepentant sheep would pass on by, happy with another successful encounter. The family felt this was very comical. They were reprehensible, I know, but they, like the sheep, were unrepentant. And when they could have warned the soon-to-be sufferer, they remained silent. Verbal would tell of this outlaw Buck and his shenanigans, and regrettably, we would all laugh and laugh. Thankfully, we knew laughter does good, like medicine.

Among the tales Verbal frequently shared, this one stood out as his favorite and is described here by Bro. Martyn Ballestero:

"Bro. Verbal Bean put his arm around my shoulder in a conspiratorial manner as we walked from the dining hall. For the third time that week of Hoosier Camp Meeting, he said. 'Bro. Marty, tell me that story about the devil again.'

I was an associate pastor with my father, Carl Ballestero, and greatly revered Bro. Bean. In my heart, I wasn't sure if he was having more fun laughing at me or my story. Nevertheless, I began.

I was twenty years old and preaching a revival in East Texas. One night during the altar service, a young single woman began to demonstrate signs of demon possession. Since she was a praise singer and sang in a trio with the pastor and his wife, she was always on the platform during service. This girl was well-liked by all. I was surprised at the demonstration, which was completely out of character for her. The saints were gathered around, crying and praying. Some were giving prayerful support to her astonished parents.

The pastor asked me if I would go pray for her. (I later wondered why he didn't pray for her and ask me to join him, but I was an evangelist and just did what I was told.)

I knelt beside this young woman and began to pray very earnestly. 'Satan, I command you in Jesus' name to come out of her. She's not yours; she has been bought with a price.'

Speaking through this young lady, a low voice growled back at me, 'She is too, mine!'

Without missing a beat, I said, 'How did you get her?'

'I stole her,' the voice said.

I said, 'Devil, I rebuke you in Jesus' name. I command you now to release your hold on her. You will be bound for a thousand years, and I bind you now in Jesus' name. Come out of her!'

A high-pitched, innocent-sounding little girl's voice sweetly said, 'I'm gone!'

'Devil,' I said, 'you're a liar. If you were gone, you wouldn't be talking to me. Now, come out of her in Jesus' name!'

At that part of the story, Bro. Bean started laughing so hard that he crumpled to the grass in hysterics. He rolled over onto his back while tears of laughter ran down his cheeks.

'I'm gone! I'm gone. I'm gone!' he said and then laughed some more.

I stood there grinning and looked at the most esteemed evangelist in Pentecost. He was too weak to stand and was completely enjoying my experience, my discomfort, and my spiritual ineptness.

Whenever he saw me at a convention or a camp, he would look at me with a big grin and say, in a high falsetto voice, 'I'm gone!'"

Enjoying fellowship with friends

Chapter 23

The Unexpected Call

We had known for some time Sis. Bean was struggling to make her church payments. We weren't able to help very much financially, but we were earnestly praying with her and the church for an answer to this seemingly insurmountable problem. She had labored valiantly to get through this crisis, and her precious church people had industriously raised money in every possible way. The congregation was down to about thirty members, but they were a faithful, loyal group and had walked with Sis. Bean every step of this perilous journey. However, with the best will in the world and with everyone giving and working sacrificially, they were at a stalemate. They were behind in the church payments and couldn't raise the funds to keep the mortgage current, no matter how they tried.

The bank manager called Sis. Bean to come in for a consultation–actually, it was an ultimatum. "Rev. Bean," he said, "We can no longer carry the overdraft for your loan. If you can't pay the overdue balance, we will have no choice but to foreclose on the church property." Sis. Bean was heart-stricken to hear this information and was helpless to suggest a solution. "There may be one way to avoid the foreclosure of the church," he continued as he looked closely at her, "If you agree to resign as pastor of the church, we will work with you until you install a new pastor."

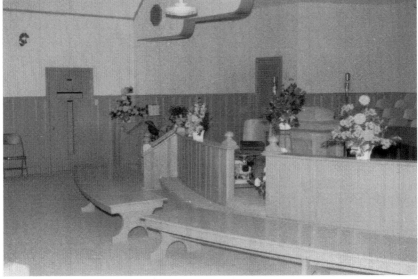

Greens Bayou Apostolic Church

Sis. Bean left the bank heartbroken and stripped of hope for a way out of this terrible dilemma. She immediately called Verbal, crying so helplessly she could hardly be understood. "Mother, what's wrong? What's happening?" he kept saying.

Finally, when she could make herself understood, she tearfully repeated to him what the bank manager had told her must be done to avoid foreclosure. She said, "I have to resign and bring in a new pastor or the bank will foreclose on the church." After she had told Verbal this horrible news, she started crying again.

Finally, she was able to speak coherently. "Verbal, please come as soon as you can. You'll have to take the church immediately. I'll call for an election at our next church service. I don't know how I can get through this heartbreak."

This was earth-shattering news to us in so many ways. We were grieving with Sis. Bean over her forced retirement because she had spent her whole ministry pioneering this church, praying most of the saints through to the Holy Ghost and baptizing them in Jesus' name. She had sat by their beds when they were sick and interceded for them, advised them, taught them, worshipped with them, and worked untiringly with them night and day. Sis. Bean had located the property and organized the church building. She had designed the church's floor plan and enlisted her brother-in-law, Vestal Foster, a master craftsman, to oversee its construction.

Greens Bayou Apostolic Church was a beautiful building with first-class woodwork throughout the interior, especially on the platform and altar areas.

We were also concerned for the saints of this church. They had been faithful and loving in Kingdom service and had given their time and money to carry on the ministry of the church. Their hearts would be breaking, too; it seemed to be an impossible situation. We had never seriously considered Greens Bayou as a place to pastor because we felt Sis. Bean would always be there for that church. Verbal was convinced his mother would continue her pastorate there for years to come.

Thinking on this transition all these years later, I wish I had been more caring and solicitous for Sis. Bean. We loved her dearly, but it has only been through the clarity of maturity that I have come to understand her loss was greater than I could have ever imagined at the time. Yet she carried on as best she could.

Verbal and I had talked occasionally about the possibility of settling down and taking the pastorate of a church. However, Verbal was still enjoying the evangelistic work, which seemed to be where we would minister in the foreseeable future. Jana was almost five and would need to start kindergarten in the fall; we weren't sure what we would do about that. Homeschooling was rarely done in those days, and we were at an impasse regarding how her education would proceed.

After receiving his mother's desperate call, we returned to Houston. Verbal had invested much of his ministry into that church and loved the congregation devotedly. He would never refuse to help his mother in this distressing and critical situation. We tied up all the loose ends, attached our trailer to the car, and headed to Houston.

The situation was worse than we had foreseen when we arrived. Sis. Bean was stricken with grief. The overdraft on the church was more outstanding than we had known, and the saints seemed crushed and defeated.

There was a ray of light in all this sorrow. Though still grieving, the saints were relieved to have Verbal come home. While they still wept with Sis. Bean, they were holding onto hope that brighter days lay ahead. The election was held at the appointed time, and the votes were counted. The outcome was unanimous, and Verbal became their pastor. Verbal met with the bank officials as soon as possible, and they granted a space of time for the church to bring the loan up to date. How this was to be done was unclear to Verbal. We would pray, the church would pray, and we would trust God to see us through. But as always, God had a plan involving His wonderful people.

As news of the hardship Greens Bayou Pentecostal Church faced became public, God's family came to our rescue. The pastors of other Pentecostal churches in Houston organized a rally to be held in our church to raise money for us. Many ministers and churches in the area attended, bringing much-needed support and fellowship. At the close of the message, Bro. James Kilgore made an appeal to the audience for an offering. People began to pledge the amount they would give; others brought their offering to the altar, and when the service was concluded, a large part of the necessary funds had been raised. This outpouring of love and support humbled Verbal and me, and once again, we thanked Jesus for allowing us to be a part of the Body of Christ.

This timely and generous offering gave us some breathing space, but there were still several issues we weren't sure how to correct. The tithing from the church was small, but we felt we must contribute to the care of Sis. Bean. She received a meager amount from Social Security, but it wasn't enough to live on. Verbal pledged to help her monthly, and he did as long as he lived.

We soon moved out of our travel trailer into the evangelistic quarters in the back of the church. It had one large room, a closet, and a bathroom. We would share the church kitchen with the saints who used it occasionally. It was large and very well-equipped. A bed was set up in the bedroom/living room, and we arranged another bed for the girls; we all lived comfortably there for a few months. It was also very convenient to be on location since so much was happening there.

Several of the pastors for whom Verbal preached had also heard of our struggles, and we received generous offerings from them. Verbal's close friends also contributed what they could, and gradually, things began to look up financially.

Other problems also needed immediate attention. The roof of the church had to be replaced, which was considered essential in a rainy place like Houston. I'm not sure how Bro. Ray Majors, pastor of Melville Pentecostal Church, heard about this situation, but he had the answer for us. He brought men from his congregation and all the necessary supplies. Greens Bayou Church was only asked to provide meals for the workers.

This was a joyous occasion for all of us. Bro Majors brought fifteen men and began the work. The men from our congregation joined in as their jobs permitted. Our church ladies were so pleased the roof would be replaced they happily met with me in the church kitchen, and we cooked our best meals for these excellent men of God.

These victories and blessings from God seemed to pour in daily, and our hearts were lifted immeasurably. The water heater had gone out, and someone anonymously donated money for a new one. I asked the church to pray that God would supply an organ for us, and again, one was delivered to the church; we didn't know who had arranged this. A spirit of giving seemed to fall on us all, and somehow, every need and many desires were supplied by the hand of God and His wonderful people.

Verbal's girls

Chapter 24

Settled In Houston

Looking back, I believe our move to Houston was a relief to both of us. Verbal had evangelized five years before we were married and continued another five years afterward. We both loved the evangelistic field; we had seen many wonderous works of God and experienced great victories. In addition, we connected personally with many upstanding pastors and their families. Our lives had been enriched immeasurably by these servants of Jesus Christ, and we were sure the relationships we had forged would stand the test of time, which proved to be true. Although he didn't complain, Verbal was weary of the constant change that evangelism requires.

When Verbal had planted his church in South Houston, it was the first time he had been in active ministry. It seems astounding now to think of a seventeen-year-old pioneering a church and then, after five years, entering the evangelistic field. He had been highly successful in both areas of his ministry.

It was during his evangelistic years that the high anointing, which was to rest on him until the end of his life, was revealed. The undying effects of that ministry will never be completely known in this life. Only eternity will reveal all that was done for the cause of Christ during this period of Verbal's life.

Having said that, it was clear when Verbal assumed the pastorate of Greens Bayou Apostolic Church, the hand of God on his life was not lessened in any way. Pastoring the church fit him perfectly. He had a natural ability to work with people; he was always led by a great vision and a compelling burden for revival. As he stepped into the pastorate, he was blessed with the same anointing and drive he had shown on the evangelistic field.

During one of our first Sunday night services, the Huffmans, a lovely family with five young sons, came to visit. As always, when Verbal saw sinners in the congregation, he was compelled in the Spirit to reach out to them. That night, he preached a masterful sermon, directed to the lost, and finished the message with a powerful altar call. The whole Huffman family came to the altar, including their young boys. The father and mother both received a beautiful infilling of the Holy Ghost. This family was a blessing to the church in many ways. Bro. Huffman had led a very ungodly life and was now ready for the righteousness of God to cover him and his family. He had a well-paying job, and they became faithful and loyal to the church. Thus began the Holy Ghost revival we were to experience during the ten years we were in Houston. This revival Spirit covered us all the years we were there.

We assumed the pastorate of Greens Bayou Apostolic Church in the early fall, and that Christmas season, we organized the first banquet the church had ever experienced. We reserved space in a local cafeteria, sold tickets at the lowest possible cost, arranged a few games and songs, and enjoyed beautiful fellowship while wearing our most attractive clothes. It was a huge success, although probably only twenty-five of us were there.

I clearly understand we were the recipients of years of intercessory prayer and seed sown in Houston. God graciously allowed us to participate in the harvest of the ministry of Sis. Bean and her faithful congregation. To paraphrase a favorite scripture, one sows, another waters, but God gives the increase. Our first year in Houston was exciting in many ways, and Verbal and I both were cherishing this new type of involvement in Kingdom ministry. Verbal began organizing and instituting the Center of Interest, a new type of presenting the Gospel to children in our Sunday school. When Sis. Bean had designed the church layout, she included several Sunday school rooms, which were on the second floor. They were roomy, filled with light, and perfect for the Center of Interest plan. It was evident Verbal was enjoying a facet of his ministry that had not been utilized while he was evangelizing. It was also touching to see how satisfying it was to him to rebuild the Sunday school into a new, more useful arrangement.

Verbal always had a strong love and appreciation for children. He was drawn to them, and laughter was usually involved in some way. He gave many of the children in our congregation nicknames. One family had three adorable young boys, and he would pay them to sing for him. We didn't have many children at this time because the congregation was still so small, but Verbal's visionary view of these changes put us in an advantageous position when the church began to grow.

Though we were a small congregation, the Sunday school teachers in place were very good and devoted to their ministry. When our toddlers were old enough to attend Sunday school classes, Sis. Brooks was their teacher. She taught them in a very simple but highly enthusiastic manner, with bright smiles and dramatic depictions of the Bible characters. She welcomed each child with open arms, and they fell in love with her and their class. When it was time for promotion, they were sad to leave Sis. Brooks and the wonderful experiences they had enjoyed. A few even cried a little. As the congregation grew, our Sunday School flourished as well.

Sis. Everhart had been leading the youth group when we arrived at Greens Bayou. She continued in this ministry and was truly a devoted anointed teacher of the Intermediate class. The Everharts were one of the foundational families of our church, along with the Stanleys, Mortons, Browns, DeMents, Owens, Moores, Brooks, and Waldrips.

I began teaching the youth class and continued in that position for the entire time we were in Houston. After a few years, a new family joined our church, the Biscamps. Sis. Biscamp became a team teacher with me, and we truly treasured our Sundays together in our upstairs Sunday school room.

Revival fires burned brightly in nearly every service within the first two years in Greens Bayou. Families were coming to God and falling in love with the Apostolic message and with our saints. Many backsliders prayed back through, and it seemed we were continually growing week by week. Verbal loved to tell the story about baptizing a man one night whose fingers were stained yellow from smoking cigarettes. When he came up out of the water, looking at his hands, the man said, "Not only did God take the desire of smoking away from me, but He also took the stains away, too."

During this time, we began to look for a home in earnest. A couple who had moved from Greens Bayou to Louisiana returned to Houston to visit our church and put their house up for sale. The house was in a modest neighborhood across the street from the elementary school. We inquired about the price, and with a little help from Mother and Daddy, we got the money together for a down payment. The transaction was completed, and we became homeowners once again.

Our new home had three bedrooms, one bath, a combined living/dining area, and a small kitchen. It was in good condition and had large front and back yards. We were ecstatic to be moving into such a wonderful place in a good location and close to the church.

We set up one bedroom for Jana and Jennifer with twin beds, one bedroom for ourselves, and one bedroom for guests. A bonus to us was that one of our precious saints, Sis. Brooks, lived with her husband next door. She proved to be a blessing to us through the years, and we were grateful for the help she gave. Her husband, too, was very kind and helpful, although he was not a church member.

Bro. and Sis. T J Marshall moved to Houston and became committed and valuable church members. Their faithfulness was unflagging, and all their children still serve God today. Bro. and Sis. Buxton, backsliders from Port Arthur, came back to God, and in due time, Bro. Buxton was called to preach. They were soon followed by Sis. Buxton's brother and sister-in-law, Bud and Jo Desormeaux. The Sanders family prayed through, and the Tienda family was added to the church shortly after. The Richardsons, along with their three children, prayed through and became a blessing to the church and us personally. These families all had children, from toddlers to teenagers, and our growth was powerful and thrilling. These are just a few examples of the mighty harvest we were experiencing.

With so much happening in the church and many newcomers, we were soon almost overwhelmed keeping up with these new converts and enlarging our Sunday school classes. Before long, some of our young people met with their pastor, seeking his approval for their marriages, and asked him to officiate at their upcoming wedding. We were having a baby boom, and there didn't seem to be enough hours in the day to accomplish all that needed to be done. Soon, Verbal was praying about bringing in someone to assist him and help us with this growing congregation. Verbal had been friends with the Yeats family from Monroe, Louisiana, for several years. He had preached for them a few nights but not a

**Verbal performs the wedding for Mike and
Debbie Everhart**

full-length revival. Bro. and Sis. Yeats had three children, Libby and twins Kenneth and Mike. Libby was married to Ralph Endsley, and the brothers were not married. Verbal invited the family to come and be with us for a special service devoted to music and ministry. I had not yet been privileged to meet this family, but I stopped by the church one afternoon to ensure everything was in place for the night's service. The Yeats trio, Libby, Kenneth, and Mike were practicing their songs for the night; I was amazed to hear the song "Pity the Man" for the first time. Their harmony was perfect, and anointing seemed to cover every note they sang; I immediately became the most devoted member of their fan club.

The service that night only confirmed what I was already feeling; this family was extraordinary in their talent and anointing. Shortly after that, Verbal invited Ralph and Libby to come and assist him in our church. They had two adorable daughters, Teresa and Dana, who became friends with our girls. The Endsleys proved to be a great blessing for us and the congregation. Ralph was a teacher, Libby was musically talented, and they were both very dedicated and hard-working. They stayed with us for two years until Bro. Yeats resigned from his church and invited them back to Monroe to follow in his pastorate there. We certainly missed them when they left.

The revival we were experiencing brought in many young people with enthusiasm and talents. I'm sure there were renegades among the group; in fact, I know there were. However, they were soon overshadowed by our Holy Ghost young people. We kept the victory and rejoiced to experience the great works Jesus Christ was doing in our church.

Verbal, as you would expect, was the Bible class teacher. The saints always looked forward to those Sunday lessons. The only possible negative to this arrangement was that often Verbal would get caught up in his lesson, which could become a sermon on any given Sunday. When that happened, the dismissed classes would have to wait in the corridors until the pastor felt it was time to finish his lesson; he might then end his class or have an altar call; we never knew which.

Early on in our pastorate, I had decided we should, as a family, try to display moderation in our lifestyle and dress, remembering Verbal had asked that our wedding not be lavish. On Easter Sunday morning, it was a custom for everyone to wear new outfits, and for the girls, this included dresses, hats, purses, shoes, and gloves. It occurred to me that some in our growing crowd may be unable to afford new clothes and would feel left out and embarrassed. I had not worn new clothes on Easter since I was a young girl, and I felt it would be helpful for Jana and Jennifer to join me; I didn't want to be guilty of causing any hurt to our precious people. With this in mind, I decided our daughters should not wear brand-new dresses on Easter Sunday.

The girls were not as enthusiastic about this regime as I hoped. Jana tried to accept this edict humbly and gratefully, and after several years, she was successful. She now fondly remembers that we were conscious of our families living on tight budgets and wanted to ensure no child felt inferior to the other children.

Jennifer was not so spiritually mature. For years, she sadly reminded me, "Every child in our congregation had new clothes for Easter, except me and Jana. Even the poorest families were able to buy their children new clothes." I believe Jennifer has reached a mature spiritual understanding and a level of forgiveness for this hurt to her pride. She finally confessed that she is thankful she and Jana had this opportunity to sacrifice for the Kingdom in their small way.

These were stellar days. Our people were extremely thankful to experience the revival and growth they had earnestly prayed for. During one of our Saturday visitations, we knocked on a door and were invited into the home by a very kind lady. She was living with her daughter and two grandchildren in their early teens. We invited them to come to church, and they gladly accepted. Soon, they all were at the altar, received the gift of the Holy Ghost, and were baptized in Jesus' name. We were thrilled to have this whole family become a part of our church. They were faithful for some time but gradually started missing services and, before long, didn't attend church at all. The granddaughter remained faithful and committed to the Lord.

In a few weeks, we received a heart-wrenching call. We were told the grandson was found dead late one night of a drug overdose. Verbal and I both were stricken with grief; this was such a needless death.

The funeral, the first since we had taken the church, was somber. We were all in tears, grieving for what might have been. Verbal's funeral message was difficult to finish. For the closing song, our lady's trio sang the Andraé Crouch song, "Jesus Is the Answer.

We all struggled to contain our tears, singing with broken hearts. I'm thankful for Diane, the granddaughter. Even though her life was sometimes difficult, and she was away from God for a period of time, she is living a victorious life, and her son and his beautiful family continue to serve God after all these years.

Verbal's spiritual life was molded by his mother. She was a strong, dynamic Christian, and Verbal had total faith in her walk with God. Consequently, he believed in and appreciated women of faith. Because of this, he trusted me to fulfill my desire to do what I could to help our congregation.

We were unbelievably busy selling peanut brittle, going on Saturday visitation, visiting the sick, getting acquainted with our newcomers, and happily trying to stay ahead of our obligations.

I learned how to conduct prayer meetings from Verbal's prayer sessions during our revivals, and one of the first things I started was Tuesday morning prayer meetings for the ladies. This time was rewarding to me personally and a powerful blessing to the church. We would gather at 10:00 a.m. on Tuesday mornings and pray. Often, anointing would fall on us and inspire our petitions and praise. After this, I would share my thoughts on simple Biblical truths, focusing mainly on how to be a good wife and mother. Many of our new converts had been saved and delivered from difficult situations, and we strongly encouraged them to participate in these meetings. It would soon be apparent how their spiritual growth and fellowship in the body were blessed by this time with their sisters in the Lord. These were sacred and cherished days.

After prayer meetings, we would visit and talk and sometimes go to lunch together. Lasting friendships and connections were formed in this atmosphere. Just being together was an essential part of all our lives, and it helped bond us into one body for the work of the Kingdom.

Along with the established faithful saints in the church, we also had a few who had special challenges in their lives. These were people who loved the Lord and the church, and most had been filled with the Holy Ghost but were somewhat limited in their capabilities. Our church was truly remarkable. We showed the love of Jesus Christ to these people, helping them, loving them, and recognizing the value and blessing they brought to us all.

One of our young men, Ricky, attended school with Paul, a student with special needs, and offered to pick him up for church. Paul was thrilled with the invitation and came to the service; from the first, he fell in love with the church, and before long, we all loved Paul, too.

Paul was a member of our Sunday School class and soon became my close friend. He would call me from time to time to discuss what was happening in his life. He usually began his conversations like this: "Sis. Bean, I hate to bother you, 'cept I need to talk to you." Then he would share some concerns he had, and I would try to reassure him that everything would soon be all right.

One day, he called, and when I answered the phone, he started the conversation as usual, "Sis. Bean, I hate to bother you, 'cept I want to tell you about my brother Carl. He's my identical twin."

I was surprised but happy to hear Paul had a twin brother. "Where is Carl, Paul? I've never heard about him."

Paul went on to explain that Carl had been in reform school but was soon coming home. "He wants to go to church next Sunday, but I can't be there with him. Is it okay for him to come with Ricky?"

"Absolutely, Paul," I replied. "I can't wait to meet Carl."

Sure enough, the next Sunday, Paul was absent, but his brother, Carl, came with Ricky. I was shocked when I saw Carl because he was identical to Paul but very withdrawn and sullen. Paul was always outgoing and friendly, so it was a surprise to find Carl so unlike him. I was happy to introduce Carl to our Sunday School class, and everyone gave him a warm welcome, but he was completely unresponsive to us all.

On the front porch of the church, after Sunday School was dismissed, I had the opportunity to introduce Carl to Verbal. "This is Carl," I said, "He is Paul's identical twin brother."

Verbal took one look at him and said, "That's Paul; that's not Carl."

"No, Verbal," I said, "Paul wasn't able to come today, but Carl wanted to visit his church, so here he is." Verbal still wasn't convinced, but I was. Carl looked exactly like Paul but was different in every other way.

Carl never came back to church, but Paul would give me an update on him from time to time. Paul would explain that Carl was living in another town with a relative and wouldn't be back in Houston for a while.

A few weeks after the Carl experience, we had a fearful, judgment service one Sunday night. We were all at the altar and spent a long time searching our hearts and making sure we were right with God.

The next morning, Paul called again. "Sis. Bean, I hate to bother you, 'cept I need to talk to you about Carl."

"What's happening, Paul? Is Carl in trouble?" I asked.

"No, Sis. Bean. You remember when my brother Carl came to church that Sunday?" he asked.

"Yes, Paul, I remember," I replied.

He then announced, "Sis. Bean, that wasn't my twin brother; that was me."

Verbal never let me forget the 'Carl episode.' He would laugh and say, "I told you that was Paul!"

During our evangelistic years, Verbal told me about a 'stalker' who had troubled him during a few of his revivals. She would turn up unexpectedly and stare at him fixedly wherever he was in the auditorium. She didn't say anything, but it was unnerving to him to feel her unwavering gaze. He said he didn't know where she was from or how she knew where he was preaching. He told me she even sent him a letter once which stated she felt God had chosen her to be his spiritual wife. I laughingly replied, "I believe I would have something to say about that."

One day, I heard a knock on the door of our house, and when I answered it, a strange, tall, thin lady with dark hair was awkwardly standing there. I had never seen her before. She told me she wanted to talk to Bro. Bean, and I went to tell him he was wanted at the door. When he saw her, he was utterly dumbfounded; it was his stalker. He was almost speechless, which was rare for my friendly husband. He didn't invite her into the house but spoke briefly with her and closed the conversation as quickly as possible.

This uninvited lady started coming to church faithfully. She would come early and stay late; while she said little, her presence was keenly felt. Verbal was troubled by her attentions. It wasn't long before she would not only stare at him but would follow him around the church while he was speaking to the saints after service. First, he kindly asked her to leave and told her she was a distraction. She paid no attention to his request but became increasingly intrusive. Finally, at the end of his patience, he told her, "You have to leave and never come back. If you don't, I will be forced to ask the police to intervene. Now, don't cause any trouble, but please go away." Evidently, he made a believer out of her; she left and never returned.

Verbal's mother was an integral part of our lives, and we were often together. One day, I received a tearful call from her, "Nita," she could hardly speak for crying, "I stepped out of my trailer, missed the step, and landed on my ankle. I know it's broken. Please send Verbal to help me."

Verbal left as soon as he heard the news and found Sis. Bean sitting in her living room. Neighbors had heard her crying for help and came to her rescue. She wouldn't go to the hospital, so they helped her as best they could back up the steps into her trailer. She was weeping with pain when Verbal arrived, and as was their custom in any dire situation, they began to pray. Verbal and the neighbors helped her back down the steps and placed her in our car. When she and Verbal arrived at our house, some men from the church had come to help, and they carried her into our guest room and put her on the bed. We were all praying desperately by this time and were heartbroken to witness her suffering.

She began to entreat the Lord for healing and started praying in the Spirit under heavy anointing. We were all doing our best to agree with her in faith for her complete healing. Her recovery took a few weeks, but the agonizing pain was gone, and this was a time for healing. Verbal found an old boot, carved the opening out a little, and used it as a cast to hold her foot and ankle firmly. One day, as we were all praying, Sis. Bean felt and heard her bones coming back into place. For years, she would recount the miraculous story of this healing. When her recovery was complete, she never had another problem with her ankle. The master healer had done His work once again.

Sis. Bean experienced another notable miracle during this time. She had just gotten a pair of new eyeglasses, and one day, for no apparent reason, they exploded, filling her eyes with tiny fragments of glass. Although her friends tried to convince her to return to the optometrist, she decided to fast and pray for three days instead. Soon after her time of prayer and fasting ended, as she was washing her face, her eyes filled with water, and the shards of glass began to wash completely out of her eyes. There was never a problem with her eyes after that day; they were completely healed.

Sis. Johnson (a pseudonym) was a faithful and loving middle-aged saint in the church. Ordinarily, she was modest and very shy. Occasionally, she would lose her grasp on reality and would enter a place that was non-existent but very real to her. None of us knew how to deal with her while the delusion lasted. While in this state, she was happy and talkative, although it seemed she felt something wasn't quite right. During one of these episodes, she confessed her love for Verbal. Sis. Johnson spent a lot of time visiting Sis. Bean, telling her how wonderful Verbal was and how much she loved him. We tried to keep Verbal out of sight during these spells, but occasionally, she would ask him for prayer. He would pray for her and then try to exit quietly. It was always special for her when she got to see him, and she would say, "Ain't he purty? He's so purty." It was probably wrong to laugh about this matter, but he had teased us all so much that we felt a little reaping on his part would do him good.

After these first few years of pastoring in Houston, we began to see real growth in the congregation. Much of the credit can be given to our Sunday school staff. While Verbal was the epitome of an old-fashioned preacher, he was also a superb example of a revival-minded pastor who never stopped looking for avenues to reach the lost. As our Sunday school grew, so did our efforts to bring in newcomers, children, and adults.

Ronnie and Marcella Wilhoite helped us arrange a candy rain, which was exactly as its name implies. The rainstorm of candy was promoted for several weeks; the children who came on the church buses were encouraged to bring visitors that Sunday. Only children could participate, and they eagerly waited for that day to arrive. As soon as the service was dismissed, our young men carried bags of candy onto the roof of the church and threw them down by the handfuls for the children to gather. This event was noisy and messy but also very exciting. We had the largest attendance of children that Sunday since we had been in Greens Bayou.

Another time, we had a country store for our Sunday school children. They were given play dollars each Sunday for attendance, but if they brought a visitor, they and the visitor were given more dollars. And if a child brought an adult visitor, they were given even more money. After six weeks of collecting money, our children were allowed to spend their 'money' in the country store. Bro. and Sis. Mundy had spent weeks gathering candy, games, and sports equipment and arranged everything in our fellowship hall to look like a country store. We also served hot dogs, hamburgers, chips, cookies, and drinks. This was a great success, and the children had almost as much fun as their spiritual pastor.

The absolute joy for Verbal and all of us was the large number of visitors, children, and adults we had in church on that Sunday. Many of them returned Sunday night, too, and we saw many of them receive the Holy Ghost.

Our fun-loving pastor

Chapter 25

The Hippie Revival

One of the most fruitful times of revival came after we had been in Houston for five years. We all resented the Hippy movement, but it was especially painful to Verbal. He felt these people were profane, ungodly, uncouth, and unrepentant. The long hair on the men seemed to be an insult aimed directly at him. He prayed for them but found it difficult to believe there was enough godliness in them to build a spiritual platform in their lives so they could be saved.

Then, God showed us how mistaken we all were. A young man from Missouri had heard about Verbal's ministry and wanted to experience it for himself. Jim Forgey had been brought up in a godly home but had strayed far from God and became a victim of the hippy lifestyle and drug culture. However, God mercifully brought him back to the altar, refilling him with the Holy Ghost. When he came to Greens Bayou, he brought with him a burden for those who had been caught up in the same pitfall. Rock and roll reigned supreme in this counter-cultural environment, and the whole nation seemed to be headed down into the depths of sin and despair. But somewhere in this process, Jesus Christ replaced what could be called disdain for these people in Verbal's heart with love and compassion. Verbal talked about this experience in one of his messages.

"I came to understand Jesus Christ loves hippies, as He loves all of us. This spiritual awakening changed my life."

He understood the Savior was talking to his heart, and this voice was familiar and loved by him.

With this new revelation, Verbal was determined to reach into the hippie community. Jim Forgie was instrumental in locating the place hippies could most likely be found, an area called Allen's Landing. He would take a friend or two and visit the area, preach a little on the street, and try to connect with anyone who seemed hungry for the Lord. Verbal also went along on some of these visits and became acquainted with a group who were having services in their apartment. He introduced himself to them, and when they learned he was a pastor, they invited him to join them in their next meeting, which would be the following night. He accepted their invitation, and they gave him the address.

The next evening, after he arrived home, he gave me this report. He took a few minutes to gather his words, then said, "Nita, you won't believe what that meeting was like. The room where we met was so dark, we could hardly see, and then we were asked to stand in a circle and hold hands." Here, he shuddered to indicate the discomfort he felt in this arrangement. I stood quietly and suppressed a smile as he related this odd experience.

Then, he told me that while he was suffering the embarrassment of holding hands with two strangers, it got worse. He continued, "They began singing, 'Kumbaya, my Lord, Kumbaya.'" We didn't use the expression 'comfort zone' in those days, but it's safe to say he was out of it that night.

That experience didn't lessen Verbal's burden of reaching these young people, and the ministry to Allen's Landing continued. While there, Jim found other religious groups making inroads into the community. He started visiting some of their meetings and made connections with Brenda and Marty Gibson. They had become acquainted in a hospital that treated mental issues and drug dependency and were both seeking some connection with the Lord. Jim brought them to church, and they were touched by the Lord during the service. They wept and repented with a sincere desire for deliverance, and God graciously filled both of them with the Holy Ghost. They were soon baptized and became pivotal in our outreach into the hippie community. The Gibsons were a work in progress, for sure. For one year, Jim Forgey spent every Friday evening with this couple, taught them Bible studies, and brought them into the fellowship of the congregation. Marty was later called to preach, and his testimony is in the Ministerial Testimonies.

Verbal was touched and moved by the willingness of these former hippies to humble themselves before God and turn their lives over to Him. The Biblical teaching they received was accepted and treasured, and they loved the worship. Many of these young people had no knowledge of spiritual matters, but they hung on until they received some understanding of the things of God.

Our church didn't seem to know how to deal with this new breed of people. This was a testing time for the congregation. These young people were absolutely unchurched, so naturally, they were untrained in proper conduct when they came to church. In many ways, they fit right in. Occasionally, they fit in too well. One night, one of these exuberant visitors mimicked our pattern of worship. He raised his hands, jumped about as if touched by God, and before anyone could stop him, swiftly turned around in his pew and kissed one of our beautiful girls in the row behind him. This was dealt with along with other breaches of conduct contrary to Christian behavior, but God still moved in a mighty way despite it all.

Many people came in during this time and received the Holy Ghost. Establishing them in truth and consistent Christian living was difficult. Part of the problem was they were easily swayed from day to day and found it difficult to make the commitment needed to walk with God. However, many of these young people were filled with the Holy Ghost, baptized in Jesus' name, and completely surrendered their lives to Christ. They had much to learn but were hungry to grow in grace. It was a challenge as well as a joy to work with them.

We were experiencing great church growth and revival at this time. Along with bringing children to Sunday school on a church bus, many saints regularly witnessed to their neighbors, friends, and relatives. Backsliders returned home and prayed through to the Holy Ghost.

Ronnie and Marcella Willhoite had just created the first home Bible study we had ever known, called *Search for Truth*. This was revolutionary to us. The Willhoites met with Verbal several times while developing this innovative soul-winning tool. They also enlisted his help to write some of the material, and he felt very privileged to be a part of this venture. Verbal was a revivalist at heart, and he greatly valued anything that furthered outreach or soul-winning efforts.

Search for Truth home Bible study was an incredible asset in soul winning. The Willhoites wrote a study guide and then created a beautifully drawn and colored flipchart to depict what was being taught. A breakthrough in soul-winning, this Bible study is still being used throughout the United States fifty years later.

After the Endsleys moved back to Louisiana, we were without an assistant for two years. Verbal contacted Mike Yeats, the brother of Libby Endsley, and he agreed to come and help in the ministry of the Greens Bayou church. He moved into our travel trailer, which we had parked by the side of the church and was a tremendous help. Mike was totally dedicated to the Lord, and he enthusiastically carried out the responsibilities Verbal had given him. During this time, he began to call Jan Williams, the daughter of Bro. and Sis. John David Williams.

Mike was soon head over heels in love with this wonderful young lady, and before long, they were engaged and planning a wedding. I had seen Jan occasionally through the years and was very impressed with her loving, godly nature. Jan took on the conviction of her parents and grandparents and trusted God for her healing. Mike loved and supported her and shared this same conviction. Verbal was asked to participate in their wedding ceremony and was honored to do so. This was a sterling couple, and we knew they were perfectly matched. Verbal and I were both thrilled to know Mike would bring his new bride to join him in ministering in our church, and they were all we could have hoped for. Jan was an outstanding musician and had written many beautiful songs. We loved this couple dearly, and it was a joy to work with them.

Their time with us was a blessing from start to finish. Their first child, Robbie, was born while they were with us in Houston. After a few more years, they moved on to start a home mission work in Louisiana.

Many times, since those days, I have longed to hear Mike lead in an altar service again. Jan would be on the organ, and they would begin to sing together under God's anointing touch,

> *"Must Jesus bear the cross alone*
> *And all the world go free?*
> *No, there's a cross for everyone,*
> *And there's a cross for me."*

It seemed to me angelic voices must have joined in because the holy presence of God would cover us as His Spirit filled our hearts with overflowing gratitude for these priceless moments.

Years later, I heard that Jan was fighting a battle with cancer. Libby Endsley called to tell me Jan's health was declining rapidly and invited me to Monroe to be with the family during these harrowing days. When I arrived, Jan was weak but still smiled her beautiful smile. She had written a song based on this scripture.

"It is good that a man should both hope and quietly wait for the salvation of the Lord."
(Lam. 3:26)

That song came to my mind as I was sitting by her bed. She was living what she believed as she hoped and quietly waited for the salvation of the Lord. It was not long before heavenly angels came to escort her into her eternal home.

I was reminded of the heroes of faith in Hebrews 11. Towards the end of the chapter, the author talks about 'others' who were tortured and had trials of cruel mockings and scourgings; they were stoned, sawn asunder, and slain with the sword. Then, a phrase is inserted within parenthesis "(of whom the world was not worthy.)" I thought about our precious Jan and was comforted by the knowledge that she was now in a place worthy of her. There would be no more sorrow or death, no dying or sickness, no separation or pain, and she would forever be with our Lord. The comforting Word is forever settled in Heaven. Thank you, Jesus.

Chapter 26

Revival and Fellowship

While pastoring in Houston, we were blessed to develop strong friendships among the ministers in our area. Bro. Tommy and Sis. Ann Jackson moved to Highlands, Texas, six years after we settled in Houston. They took the pastorate of Highlands Apostolic Church and started with a small handful of people, and soon, the church began to grow. One Friday night, we had a packed house at a rally in Greens Bayou. Chairs were placed down the aisles and in the vestibule. I noticed a beautiful lady with her three young children sitting there. After service, I approached her and introduced myself, and she replied that she was Ann Jackson. I surmised we were about the same age and hoped to build a friendship with her, especially when I realized how close we lived. We soon arranged to meet for lunch, and that was the beginning of a close relationship that has continued and strengthened through the passing years.

Verbal and Bro. Jackson also became close friends and comrades in the gospel. Bro. Jackson had received the Holy Ghost in a revival Verbal preached for Bro. Henry Dunn several years previously in Silsbee, Texas. Highlands Apostolic Church was experiencing revival services, and many people were being saved and discipled. Before long, our two churches assembled for various meetings, which was always a blessing. Occasionally, Verbal and Bro. Jackson would trade pulpits for the Sunday night services, a welcome change for both congregations. Greens Bayou Church enjoyed those exchanges, especially when Bro. and Sis. Jackson would sing for us before he preached. There is an account of the Silsbee revival in the Revival Testimonials.

One afternoon, Bro. Jackson called Verbal and asked if he would preach for the Highlands Church three nights in the coming week. He explained, "One of our precious ladies has never received the Holy Ghost even though she has lived righteously for sixteen years. Sis. Hopson is faithful in every way, and I'm unaware of a blemish in her life. But I'm burdened for her. She needs the Holy Ghost."

Throughout Verbal's ministry, God had given him faith to pray people through to the Holy Ghost who had been seeking for months and even years. He was happy to accept the invitation to preach for our neighboring friends.

Bro. Jackson described those services this way: "Bro. Bean came and preached the first night. It was a good message on faith, but he never mentioned Sis. Hopson or her need of the Holy Ghost. The next night, we had a powerful worship service, and while everyone was praising the Lord, Bro. Bean walked back and knelt by Sis. Hopson, who was sitting at the end of the pew about four rows from the front. He talked quietly to her for a few minutes, then stood, placed his hands on her head, and began praying. Immediately, she was filled with the Holy Ghost and began to speak with tongues. She never wavered in her walk with God and still lives for the Lord today."

"No friendship is an accident," O. Henry wrote, and I firmly believe the fellowship we shared with Tommy and Ann Jackson was not accidental but arranged by God. This friendship has enriched my life in too many ways to count.

After a few years, we organized a local youth camp with the Jacksons. Bro. Johnny Hair and his youth group joined us after a year, which became a tradition for the three churches.

We rented a nearby dude ranch; the kids rode horses, played baseball, took hikes, and had a great time. Because she was afraid of horses, Jennifer fondly remembers her daddy walking beside her the entire trail ride, holding the reins and reassuring her as she rode. There was a swimming pool on the property, and we selected a time when the boys could swim, and afterward, the girls would have their turn. Jana and Jennifer still have fond memories of those days.

After supper, we would have a fireside consecration service for the young people. The presence of Jesus Christ felt tangible, drawing nearer to us as we sat beneath the shining stars, blanketing the heavens. These meetings were profound and life changing.

Verbal and Bro. Jackson had many things in common. They both were outdoor sportsmen and enjoyed hunting and fishing whenever they had the opportunity. They made many trips to the Hill Country, where they would sleep in tents and hunt deer. Verbal was always careful to locate a deer lease where he could hunt, but increasingly, he wanted his own acreage. Finally, he was able to purchase several acres on a hillside outside of Bandera, and he set up his hunting camp there. We would go with him each year during Thanksgiving when deer season opened, sleep in our tents, and cook on the Coleman stove. We didn't mind the inconveniences brought about by this rough living because we loved the outdoor life. Sleeping under the stars in God's heaven brought its own sense of peace and awe at the majesty all around us.

During this time, several pastors organized an annual youth camp at Dry Creek, Louisiana, to serve the Texas and Louisiana areas, and Verbal was often asked to be the camp evangelist. There, powerful messages were preached, intensive prayer meetings took place before service, and we enjoyed the fellowship of people of like-precious faith. Sis. O'Brien led the youth camp choir, and it was marvelous to hear the young people singing under her Holy Ghost anointed and exuberant leadership.

That Friday night, Sis. O'Brien chose to lead the song "If You Miss Heaven, You'll Miss It All." At the beginning of the song, a musician stood in the back of the auditorium, playing "Taps" on his trumpet. Then, the choir began to sing the song, "If You Miss Heaven, You'll Miss It All." None of us knew that this song was ordained of God, especially for this night.

As Verbal prayed for this camp earlier in the month, he was impressed to portray hell in all its anguish and as realistically as possible. He assembled a small group, and they made a recording of the sounds they imagined could be heard from hell: crying, screaming, and begging for help, along with the sound of crackling fire. Verbal prepared to depict the lost soul condemned to that eternal inferno.

The recording was turned on as somber music played, and Verbal stumbled in from behind the platform. Wearing an old, tattered robe, he was covered with clanking chains of all descriptions. They were around his neck, holding his feet loosely together and draped over his shoulders, dragging the ground until he could barely walk. As he entered the auditorium, he was crying, "Please, God, don't send me to hell! Forgive me! Forgive me! Forgive me!" he pleaded. "I'm sorry! Save me, Jesus; save me from the devil's hell! Save me!"

In desperation, people immediately started running down the aisles, filling the altars, and packing the front from wall to wall. When Jennifer saw her daddy staggering in, wrapped in those horrible chains, she immediately started crying because she thought he was going to hell. When I was aware of her distress, I comforted her as best I could, "It's not real, Jennifer. I promise. Your daddy is not going to hell. He is not going to hell."

The camp meeting was filled with people repenting and searching their hearts; many were filled with the Holy Ghost. We were all in agreement that night; no one wanted to go to hell.

Our life in Houston was unbelievably busy, but each day was treasured. Verbal continued to preach at various conferences and meetings but was careful to stay close to our congregation. He wanted our people to know they were his primary concern and understand that he would give witness at the Judgment Seat of God to their faithfulness. This sense of responsibility to the flock of Jesus Christ remained with him all the time we were in Greens Bayou. While teaching the young preachers in our church, he said, "Pastors should always stay close to their saints."

During our years in Houston, God added many wonderful saints with various talents and abilities. Verbal, having a genuine love for music, quickly learned who among them could sing or play a musical instrument. They were invited to be involved in the church music ministry when it was prudent. God gave us talented musicians and singers, and soon, we were enjoying trios, solos, quartets, and, best of all, our choir.

Ann Jackson and I were privileged to attend some music conferences held in Jackson, Mississippi. We took our portable recorders, which were cutting-edge technology at that time, and recorded the sessions. When we arrived home, we had many new songs to teach our choirs. Among those were:

"The Cross Is My Statue of Liberty,"
"Move Me with Your Message Once Again,"
"Soon and Very Soon."

This proved to be a great blessing for us all. On many Sunday nights, the Holy Ghost would fall while the choir sang, and people would shout and run the aisles. At other times, conviction fell, and backsliders and sinners would start seeking the Holy Ghost from their pews. Bro. Ted Buxton and his talented wife, Karen, began to help with the choir, teaching parts and selecting songs.

Another aspect of this music ministry was many people could bring their talents and abilities to the Lord. As more and more were involved and included in the music of the church, they were blessed in a personal way, with anointing on their lives.

I organized a ladies' trio and asked Karen Buxton and Rhonda Forgey to sing with me. They were both gifted singers, and we loved getting together to learn new songs. When we heard the song "Jesus Pilots My Ship," we were all touched by the lovely melody and lyrics and practiced until we felt confident enough to sing it in church.

This became one of Verbal's favorite songs, and he would often say, "Come on ladies, sing my song."

Verbal also arranged for Karen Buxton to sing with us in a trio. The song we sang the most was "I'll Have a New Body (I'll Have a New Life)." We used some of the newer music for choirs and specials, but Verbal never strayed far from his gospel music roots.

The Greens Bayou Apostolic Church was remarkable in many ways. No one ever opposed or criticized their pastor's plans, burdens, and vision. Verbal commanded outstanding respect and love from the congregation. We didn't have 'church trouble' as such; however, we did have 'people problems' to deal with. People brought issues to us that needed to be resolved. Since many of them were brand new members and were quite spiritually immature, they needed extra care and counseling. We spent significant time working with their personal, financial, or marriage problems.

Many of our saints had come from complex and troubled backgrounds. Verbal prayed and studied for hours preparing messages and lessons concerning practical things: learning to be consistent in prayer and church attendance, being kind and loving to their families, and recognizing the importance of holding down a job. Some also had to understand the value of maintaining a clean, organized home or teaching their children to be respectful and obedient. It was a 'work in progress' for sure. Occasionally, Verbal would laughingly say to me, "What this church needs is a good old-fashioned Verbal Bean revival." However, it was extremely rewarding to see these new converts grow in grace and in the knowledge of Jesus Christ; we counted the effort as definitely worthwhile.

One day, Verbal came home and said, "We have a new tithe payer in the congregation. They turned in their first tithing offering last night." Then he held out his closed fist. He smiled and continued, "I'll give you this tithing envelope to keep, or you can have a twenty-dollar bill."

I have never placed a bet in my life, and gambling should be abhorrent to me at all times, but I was tempted. "I'll take the tithing envelope," I responded. Still smiling, he handed the envelope to me, and I quickly opened it to discover thirty-two cents. One of our young Sunday School boys had been given a little money, and he faithfully brought the tithe to his pastor.

During these years, we were blessed to have many evangelists come to Greens Bayou to preach for us. We enjoyed the ministry of Bro. Joe Duke, Bro. Scotty Teats, Bro. Robert W. Cavaness, Bro. Johnny Hair, Bro. Johnny Willhoite, Bro. Vaughan Morton, Bro. Hanchey, Bro. Carl Ballestero, and many more. Of course, they often brought their families with them, which was an added blessing to Verbal, me, and our girls.

One Sunday, while Bro. and Sis. Duke were with us in revival, I prepared a roast dinner for them and brought it to the evangelistic quarters after the Sunday morning service. I planned to feed my family when we got home. Bro. Duke said, "Why don't you folks stay and have dinner with us." I was reluctant to impose our family into their quiet Sunday, but he persisted. "We want you to stay and eat with us."

At this time, Jana, who was usually a little shy, piped up and said, "Please, Mama, let's stay and eat; all I've had all day is one little biscuit." Of course, after that remark, I felt the least I could do was assure Bro. and Sis. Duke that I did feed my girls, and we stayed to share their Sunday dinner. Bro. Duke thought her remark was very funny, and throughout the rest of the revival, he would remind me that Jana only had one little biscuit to eat that Sunday morning.

Our church growth remained steady, and Verbal continued to take pleasure in the role of pastor. People were filled with the Holy

Ghost in almost every service, but not all of them survived spiritually. Looking back, I realize that Verbal was very progressive in his thinking about church health. While he never varied in his teaching on the essentials of doctrine and holiness, he sought effective ways to bring new people to church, see them baptized, filled with the Holy Ghost, and grow to spiritual maturity.

Because of this, Verbal recruited as many of our saints who were willing and engaged them in church ministries. He organized a committee which he called "Save the Baby." The saints were invited to be a part of this plan, and during the first meeting, he explained the purpose of this committee. "We have many new people praying through in our services. Most of these people have never been schooled in the things of God. If they are to live spiritually, they must be cared for, just as we would care for our newborn babies. My challenge to you is to seek out newcomers and spend time with them. Entertain them in your home if you can, or take them out to eat. Check on them and find out if they have a need that you can help them with. Please love them and mentor them. We've seen too many of our newcomers go back into the world. We must protect them."

This dynamic plan was entirely new for most of us but effectively established our new converts. Many of the saints took this responsibility to heart and were instrumental in strengthening the body of Christ.

Verbal also enlisted the young men who felt called to preach to expand their ministry beyond the pulpit and help take on the care

Anniversary celebration

of God's people. Some were sent to make hospital visits; others were invited to sit in on various Sunday school classes to learn the essentials of ministering to children. They were encouraged to assist with the bus ministry and help entertain our visiting evangelists and their families.

We focused on bringing the saints in the congregation into close fellowship with each other and encouraged them to include our new converts in their friendship circles. We had social events in our fellowship hall regularly. We would serve food after Sunday night services, organize countless showers, and use any excuse we could find to encourage love and friendship among the congregation.

The Lord was also faithful to move miraculously in healing and deliverance. Although her husband didn't attend church with them, Sis. Flowers and her five daughters became an integral part of the congregation. Her mother, Sister Cash, had been suffering from a cancerous growth on her back that had spread to the bone, causing her severe pain. In her distress, she said to her daughter, "Please ask Bro. Bean to pray for my healing."

During our next service, Verbal became very burdened and started crying and praying; finally, he looked up and said, "God wants to heal someone of cancer."

Sis. Flowers said she immediately thought of her mother and searched her purse for a handkerchief. When she located one, she went to the front and said, "Bro. Bean, it's my mother. She is suffering from a cancer on her back, and it has grown into the bone."

Verbal took the handkerchief, anointed it with oil, and said, "God wants to heal her." He prayed over the handkerchief, and Sis. Flowers took it home and mailed it in a letter to her mother the next day. In the letter, she told her that Bro. Bean said God wanted to heal her of cancer. When Sis. Cash read that, she shouted all over the house. Immediately, she put the handkerchief on the growth. Three days later, while she was taking a bath, the cancer fell off into the bathwater. She was completely healed!

During this time, Verbal received a call from his good friend, Bro. Ballestero. The Ballestero family had been in Salt Lake City for three years, starting a new church there. Bro. Ballestero felt it was time to resign from the pastorate there and return to the evangelistic ministry. He wanted his family to become a part of a church in the South where most of his revivals would be held. He said, "Bro. Bean, I'm going back into the evangelist ministry, and if you feel it's the will of God, my family and I want Greens Bayou Apostolic to be our home church."

Bro. Ballestero couldn't have expressed anything more welcome to Verbal than those words. He quickly replied, "Oh yes, Bro. Ballestero, I'm honored you're choosing Greens Bayou as your home church.   Please bring your family to Greens Bayou; we'll love them as one of our own. I know they will be a blessing to us all."

Bro. Ballestero was a preacher's preacher, and his ministry was known and treasured in Apostolic churches from coast to coast. Sis. Ballestero was a saint in her own right. She was an excellent musician and singer, and God often used her in intercessory prayer. Having this family join our ranks in Greens Bayou proved to be a blessing to us all, but especially to me. Ramona and Carlene both helped with my girls, who absolutely adored them, and Ramona became my hairstylist. Nila traveled with her parents when they evangelized, so she was only with us periodically. But she, like the rest of the family, was absolutely sold out to the Kingdom of God. She and her sisters sang in a trio when she was there, and they were powerfully anointed as they ministered to us all. In addition, all the ladies of the family were exceptionally gifted cooks. We were always delighted when invited to share a meal with them.

There was a period of time when all the Shoemake siblings lived in Texas. Dayna and Jimmy pastored in Austin, Regina and David pastored a church in Seabrook, and Jimmy and Bobbie were pastoring at Spring. We were together for just about two years, and I look back on those days as treasured memories. We all had so much in common because of the ministry and our backgrounds. Verbal and the guys would discuss pastoral issues and plans for church growth, and inevitably, we would all begin to tell funny stories about our children.

David and Regina had been close to my heart for many years. She was my confidant, and we spent many happy hours discussing ministry and family matters. David was always loads of fun, and we could count on him to make us laugh.

One of my favorite memories was when I took Jana and Jennifer to visit with Dayna and her boys while our husbands were on a hunting trip. They ranged in age from three to eight. After our husbands left one day, Dayna and I decided to take the kids on a picnic at the lake and put a lot of effort into making the day special. We packed a lunch of their favorite foods and brought along balls, bats, and various toys for them to enjoy. Dayna's youngest boy at the time was Loren. He was too cute for words, had bright red hair, loads of freckles, and wore glasses. He was then, and always remained, a favorite of us all.

Loren was a lot of fun but also prone to falling into moods when everything irritated him. This was one of those days. He complained about how crowded the car was and wasn't happy about sharing the toys. We tried to make things better for him, but nothing seemed to work. Finally, Dayna had had enough. She looked sternly at him and said, "Loren, if you don't get happy right now, you're going to get a spanking!"

By this time, Loren had gotten the message. He turned his scowling face up to us all and said, "I am happy! I am happy!"

Bobbie, more than Jimmy, who was solemn by nature, shared some of the babysitter escapades her boys, Jimmy and Jon, instigated. One night, she told us that she and Jimmy had an appointment and had arranged for one of the teenage girls from their church to babysit the children. Soon after she arrived, they left for their meeting. Before Jimmy and Bobbie were hardly out of sight, Jimbo, as he was called, and Jon were entirely out of control. They ran in and out of the house, fought with each other, and generally created havoc. Nanci, the older sister, did her best to help keep her younger brothers in check, but this time her warnings fell on deaf ears.

The babysitter tried to reason with them, then threatened and scolded them roundly and sent them to their room for 'time out.' Finally, peace and quiet were achieved. While the babysitter and Nanci sat in the living room talking together, Nanci thought she heard the sound of a window opening. Jumping up, she rushed through the hall to find the boys. She saw a light in the bathroom, went to investigate, and discovered Jimmy and Jon had climbed out the bathroom window and were on the loose. The boys were finally rounded up and brought back to the house and were sternly told to sit and contemplate what their fate would be when their parents arrived home.

Chapter 27

Family Matters

As a teenager, we had an open discussion during one of our Bible studies at the San Jose church. One of the mothers stood up and said, "My husband and I try to have a family vacation every year with our children. I noticed that as children grow up and become teenagers, family time is not as important to them as it was when they were younger. So, we decided that while our children were still young, we would make the time to take them on trips with us. These vacations are very precious in our lives."

That discussion stayed with me. Shortly after we moved to Houston, I explained to Verbal that I thought getting away from the city and taking trips with Jana and Jennifer each summer was very important. He was in complete agreement, and we would plan a special vacation time for our family every year. Some years, we would take camping trips with Verbal's family, and we all had fun fishing, hiking, or playing in the water. We had a campfire each night and roasted hot dogs and marshmallows while we shared funny stories with the family. We sometimes would sing a few songs together before we went to bed.

Verbal and Hobart

As the girls got older, we were privileged to take several memorable vacations. One year, we traveled to Yellowstone Park. We rented a cabin located on the banks of a river, and during the night, the sounds of the moving water lulled us to sleep. Jana and Jennifer were excited to see the moose, elk, and bison roaming freely in the park. The geysers were magnificent, especially Old Faithful. We learned it is renowned for its predictable eruptions, which occur roughly every ninety minutes to two hours. We had never seen anything like that in our lives. We also visited Jackson Hole, Wyoming. This beautiful town lies between the Teton Mountain Range and the Gros Ventre Range. The valley had stunning landscapes, majestic peaks, and lush forests. Verbal remarked it was the most beautiful place he had ever seen.

One year, we also took a road trip to Tennessee, where Verbal was scheduled to preach at a conference. After the meeting was over, we spent time exploring the surrounding area. We were captivated by the natural beauty of the Appalachian foothills. Fertile valleys and dense forests mark this area, and the hills are dotted with farms, vineyards, and orchards. It is a feast for the eyes.

We had been told about an outdoor drama, *Unto These Hills*, in North Carolina, so we drove there to see it. The drama told the story of the Cherokee tribes, which can be traced back to the years before the anguish of the *Trail of Tears* to the present day. The Cherokees who survived the forced march were relocated to the Indian Territory, which later became Oklahoma. My family was from Oklahoma, and we had all inherited a share of Cherokee Indian blood. Daddy's older brothers received reparation money from the State of Oklahoma, which was given to members of the Cherokee tribe. This story was pertinent to me because of our connection with the Cherokee nation.

This historical drama, which clearly displayed the heartbreaking treatment of these Native Americans, some of whom could have been our ancestors, was sobering to us all. Jana and Jennifer had many questions which were almost impossible to answer.

Although we were somber for some time after this event, we were thankful to have seen this historical drama.

Some summers, we would take a road trip to California to visit my family. My girls have wonderful memories of those vacations. Mama Blanche and Papa, as Jana and Jennifer called my parents, rolled out the red carpet for our visits. Every conceivable candy and snack, always including Dr. Pepper, was available for us all, and Mother had stocked the freezer with cartons of ice cream, a family favorite.

Mother was an incredible cook and filled us up with her delicious meals. Our favorite was when she fried chicken. In addition to the chicken, we enjoyed biscuits, gravy, and mashed potatoes. Then, Mother also made a chocolate pie for dessert to give the crowning touch to the meal. This was from a recipe handed down to her by her mother. We all agreed: This was the most delicious chocolate pie ever.

Daddy always asked Verbal to preach while we were in town, and it was a pleasure to visit with friends and relatives we hadn't seen for a long while.

Our trips to San Jose always included at least one day spent in Santa Cruz. A museum there housed the life-sized wax reproductions of Jesus Christ and His twelve disciples. They were copied from Leonardo de Vince's picture of *The Last Supper*. The lighting was low, and soft music played while we sat and tried to absorb the importance of this occasion. I'm sure depictions of that last night before Jesus was taken to be crucified were far from accurate, but those are the images carried in my heart when I think about that time.

One of our vacations left an indelible mark on me. Verbal and I researched and located a family-friendly dude ranch in the Texas Hill country. This was a dream vacation for Verbal and the girls, too. We were excited to visit a working ranch for the first time. It was located at the base of some lovely hills, had a sparkling creek, and boasted a swimming pool, ping-pong tables, and a basketball court. Three meals were served every day.

One unforgettable morning, we signed up for a trail ride. Verbal and Jana were thrilled about this opportunity; Jennifer and I were more skeptical. We were both uncertain of our horseback riding abilities and not sure this would be the fun Jana and Verbal declared it would be. We went to the barn and were allowed to choose our mounts. Verbal oversaw this operation because he had some knowledge of horses and a lot of knowledge of his 'girls,' as he called us.

Verbal and Jana were quick to choose their horses, but Jennifer and I carefully looked over those Verbal and the trail boss thought would suit us. Mine, especially, seemed very large and menacing. Finally, however, we were helped onto our horses, the stirrups were adjusted to fit, and we were on our way. The first part of the ride was through scenic foothills, which were truly stunning, and I was beginning to relax a little and enjoy the picturesque trail we were on. Our ride took us down a slight incline, which led to a small creek we would pass through.

Cautiously, I rode my horse through the creek, and when he stepped out on the other side, he started bucking violently. This was so unexpected and horrifying that I was scared nearly out of my wits or what was left of them. He would kick up his hind legs and then land back down with a thud. I was hanging on for dear life, and when I could get my breath, I would scream, "Jesus! Verbal! Jesus! Verbal!" Verbal got to me as quickly as possible, grabbed the horse's bridle, and held on tightly. Apparently, the horse felt he had adequately shown his bucking ability and stood quietly while I tried not to have a nervous breakdown. Wrongly, thinking I had suffered enough humiliation through my horrible horsemanship, I realized my hairdo, which I had carefully piled on top of my head, had fallen onto the side of my face. The other riders gazed round-eyed as I painstakingly pulled out every bobby pin and the crepe wool holding my hair in place. I threw the bobby pins away, but Verbal kindly stuffed the indispensable crepe wool into the front of his shirt.

When Verbal recounted this event to every friend or relative he could persuade to listen, he would state, "I would have helped Nita sooner, but I didn't know if she wanted Jesus, or me, to come to her rescue."

Early one spring, Verbal asked if I would like to visit The Texas Hill Country. Because I was always happy to be with him and loved having his undivided attention, I arranged for the girls to stay with Sis. Bean. I packed a small suitcase, and we started on the road to Fredericksburg. Verbal wanted to discuss issues and plans for our congregation for a while but soon became quiet and concentrated on the road. I never minded his silent times and always had a book handy to keep me occupied while he was lost in his thoughts.

I loved to read, and though Verbal didn't read fiction himself, he never objected to my reading habit. The book I chose to bring on this trip was *Hannah Fowler* by Janice Holt Giles. This was a beautifully written account of a young lady, Hannah, who married a woodsman named Tice on the Kentucky Frontier. The author tells of their challenging but fascinating struggle to endure the hardships of frontier life. Tice and Hannah managed to build a log cabin, and Tice furnished it with his woodworking skills. Hannah had brought enough supplies from her home to set up housekeeping, and soon, they were enjoying their small but comfortable homestead.

Before long, Hannah realized she was pregnant but was too embarrassed to discuss this private matter with Tice. She was in a quandary and had no womenfolk around to confide in. While mending some socks in front of the fireplace one night, she noticed her husband was working on a new piece of furniture. She looked closely at his handiwork and realized Tice was constructing a cradle.

When I reached this part of the story, it was so sweet, and the love and tenderness between Hannah and Tice reminded me of my relationship with Verbal; I felt I had to share it with him. "Verbal," I said. "Would you mind if I read a few pages of this book to you? It's so touching, and I think you would enjoy it. It's about a young frontier couple." He kindly agreed to listen to me. It wasn't long before Verbal was caught up in the lives of this hard-working couple along with me. Since the sun was going down, I turned on the dome light to keep reading.

After a while, I asked if he had heard enough, but he said, "No. Keep reading." At this juncture in the novel, a heart-wrenching event occurs; Indians kidnap Hannah while Tice is in the woods, hunting squirrels for their supper.

We traveled through the night, with only the sound of my voice to break the silence. I continued to read; I certainly couldn't close the book while Hannah was in danger of her life. Finally, we reached Fredericksburg, and Verbal located a motel where we would stay. We quickly unloaded our belongings, prepared for the night, and climbed into the bed. We were tired; it had been a long day, but neither of us was ready to sleep. I turned on the bedside lamp and continued reading. It wasn't until after midnight before Hannah was rescued, brought home to her loving Tice, delivered her healthy baby boy, and life returned to normal for our frontier couple. This is a memory I still treasure and bring out from time to time to remind me of our Fredericksburg journey.

The time on Emporia Street was truly blessed. Jana started kindergarten soon after we moved into our house and attended the elementary school across the street for the four years we lived there. After three years, Jennifer followed in her steps. We attended as many school functions as possible and were grateful to live nearby. Our neighborhood was safe, and the girls and their friends spent countless hours playing in our large backyard.

Jana Kay   *Jennifer Ellen*

One sweltering summer, Verbal bought an above-ground swimming pool for Jana and Jennifer. It was a joy for him to see his girls happy. Maybe because, as a boy, his family had lived with only the bare necessities of life, he wanted something more for his family. He was a doting father and never questioned me when I felt Jana or Jennifer needed new clothes, piano lessons, or a visit to the zoo. I understood our financial limitations and was careful to stay within our budget. We didn't have arguments about money and how we spent it. Verbal was a generous and loving husband and father, a true example of godliness in every way. A Verbal Bean quote:

> *"I believe preachers should live righteously and godly every day of their lives. I believe we should be kind and loving to those around us, especially our families. If I was ever frustrated with my wife and spoke unkind, hateful words to her, I could not enter the pulpit that night until I had apologized and made it right."*

Through the years, Verbal mentioned his admiration for Spitz dogs; he felt they were very smart and beautiful. I remembered this when considering a special birthday gift for him one year. Looking through the want ads in our newspaper, I found a lady selling Spitz puppies and visited her home to look them over. They were all adorable, but I chose the most alert male of the litter. I left this puppy with its owner for another week until Verbal's birthday.

That day, I brought the puppy into the house and happily presented it to Verbal. Though it was challenging, I was thrilled, knowing I had surprised him. He was very pleased with this living birthday gift and happy to have his own beautiful little Spitz puppy, which he graciously shared with his family. We all loved Prince, as Verbal named him, and he became a favored member of the Bean family. Prince proved to be very smart, and Verbal spent many hours with him, training and teaching him tricks.

During this time, Mike, Verbal's adopted brother, was often in our home, sometimes for months at a time. Jana and Jennifer loved him very much, and we enjoyed having him in our family circle. He was helpful and always willing to run errands for us or share in the chores around the house. He was a teenager, and I think he enjoyed the busy lifestyle we were living then. His relationship with Verbal was more like a father and son than brothers, and we were glad he was a part of our family circle.

Our home seemed to become smaller with time, so we searched the area and tried to locate a larger place to rent. We found a beautiful four-bedroom, two-bath home in a nearby subdivision named Woodforest. We negotiated with the owners and agreed on the rent. We were happy to move into this lovely home and have a comfortable space available when evangelists or friends would stay with us. Jana and Jennifer had their own bedrooms now, and although they still slept together, they had room enough for all their clothes and toys.

The furniture we used in our former home was mainly second-hand and showed signs of wear. We couldn't afford new furniture for the whole house, but we got several new pieces, including a beautiful bedroom suite with a king-size bed. Verbal was especially grateful for this because now he could stretch his long legs to their full length.

Our new dwelling proved a tremendous asset in our desire to stay close to our saints and new converts. We invited various groups to use our home for social events. We hosted showers, parties, potluck dinners, birthday parties, Bible studies, and prayer meetings. This continued as long as we lived there.

Verbal and I both loved to have friends and family visit us, and to cook a company meal for them was one of the great joys of my life. People in the church would also have us over for meals, and I nearly always left with a new recipe to use for special occasions. It was while we lived in Houston that I learned to make shrimp gumbo. This was one of Verbal's favorite dishes, and I was determined to master this Cajun specialty if I could. While talking to one of my friends on the phone one day, I remarked, "I would love to be able to cook gumbo."

"Well, it's not that hard. I can tell you how to make it if you want me to," she replied.

"Please do," I replied, "My husband would be so happy if I could make gumbo."

I didn't have a tablet to write on, so I took the cover off one of our long-play records and used that to copy down her instructions carefully. Following her directions to the letter, even browning the flour in oil to the darkest brown possible, I made my first-ever gumbo. Verbal and the family loved it, so it became one of our favorites.

In addition to the church events we held, we were blessed to have the Wheeler family live with us for several weeks. Bro. Wheeler, his wife, Patsy, and their toddler daughter, Michelle, were a joy to have in our home. Verbal thought Michelle was cute and spent a lot of time teasing and playing with her. He would say, "Your Daddy can't even steal sheep!"

She would angrily reply, "Yes, he can. My Daddy can, too, steal sheep!" We would all laugh about her vehement response to defend her daddy. Bro. Wheeler was a skilled Bible teacher, and he and Verbal spent many hours working, studying, and praying together; they also spent time camping and hunting. I loved having Sis. Wheeler with us; she was witty and helpful in every way.

Even though our home was a rental, we felt blessed to be able to live in such a comfortable place. The school Jana and Jennifer attended was nearby, and they walked there each day with their neighborhood friends. As the girls left for school, we would stand at the door and pray with them. Along with our personal devotions, we found there was always a need for more prayer in our lives. Whenever life presented challenges, prayer was our solution. We recognized the constant need for God's presence, and He was always there to help us.

These were comfortable times, with little concern about danger or crime. We all looked out for each other's children, and they were welcome to play in our homes nearly any time.

The Verbal Bean family

One day, as I was talking with the lady who lived next door, she said, "How is Donna?"

This was puzzling because I knew nothing about Donna. "Who is Donna?" I asked.

She looked at me closely and said, "Your daughter, Donna."

As the mystery deepened, I said tentatively, "I don't have a daughter named Donna."

By now, we were both puzzled and a little embarrassed. "Isn't your youngest daughter a blond?"

"Yes," I replied, "but her name is Jennifer."

"Well," my neighbor said with a laugh, "she told me her name was Donna."

It took Jennifer a little while to live this down, and occasionally, we would call her 'Donna' just for the fun of it.

During this time, Bro. Molander came to preach for us for several weeks. As was his custom, he instituted 5:00 a.m. prayer meetings. These were blessed times. Granted, it was difficult to get up so early, but once we got to the church, the power of God would fall on us all. He also emphasized shouting and running the aisles during revival services. Our church freely worshipped, I thought, but Bro. Molander carried it to another level. He was never satisfied until the whole church was carried away in the Spirit.

Once, while Bro. Molander was there, Jennifer became very ill. She ran a high fever, ate only a little, and reluctantly took a few sips of water at a time. Her sickness lasted several days, and we were comforted to have a prayer warrior living in our home with us during that time. We played gospel music for hours and interceded before the Lord as we held onto God for victory. Deliverance did come, and we wept as we saw Jennifer restored to her happy self as the power of Jesus Christ fell on her.

The girls were growing up quickly; Jana was now old enough to be involved in youth events. She was somewhat reserved in a crowd, but she loved these times with her friends. Sis. Everhart was still our youth leader and planned get-togethers regularly. I'm not sure why we felt this was a good idea, but Jennifer, too, wanted to be included in everything that was going on. She was too young to be with Jana during these times, but she begged us to go, and we unwisely relented. She lived to have fun with everyone and was usually the life of the party.

Each time the girls went to be with the young people, Jana would come home furious and complain loudly about all the terrible things Jennifer had done that evening. Jennifer wasn't at all disturbed by these accusations. She had accomplished her lifelong goal of having as much fun as possible on any given night.

But one evening, Jennifer went too far. The young people were having a party at our house with Sis. Everhart in charge. They were seated at tables, playing games, and eating snacks. Jana stood up for just a minute to speak to a friend, and while standing, Jennifer decided that her sister didn't need her chair and moved it away from the table. Since Jana didn't know about the chair removal because it happened behind her back, she sat down and landed firmly on the floor. For Jana, this was the final humiliation; she felt Jennifer shouldn't have been at the party at all. It seemed clear to her that Jennifer knew it was Jana's chair and wanted to embarrass her. Jana was ready to die, just after she killed Jennifer. Well, all the king's horses and all the king's men couldn't have brought sisterly peace that night.

Verbal had a serious discussion with Jennifer, who maintained her innocence. "I thought Jana was through with the chair," she said tearfully, "and she wasn't hurt at all." Verbal reminded her she probably shouldn't have been at the party, but if she were going to be allowed to participate in these events, she would have to be more careful and not cause any more problems.

Jana was also in line for a stern conversation with her daddy. Verbal agreed Jennifer was out of line and should be more careful in the future, or she wouldn't be included in these groups. But Jana, too, had to be responsible for her own actions and attitudes.

It was not in Verbal's nature to be a severe disciplinarian. He would handle business, if necessary, but it was not easy for him. Verbal was a loving, gentle man, probably much like his father. He was also peace-loving, dreading and avoiding confrontation if he could. But Verbal was also an articulate and deep thinker. He was a formidable opponent if dragged into these disagreeable conflicts, but his first choice would always be a peaceable settlement.

While living on Lantern Lane, after carefully searching the countryside near us for a suitable place to build a home, Verbal found what seemed to be an ideal place and purchased twenty acres on Miller Rd. #2. It would be three years until we moved there, but Verbal immediately started putting fences up and even bought livestock. Then, his next project was to build a huge barn on the back of the property. He was a country boy at heart and could spend endless hours working with the cattle, planting hay, and riding a horse. This life fit him like a glove. The barn became his favorite place to pray and meditate, and he spent many hours there, seeking the Lord.

The years we spent in our home on Lantern Lane are priceless in my memories. One Christmas is especially poignant and sweet to me. Verbal had bought three horses and had a barn ready for them to occupy. We would spend hours on the Miller Road property whenever we had time to spare, and Jana had taken to horseback riding with her daddy like a professional. Jennifer, too, could be persuaded to mount a horse with promises from her daddy that she would be safe with him beside her.

Verbal and I didn't exchange gifts for Christmas and gave the money we would have spent to Christmas for Christ. But we did give gifts to the girls. Usually, I was in charge of buying all the gifts, but this year was different. Verbal found a beautiful saddle, just the right size for the girls to use, and bought it for them for Christmas. He put it on a room divider and let the girls take turns sitting in their new saddle. After searching diligently, I found a beautiful manger set made in Italy and placed it in the living room of our house. We didn't put up a Christmas tree but modestly decorated for the holidays.

The Christmas saddle

Chapter 28

Division

For years, it has been astounding to me to observe how Jesus Christ brings His children together into one body. It seems impossible when I consider how many differences there are among us: language, customs, culture, perceptions, nationalities, backgrounds, and individual personalities, to name a few.

Yet over and over, countless times, I have been a participant and an onlooker to this amazing miracle God made come to pass. My Bible studies have confirmed what I have witnessed in my own life.

However, I must state that this can only happen because God allows us to partake of His divine nature in this process. We could never see this accomplished by our own efforts and abilities. My conclusion is that the love of God enables us to partake of His divine nature, and that, in turn, allows us to become an integral part of the body of Christ.

> **"And hope maketh not ashamed; because**
> **the love of God is shed abroad in our hearts**
> **by the Holy Ghost which is given us."**
> **(Rom. 5:5)**

I am convinced we could never share enough of our human love to enable the body of Christ to function in unity. That purpose requires a supernatural infusion of God's love to accomplish this monumental yet necessary requirement. So, God, in His infinite mercy and care, teaches us throughout the Scripture how we can take on His nature enough to bring about this miracle.

The Old Testament taught that we are to love our neighbor as ourselves (Lev. 19:18), but the New Testament tells us we are to love one another as Jesus loves us (John 13:34). Because the love of Jesus Christ is a necessary element to our personal salvation and the salvation of the world, He poured out that love in unfathomable measures to mankind. As we follow in His footsteps, we, too, are to share in the nature of God by loving all mankind, but especially those of the household of faith.

In the New Testament, the saints are instructed to love one another Fourteen times. Fourteen times. We are instructed to apply the love of God in our daily lives. These admonitions are clearly stated: Husbands love your wives, wives love your husbands, wives love your children. We are to edify one another, receive one another, salute one another, serve one another, comfort one another, minister one to another, be hospitable one to another, have compassion one to another, be kind one to another, have peace one with another, care one for another, speak not evil one of another, judge not one another.

When this concept, "Love one another," is so distinctly exemplified in the life of Jesus Christ, even unto His death on Calvary, I cannot consider it a matter of choice in my life. It must become as integral and essential as breathing.

Disputes, disagreements, separations, and conflicts seem to also be constants in our relationships but can never be the determining factor in whether we love each other or not. Abraham and Lot discovered this in the problem they faced with their hired help. There was strife between their herdmen, which became a difficult problem to correct. Abraham took the first step to reconciliation.

> **And Abram said unto Lot, let there be no strife,**
> **I pray thee, between me and thee, and between**
> **my herdmen and thy herdmen; for we be**
> **brethren. (Gen. 13:8)**

Sadly, divisions had been building in the brotherhood for several years. Verbal and his friends were disturbed by what they saw as a growing trend from the leadership of the United Pentecostal Church to take on more authority than they should. Our district leadership was excellent in many ways but could be authoritative. It was expected that pastors and ministers in the district were to be obedient and compliant with not only teachings on doctrine but also on organizational matters as well. In my view, the breaking point was when officials felt they had the authority to assert that only UPC ministers would be allowed to preach in UPC churches.

This discord among preachers was troubling, and no one seemed to have an acceptable solution. Instead of growing closer, the split between differing factions seemed to be driving a larger wedge between the brethren with every passing day. A few other districts experienced the same problems as we in Texas and Louisiana.

This was extremely painful because virtually every pastor or preacher involved in the separation seemed to feel that their position on the matter was right. Soon, communication was difficult, if not impossible, between dissenting ministers. Instead of seeking common ground and reaching conciliation, the battlelines were drawn, and no compromise seemed possible. In my humble opinion, even Biblical teachings regarding fellowship between brethren were not always embraced. I would be the first to say that I am probably not qualified to discuss this matter, but it was the elephant in the room to us. The problem was too big to ignore.

I had watched Verbal, this righteous, sacrificial man, pour his life into the Kingdom of God. He was not involved in politics. His character would not allow him to harbor bitterness or unforgiveness, yet here we were, verging on separation from our precious brothers and sisters.

I give no judgment as to who I think was right or wrong. I am simply sharing my observations of those heartbreaking months and years. These Holy Ghost-filled brothers and sisters had lived godly and righteously. Many hearts were broken in this unhappy season, including mine. Most of our friends, and certainly Verbal and I, had never known or been a part of any organization other than the UPC.

Mother and Daddy came out to be with us when the battle seemed most heated. Daddy had always been level-headed, wise, and capable enough to see both sides of many problems, but this division perplexed him. He could not understand why we couldn't just take the humble side and stay in the UPC. We were made to understand that if Verbal left the organization, family fellowship would be difficult, if not impossible.

Daddy and Verbal were two of the most honorable men I knew. They both influenced the fellowship because of their holiness and doctrinal principles. I had grown up in a home where integrity and honesty were taught as necessary in godly living. Daddy would not have told a lie in a business transaction even if it would have made him a million dollars. Most mornings of my childhood, I was awakened by Daddy praying and walking the hall in our home. He was generous and giving to the work of God, especially missions.

Verbal's life was also spotless before God. His convictions were true and unchanging. Since childhood, he had developed a personal relationship with Jesus Christ, who ordered every decision made in his ministry. It was difficult for me to comprehend how this division had come about between these two men of God.

We soon found out that Verbal couldn't stay in the UPC because there was a more difficult problem than he had realized. Just before Mother and Daddy arrived, Verbal was dropped by the Texas District Board. He had been late with his annual dues, so he went to the district office to meet the board and try to come to some understanding as to how this problem might be fixed. When he addressed the board, Verbal said he was sorry his dues were late and asked for their consideration for his reinstatement. He was immediately dismissed from the room and learned later that the board had met before he arrived, dropped him from the Texas District, and had not told him of this decision. However, this settled the issue as to whether he would join his friends in the new organization.

The Apostolic Ministers Fellowship was established soon after this. Some ministers were dropped from the UPC under various charges, and others voluntarily turned in their membership cards. This was a sorrowful time, though we tried to be hopeful. Verbal preached at many of the conferences and meetings held by this group. We all had mixed feelings because we were not sure what this turn of events would mean for us. Verbal was under high anointing when he would preach; the presence of the Lord was powerful, and we felt the touch of God in these services. There was much comfort in His presence.

I am unsure how eternity will judge all the events that happened through these months. I believe there were righteous, God-fearing men on both sides of the issue. I also am convinced that most, if not all, of the Holy Ghost men seeking guidance for their families and churches' future, were sincere and humble before the Lord.

Although this disagreement seemed widespread, it affected only a small portion of the UPC ministers. I know I have only described an insignificant part of all that occurred during that time. There were arguments to support the position of preachers on both sides of the equation, and I am not qualified enough to sort out all the matters in question at that time. I am not convinced any of the participants could clearly hear or understand the concerns of those who did not agree with them. But I believe there was a separation between brethren of like precious faith, which was detrimental to the cause of Christ.

My dilemma was that most of the spiritual encounters I experienced since childhood had happened under the auspices of the United Pentecostal Church. I couldn't imagine how we could manage being ostracized from the organization that had birthed, taught, and loved Verbal and me. My heart was broken. I cried until I had no more tears to shed. Verbal, too, was feeling the loss of companionship of men he had fellowshipped, loved, and preached for. The hardest part for both of us was the separation we felt from my family. I knew they still loved us, but knowing we would not be worshipping and enjoying conferences together was almost impossible to accept.

It was good to know that we would have wonderful, dedicated ministers and churches with whom we would be associated. I was grateful for this and utterly trusted Verbal's ability to find the will of God for our lives. I believed then, and still believe today, that there should be no separation or division between Apostolic people who love the name of Jesus Christ and live according to His laws. Verbal and I still loved the UPC and the people in it. I know countless people in the organization still valued and loved us, but fellowship was very limited.

The hardest part was the knowledge that Verbal would not be welcome or allowed in the pulpits of many of our friends and family. I struggled and wept dealing with these issues, but with time, God granted me peace and a level of understanding. Not for the first time, I was so very grateful Jesus Christ was the captain of our lives, and it was not necessary or even possible for me to discern who was right or wrong. It was essential for me to hold and cherish my relationship with our Savior because I knew our steps were "ordered of the Lord."

Looking back through the lens of time and countless tears, I believe I must do my part to live sincerely and righteously before God and leave matters too difficult for me to understand in His loving hands.

I had been taught for years that God instructs His children to be reconciled with each other whenever there is a disagreement or separation between them.

> **"Therefore if thou bring thy gift to the altar, and there rememberest that thy brother hath ought against thee; Leave there thy gift before the altar, and go thy way; first be reconciled to thy brother, and then come and offer thy gift."**
> **(Matt. 5:23-24)**

I have always been intrigued by the teachings of giving our coats in addition to our cloaks or going the extra mile. These teachings have challenged my thinking regarding possessions or convenience in relation to others and their needs.

The separation from friends and loved ones seemed interminable, but it was only a few years. One day, during these difficult times, Verbal received an unexpected phone call from Bro. Carl Ballestero who said, "Bro. Bean, I need to discuss some troubling information. I just received a call from a friend who pastors nearby." He explained, "My friend called to tell me he was planning to move to San Jose and start a church. He told me that he had close friends he had won to the Lord living there, and they were members of Bro. Shoemake's church. My friend believes they would want to join him to start another church in that city." Verbal and Bro. Ballestero discussed this troubling information for some time, agreed to pray about the situation, and said their goodbyes.

Verbal immediately joined me in the kitchen and related the information he had received from Bro. Ballestero. This was disturbing to us both, and since my family's relationship was troubled at the time, we were puzzled as to how and if we should pass this news on to Daddy. After we had discussed the matter for some time, we agreed that Verbal needed to call Daddy and let him know that his church might be in danger of a split.

It was very touching to me that although Daddy had distanced himself from his relationship with Verbal, Verbal still loved him and had his best interests at heart. So, he placed the call, and Daddy answered the phone.

"Dad," he said, "Bro. Ballestero just called and told me a pastor friend of his is planning to move to San Jose, take some people from your church, and start a new work in your area." They discussed what had been disclosed and how Daddy should respond. As the call was ending, Daddy expressed his appreciation to Verbal for the concern he and Bro. Ballestero had shown toward him.

Shortly after this conversation, Mother called and said she and Daddy wanted to come and visit us if it was convenient. This was wonderful news for us, and we gave them our warmest welcome when they arrived. This was such a precious time for all of us, and we could hardly stop hugging them. It wasn't long before Daddy suggested he and Verbal walk to the barn and check on the livestock. During their time together that day, Daddy expressed regret for the estrangement and the sorrow it caused. Verbal said how thankful and relieved he was that the wall that had separated the family was torn down. They hugged and cried together as reconciliation and love was restored. This happened just a few short months before Verbal was killed.

As it happened, the preacher who had planned to move to San Jose never did, and nothing more was ever heard about the matter. I will always believe Jesus Christ moved heaven and earth to bring about this God-ordained resolution.

Abram was willing to take the humble side in the conflict between him and Lot. He was God-called; the promise of possessing all the land wherever his footsteps fell was given to him. He was called God's friend. Abram was Lot's superior in every way, yet he allowed Lot to have the first choice in dividing the land. I believe Abram considered his loving relationship with Lot more important than any amount of land.

Let there be no strife, I pray thee, between me and thee, for we be brethren.

Chapter 29

Pass It On

For many years, Verbal had felt a heavy burden for young ministers. He was keenly aware that the love for the message and doctrine we treasure must be transmitted to the next generation. Several young men from Texas Bible College attended our church to be under Verbal's ministry, and we also had men in our congregation who were beginning to feel the call of God to preach the gospel. These, and other young preachers he knew and loved, were the reason Verbal planned to start a Bible school.

Throughout his ministry, Verbal frequently preached the sermon "The Third Generation," in which he articulated the danger of losing the truth and convictions handed down from previous generations. This powerfully anointed message was delivered from a burdened heart. Verbal knew that if the younger preachers didn't hold on to the miraculous and life-changing ministries of the past giants of faith, everything we hold dear could be lost in one generation. He drew his message from this passage in Judges:

> **"And also all that generation were gathered unto their fathers: and there arose another generation after them, which knew not the Lord, nor yet the works which he had done for Israel." (Judg. 2:10)**

Verbal was consumed by a desperation to hold onto all the truths he had been taught and loved. The commitment to start a training ministry for young men was birthed out of this deep-seated love of Jesus Christ and His salvation plan.

He named this school *Apostolic Ministers Training Institute*. He had been in conversation with Bro. Roy Lawrence, for some time, about coming to Houston to help build this ministry from the ground up. Bro. Lawrence was a very capable, dedicated, and studious man of God, and he moved his beautiful wife and family to Houston to assume the leadership of the *Apostolic Ministers Training Institute* while simultaneously starting a new church in Pasadena. He and Verbal worked and prayed together for days to create a curriculum, compile a list of teachers, and establish a plan of action to bring their shared dream to life.

Verbal bought a large mobile home, which was then parked by the side of the church. The young men who didn't have a place to live in Houston could reside there. There was room enough to house six students at a time, and Bro. Broussard would act as house manager and take care of daily matters. Sis. Rumsey, one of the faithful ladies in the church, offered to prepare one meal a day for the students.

It was decided that the classes would be conducted in the evenings to leave the students free to continue working their jobs. They arranged to hold the sessions on the second floor of the church in one of the large Sunday school rooms set aside for this purpose. They agreed that the sessions should be recorded, and Verbal asked Bro. Lawrence to find the best reel-to-reel recorder available at the time. It was located, purchased, and set up in the classroom. These recorded lessons proved to be the reason we have access to these priceless and timely lessons today and also have the ability to transmit these eternal lessons to hungry hearts around the world. This was one miraculous reminder of how Verbal's ministry lives on still today.

We all knew this was a wonderful, innovative endeavor, but I'm not sure any of us realized the eternal value and lasting implications the *Apostolic Ministers Training Institute* would bring to the Kingdom of God.

Anointed and devoted preachers were enlisted to teach these students, usually for a week at a time. Included in the teaching schedule were Bro. Lawrence, Bro. O'Brien, Bro. Majors, Bro. Burr, and Bro. Spell, to name a few. Classes were conducted Monday through Friday evenings, except for Wednesday nights. These heroes of the faith donated their abilities to the spiritual development of these young men.

Verbal began the institute by teaching the subjects he felt most necessary for these young men: the sessions were on *Prayer* and the *Works of the Holy Ghost*. His teaching style was relaxed, with time for questions and discussion. His students said Verbal often sat on the edge of his desk, swinging his legs, and taught these men the things of God as he had received them.

Verbal had unparalleled insight into the necessity and power of prayer. Early in his life, he studied and learned how to pray effectively. He had spent countless hours praying before and during his pulpit ministry and systematically taught people how to pray throughout his revivals. He was also committed to moving into the supernatural realm in every service. Considering this, **Prayer** and the **Works of the Holy Ghost** would be the most crucial curriculum in the **Apostolic Ministers Training Institute.**

The students were astounded by the extent of Verbal's Biblical knowledge. Bro. Marshall told me that Verbal would often answer questions and cite the scriptural reference without ever opening his Bible.

Since Verbal's death, his ministry has been carried throughout the United States and around the world. The recordings of his lessons, **Prayer** and the **Works of the Holy Ghost**, have been duplicated and heard by thousands of people. These two subjects were transcribed from the recordings and printed. Innumerable copies of these books have been in circulation for many years.

While ministering to these young men, Verbal also emphasized the need for balance in a preacher's life. This is a testimony of how he learned to use wisdom in his ministry.

In one of the class sessions, Verbal described how he damaged his health and had to stay home sick for a month because of not having the right balance in his spiritual life.

> *"I spent about three hours a day in prayer. I spent many hours alone, praying, seeking God. We had morning prayer meetings, I would pray later in the day, and I also prayed before church. Sometimes, the burden for the service would be heavy on my heart all day as I became more and more desperate for a victorious service that night.*
>
> *Through experience, I learned to pray earnestly and fervently, then take time off during the day to rest, take a drive, or talk with a friend. Then I would pick up the burden again before church."*

While Verbal was teaching a class one evening, he stated, "This lesson is being taped. I am doing this for you and for those who will be taking this class by correspondence later on." He probably did not know how prophetic the nature of his remarks would prove to be. The *Apostolic Ministers Training Institute* held classes for only four years, from 1969 to 1973. Although there were not a large number of students, the influence of that school is still pertinent and powerful today.

During the last years of his life, Verbal's ministry was controversial to some. Sadly, the separation between the Apostolic Ministers Fellowship and the United Pentecostal Church lasted far too long, and there was little fellowship between these two factions. At that time, it would have been difficult, if not impossible, to foresee that Verbal's ministry would one day be accepted and revered by practically all Oneness Pentecostal movements.

Everywhere I go in Apostolic circles, when people discover I was married to Verbal Bean, they express their eternal gratitude for the spiritual treasure that was imparted to them, their families, and their churches by his ministry. They have stories, most of which I had never heard before, about Verbal's lessons and the messages' miraculous impact on their lives. Over and over, I hear words like these:

> "I have read the book on ***Prayer*** so often, it's falling apart."

> "After I listened to the lessons on the ***Works of the Holy Ghost,*** God has used me in miraculous ways."

> "I am so grateful to the Lord for allowing me to experience Bro. Bean's ministry."

> "I know he was a prophet sent by God."

> "Those tapes changed my life and ministry."

Bro. D. C. Moody expressed to Bro. Jimmy Lee, "A dead man taught me how to be used in the gifts of the Spirit."

This is the testimony from Bro. Mark Morgan, pastor of Abounding Grace in San Francisco, California:

"As a young man, very early on in my ministry, I was perplexed regarding how God was using me. I didn't fit the mold in what we would consider an evangelist to be. At that time, Pastor Larry Eddings suggested I listen to some cassette tapes by Verbal Bean teaching on **Prayer** and the **Works of the Holy Ghost**. I was driving in my car, and I put Bro. Bean's tapes into the cassette player. After I listened to those, I pulled my car over to the side of the road and wept because they really helped me understand how to begin my journey into the Apostolic ministry. I'm so thankful for the ministry of Bro. Bean and the impact he had on my life."

It is astounding and humbling to recognize that a small Bible college, *Apostolic Ministers Training Institute*, conceived in the heart of a righteous man, was the vehicle the Lord used to preserve and transmit priceless and eternal lessons. These truths were taught there by men of God, especially by a servant of Jesus Christ, my precious husband. Verbal's ability to make these immortal lessons understandable to every searching servant of the Lord has had eternal consequences. The demographics of Heaven will reveal the eternal power of God's Word spoken through the lips of mortal men.

**"But the Word of the Lord endureth forever.
And this is the Word which by the Gospel is
preached unto you." (I Pet. 1:25)**

In addition to the *Apostolic Ministers Training Institute*, Verbal also started a company called *Truth Enterprises*. This was a cherished undertaking, and Verbal had prayed and explored its potential for generating income for quite some time. He felt the need to see that the young men praying through to the Holy Ghost and leaving the hippie world were equipped to function in an orderly lifestyle. They would be taught a trade in order to provide for themselves and their families.

This endeavor was headed up by Bud Desormeaux, who was assisted by Ted Buxton, T J Marshall, and Joe Morgan. The purpose of this company was to start a business repairing barges. These experienced men, who were well equipped for this task, would teach welding. Most of these young people had never learned the discipline of working at a public job, organizing a budget, and attending to basic responsibilities. This would be a priceless opportunity for them to learn to be diligent and industrious in earthly matters.

The second purpose of *Truth Enterprises* was to raise money to construct a much-needed church building on the thirty-five acres Verbal had purchased on Wallisville Road.

Sis. Smith, one of our faithful and dedicated ladies, was a successful businesswoman who opened a bakery in our area called The Sweet Shop. She helped finance *Truth Enterprises* from the beginning, and her support was one reason it became the successful venture Verbal believed it would be.

We were all incredibly busy during these weeks, but Verbal believed personal consecration and dedication to the cause of Christ could not be overlooked or shortchanged. Prayer would not be sacrificed for convenience. Our church services were still consistently victorious, and revival fires continued to burn. Verbal believed and clearly taught that Jesus must be the author of every plan, dream, or vision. The need for supernatural guidance was essential in every way.

"Except the Lord build the house, they labour in vain that build it..." (Psa. 127:1)

Chapter 30

Blue Skies

During this time in Houston, Verbal and I realized that we needed some assistance. The Lord provided this help with a wonderful young couple, Bro. and Sis. Jimmy Lee.

About a year before we moved into our new home, Verbal had asked Bro. Jimmy Lee and his lovely wife, Cathy, to come and assist us in Greens Bayou. Bro. Lee carefully sought the Lord regarding this invitation and finally felt the freedom to bring his small family and join us. This couple, along with their active toddler, Nathan, were a blessing to us all, but especially to Verbal. Bro. Lee and Verbal had a close friendship and a deep understanding and agreement regarding Biblical truths. Bro. Lee soon led the song services with his strong baritone voice and took charge of announcements, prayer requests, and offerings. He and Sis. Cathy were totally dependable and exemplified godly living in every aspect of their lives. She was soft-spoken but was very capable and quietly ministered among us wherever she saw the need. These months were busy, filled with joy and anticipation.

In addition to his musical ability, Bro. Lee was an accomplished carpenter and spent many hours working on our future home. He confessed to me sometime later that the modifications Verbal and

I wanted to make to the house while the building was in progress were a challenge. We came to understand that maybe some of our suggestions weren't as practical as we thought they would be.

We were finally finished with nearly every detail of the house; only a few more loose ends needed to be tied up. Verbal, generous as always, told me I could purchase some new furniture for our home, and I spent hours poring over magazines and visiting decorating centers. These are happy memories. I was blissfully unaware that the final chapters of our lives were being written daily. In my mind, the future stretched infinitely before us, beautiful and filled with light.

Our only thoughts about the future were centered on the revival we believed was in store for Greens Bayou Apostolic Church, the building of a new sanctuary to house our growing congregation, and seeing the hand of God manifested on our family and saints. Maybe impaired vision regarding dangers or possible disruptions to our well-being has its benefits, I don't know, but there didn't seem to be a cloud on our horizon. Our skies were blue.

The following weeks were a whirlwind of activity. It seemed there were church events scheduled for most nights of the week. The congregation was full of young couples, and we were giving baby showers nearly back-to-back. Our new converts made up a large part of the congregation, and they required a lot of care and prayerful attention.

Verbal was preaching anointed and visionary sermons in every service. He anticipated a victorious future and taught wonderfully encouraging prophetic messages about revival and what Jesus Christ had planned for His people. My husband still carried undying faith for unprecedented Holy Ghost outpourings and firmly believed we would live to see another Acts revival when more than three thousand souls would be saved in one day.

Verbal entered a season when he focused on preaching about the coming of the Lord. The message was clear. We should always be ready because we don't know when the bridegroom will return for his bride. The condition of the world was worsening with every passing day, and we must keep our wedding garments clean, without spots or wrinkles.

Coming home one day after school, Jennifer walked into our mobile home and said, "Hello, I'm home." When no one responded, she thought that was strange. She put her books on the kitchen table and looked around the room and out of the window to see if both vehicles were there, and they were. Then, she was horrified to see Verbal's dirty coveralls, hat, work boots, and socks lying in the middle of the floor.

I always tried to make sure I was there when the girls were due to arrive home, so it was unusual for Jennifer to find an empty house. I must have gone down to the barn for some reason that day, so I wasn't home as usual. Feeling distinctly uneasy, Jennifer began to search all the rooms, but there wasn't another person in the house. Then, she had a horrible thought. The rapture had taken place, and she was left behind. She was terrified and started crying. She rushed to the telephone to call her Granny to see if she was still there. She was vastly relieved when Granny answered the phone and assured her the rapture had not taken place. She found out later that her daddy had received an emergency call to go to the hospital and pray for someone, so he dropped his dirty clothes where he stood as he rushed to change into clean clothes for the hospital call.

Sunday nights were the best. Opening the service, Verbal would loudly proclaim. "God's power will never diminish!! We will be a witness to the saving grace of Jesus Christ in these last days. The darker the night, the brighter the light of salvation will shine on our church and on our city." After Verbal's proclamation of faith, we would begin singing, "There shall be light in the evening time."

The saints would be caught up in the Holy Ghost power we all felt; we would shout on the platform, and people would run around the aisles. Those services were stupendous, and anointing would flow like rivers of blessings over all privileged to be there. Looking back on those Spirit-filled services, it seems to me that God was giving us a double portion of grace and victory to strengthen us for the dark days, unseen but inevitable, we would all soon be facing.

Chapter 31

Miller Road #2

Living on Lantern Lane was a happy time for us, but Verbal longed to move to Miller Road and build a home, which seemed to be a dream location for us all. In preparation for this project, we bought a large mobile home, which was set up in what was to be our backyard. This proved to be a mixed blessing. The mobile home was roomy and comfortable, with three bedrooms and two baths. But we soon learned that living on twenty acres of undeveloped land is a very different state of affairs than living in a subdivision.

Verbal had created a lane of sorts that went from Miller Road back to the barn. He had a tractor he called *Ol' Blue,* fitted it with a blade, and scraped out a fourteen-foot-wide road for our use. Verbal deposited yards and yards of gravel binder on the dirt after the road was leveled, and we were good to go until it rained. The mud became an unending source of aggravation and inconvenience. We were stuck in the mud several times in our vehicles and had to have someone on the tractor pull us out. Bro. and Sis. Marshall had come to visit us one day after I had just lost another monumental battle with the mud. Once, while slogging through the boggy driveway in my high heels that day, I said to Sis. Marshall, "If I ever lose the victory, it will be because of that mud!"

The mobile home was set up parallel to the 'road,' and we had a small porch with steps leading to the front door, which helped a little. Verbal had a water well dug and a pump installed. This all seems very primitive to me now, but it was primitive back then, too. In addition to the problem with mud, we struggled with huge rats, some as large as small dogs, and no matter how many traps we set or how much poison we put out, it was an ongoing battle.

Verbal was always pleased when friends would join him in his farming endeavors. One afternoon, he was on *Ol' Blue* with two of our young men from the church riding along with him. He was plowing one of the fields in preparation for planting hay. As he turned the corner heading back up to the other side of the pasture, the brakes failed just before they reached the fence. The boys told me later that instead of becoming upset, Verbal just started singing at the top of his lungs, "When We All Get to Heaven," and plowed right through the fence. They spent the rest of the afternoon marveling that they had emerged uninjured from their adventure.

One of our faithful members, Bro. Henderson, was an excellent builder, and Verbal and I spent many hours with him and his wife, Mildred, discussing what type of home we should build. We considered the size, style, and floor plan. Verbal and I decided on a simple plan: a rectangular structure facing Miller Road, featuring a full-length porch across the front.

The construction of our home was a long but enjoyable process. It was a pleasure to check on the progress each day, and after the house was framed and sheetrock put up, it gradually took shape. In my imagination, I chose colors and arranged furniture and window coverings.

Jana and Jennifer were very happy living in the country, as they described it. Verbal had selected one of our horses for Jana to ride, and she fell in love with Miss Priss, as the mare was called. This horse was a chestnut color, distinguished by the white markings on her feet and head. Jana spent countless hours riding all around our acreage. She was an exceptional horsewoman, and we loved to watch her hair flying in the breeze as she flew down the lane to the barn on the back of Miss Priss.

Jennifer had developed a strong fear of horses after an unfortunate bucking incident. While riding her pony one day, wanting to go a little faster, she flicked her reins and accidentally hit her mount in the face. The horse took exception to this and promptly bucked her off. This caused Jennifer to have a very real fear of horseback riding for many months. Being the sweet father he was, Verbal bought her a fun go-cart to enjoy instead, and she spent days driving her vehicle at full speed, up and down our lane; we never knew how many miles she put on her vehicle, but we did have to replace the set of tires once before summer was over.

Jennifer came into the trailer one day, full of indignation, and told me of a terrible offense her father had committed. She and her best friend, Holly, had spent the morning creating a village for their dolls to live in. They had chosen the bed of Verbal's dump truck as the location for their project. The girls had taken loads of toys and materials from the trailer and spent a long time creating this beautiful space for their doll families. This lengthy process involved numerous decisions and revisions to complete the delightful task. They finally had everything in order and were firmly in make-believe land. The girls were especially thrilled when Verbal climbed into the truck, drove slowly around, and checked on the condition of the livestock. Jennifer and Holly thought this was a momentous addition to their morning. After this delightful drive, Verbal returned to the barn and parked the truck.

Unbeknownst to Jennifer and Holly, Verbal had observed their project and planned this trip to inspect the cattle just for their enjoyment. But he couldn't resist giving them one more exciting thrill to conclude their day. Just before he turned off the motor, at the slowest speed possible, he began to raise the bed of the truck. Soon, the girls, the dolls, their families, the carefully arranged furniture, and all the accessories began to tumble willy-nilly out of the truck. The girls were indignant and vociferous as they began to tell Verbal what they thought of someone who would destroy a village for fun! It took a while for Verbal to get back into their good graces, but he was unrepentant, as ever, when pulling a prank on someone.

One day, while Sis. Bean was visiting me in the kitchen. She looked at me and said, "Nita, why don't you have us a baby boy?" For some time, I had thought about trying again for a boy but wasn't convinced I would be successful. I replied, "Well, if the Lord tells you it will be a boy, I just might." Jana was twelve, and Jennifer was nine, so if I was going to have another baby, it should be soon. As it happened, before long, I was carrying our third baby. I had difficult morning sickness, but otherwise, it was an easy pregnancy.

Verbal and Jennifer were thrilled with the news about a new Bean baby. Jennifer loved babies and could be seen toting one or another of them around after every church service. Jana was very unhappy when she learned the news. She pouted for a while, then ended up in tears as she said, "Our family is perfect as it is. Why do we need another baby?" I don't know if she was embarrassed or just annoyed, but try as we might, we could not convince her she would love our new baby.

One day, Verbal remarked, "Nita, I don't think we should talk about how much we want a boy because I don't want our girls to feel they are not as important as a boy would be." Though the matter was not mentioned often, I knew he would be thrilled if we had a son added to our family. Mother flew out to Houston again to be with us during the birth. As before, our baby was very late, but finally, the fateful day arrived, and on July 1, 1975, we welcomed our newborn son into the world weighing nine pounds. Verbal and both our mothers couldn't wait to get on the phone and spread the joyful news of the birth of our baby.

For years, I had decided if we ever had a boy, he would be named Verbal Winston Bean II. Verbal and I had discussed it, and though he was a little reluctant, he agreed to the name. While still in the hospital, I filled out the birth certificate with the name Verbal Winston Bean II. However, as he thought about it, Verbal began to have doubts. He really wanted this baby to have a more traditional name. Since I had already finished the paperwork for the birth and the papers had been sent to the authorities, I had to fill out another form to change the name and send it in. So, we finally agreed our beautiful boy would be Joel Winston Bean. When Verbal admitted to me a few weeks later that maybe we should have kept the name Verbal Winston for our son, I confess there were a few things I wanted to say, and perhaps a few words were spoken. However, we agreed another name change might be one too many.

After four days in the hospital, it was time to go home. Verbal had brought the girls to see Joel and me every day, but Jana was still very quiet about the baby. Jennifer was actually too young to be allowed into the hospital room, but friends carefully smuggled her in to be with all of us. Neither Verbal nor I knew Jana's feelings regarding her new brother, and we were reluctant to question her about it.

When Verbal brought Jana and Jennifer to take Joel and me home that morning, he measured the distance between our house and the hospital. Soon after they arrived, Joel and I were released from the hospital and taken downstairs. A nurse stood nearby holding Joel while Verbal carefully helped me into the passenger seat. He had arranged for the girls to draw straws to see who would first hold the baby on the trip home. Jennifer drew the short straw and climbed into the back seat, and Verbal placed Joel into her arms. She was thrilled with this tiny new brother, looked at him lovingly, and kissed his cheek. At the halfway mark on the way home, Verbal pulled the car to the curb and parked while the baby transfer occurred. He gently lifted Joel from Jennifer's arms, walked around the back of the car, and put him into Jana's lap.

Verbal returned to the driver's seat, and we continued the trip home. Shortly, we heard Jana talking to Joel. "You are so beautiful." she told him, "And I love you. You're my precious baby boy," she continued. Verbal and I looked at each other and didn't make a sound. This sweet talk continued all the way home. Jana had fallen in love and didn't care who knew it. This transformation has lasted all these years and is still in effect today.

Having a baby in our home was absolutely heaven to the Bean family. There seemed to be a race to see who could reach Joel first and pick him up every time he cried. The girls were old enough to care for our baby and were helpful to me during this time, but there may have been a few arguments to decide whose turn it was to hold Joel. I'm sure he was the most adored baby boy in Harris County. Verbal had been careful to make sure the girls knew they were just as beloved by him as a boy would be, but there was no denying the pleasure he took in being the father of this child, a gift from God. Fortunately, we didn't know this precious time would be cut short.

Since the birth of our girls, remarkable, almost magical things had been created for the mother's convenience and the baby's comfort. Disposable diapers, which actually worked, were available to everyone. After raising two babies on the evangelistic field with

Family portrait

only cloth diapers, this new invention seemed to be a gift from heaven to me. Also, being in the comfort of our mobile home with a beautiful nursery prepared just for Joel was a luxury indeed.

Joel's first birthday celebration.

One day, Verbal called me from the kitchen, where he had been working on some drawings. He was very artistic, taught himself to draw, and eventually painted a few pictures in oils. I didn't know what project he was working on then, but I joined him in the kitchen when he called my name. "Look, Nita," he said, "I've got the perfect name for our place. I'm calling it the Triple J Ranch." Using our children's initials, Verbal had drawn a very attractive arrangement of three J's and soon decided to have it crafted in wrought iron to be displayed above our driveway entrance.

Although the pace seemed slow, gradually, the house was nearing completion. The flooring was down, but there were still a few building projects to finish. During the Christmas season of 1976, Verbal became very sick with the flu and took a strong dislike to the mobile home where we were still living. He said, "Nita, I don't think I can stand to spend one more night in this place." Since our new home was nearing completion, we moved mattresses into the family room and stayed there for Christmas. A few of our faithful men and their wives came to help us with this undertaking. We gathered up bedding, a few clothes, and all our Christmas gifts and moved into our new house. This move proved to be very therapeutic for Verbal, and soon he began to feel better. We built a fire in the fireplace, sat on the carpet in our robes and slippers, and opened the Christmas presents. Verbal and I had bought a small record player and new records for Jana and Jennifer, and after these gifts were opened, we began playing Christmas records. We played games, ate snacks, and enjoyed being a family. Jana and Jennifer both recall this as a favorite Christmas.

The church was still growing. People received the Holy Ghost and were baptized in almost every service. Verbal was unbelievably busy preaching conferences, seminars, and in local assemblies. He had cut down on the invitations he would accept but also felt it was important for him to stay connected and close to his brethren in the ministry.

People have asked if any of us had a premonition of the impending tragedy. That fear had never entered my mind. I felt we were in God's perfect will, we were healthy, and it just didn't occur to me that this could be cut short in any way.

However, a few years ago, Jana and Jennifer both told me about a conversation each had had with their daddy. Although it occurred on different days, it was during the same period of time, and their stories were almost identical. Jennifer told me that one Sunday after the service was over, she went to Verbal to get his permission to spend the afternoon with Holly, her good friend. It was common for the girls to spend Sunday afternoons with their friends, in our home or theirs. Verbal usually was agreeable with this arrangement, but this time it was different. "Why don't you just come on home and be with the family today? We need to spend time together, and we never know how long we'll be able to do that." Jana's conversation with her daddy a few weeks later was almost precisely the same. I don't know if Verbal saw the girls growing up quickly and realized these days wouldn't last forever or if something was troubling his spirit.

Verbal, Jana, and Jennifer

Baby Joel

Chapter 32

Goodbye

Saturdays were busy days for us all, and usually, we were involved in some outreach or visitation, but this Saturday was different. The girls were with friends for the weekend, and Joel slept in later that morning than usual.

Although much of that day remains gray and indistinct, some memories remain clear. Verbal and I had time to be together, just the two of us, that morning. That rare occurrence made those few hours especially precious to me. We had breakfast and shared our plans for the day. Verbal had many things on his agenda, but one of the main events he was looking forward to attending was a local livestock auction. He enjoyed the occasions when he could mingle with the community and get acquainted with more of our neighbors. During that auction, he bought a prize sheep raised by a young FFA member.

Before leaving, Verbal received a phone call from Nylotis informing him that their Uncle Ross was in serious condition. He was ninety-two years old, so this news was not unexpected. Verbal told Nylotis he would get there as soon as he could. After he hung up, he asked me to be ready to go with him to see Uncle Ross that afternoon. Then he hugged me, said goodbye, and left the house.

The last picture taken at the fairgrounds

Verbal met with Bro. Lee, and they discussed and planned things that should be taken care of that weekend. In his testimonial about Verbal, Bro. Lee shared this information:

"During our meeting that day, Bro. Bean told me he, his wife, and aunt would be going to Louisiana later in the day to be with his Uncle Ross. Uncle Ross, ninety-two years old, was in a dying condition and had expressed some interest in being baptized. Bro.

Bean said he hoped he would be able to baptize his uncle before he passed. He continued, 'I plan to be back tonight. If, for some reason, I don't make it back for the morning service, Bro. Carl Ballestero is to preach. Carry on as if I were there. I'll be back for church tomorrow night, Lord willing.' This was the last conversation I ever had with him. As he left, he waved goodbye to our small son as he drove out of sight."

After Verbal left, I took Joel with me and visited the Cradle Gem, a local shop for baby clothes and nursery supplies. I bought a gift there for one of our young ladies who was expecting her first baby; we were giving her a shower the next week.

Joel and I stopped at McDonald's for lunch. He was a picky eater but always ready to eat a hamburger. We went home after we finished, and the memories of the rest of the afternoon are largely wiped away. Later, I prepared for the trip to Louisiana, putting Joel into one of his cutest outfits. We loved to show him off, and he could have been given the title 'best-dressed baby boy' in Greens Bayou Church.

Verbal returned home, and I vaguely remember feeling rushed to leave for Louisiana because he was running a little late, which was unusual for him. Soon, we were in our vehicle, an old Ford station wagon Verbal had purchased for a song that day. We had decided we needed a new car but hadn't found the time to shop for one, so he bought this Ford to use temporarily. Verbal called the man who handled our insurance and asked him to draw up the necessary papers to cover the Ford before we left on the trip, and he said he would. As it happened, the insurance man decided he could wait until Monday morning to put the insurance in place.

We drove to South Houston to pick up Verbal's aunt, who was called Auntie by her family, and she rode with us on the trip to DeQuincy. When we arrived at the nursing home where Uncle Ross lived, we met the rest of the family, who had gathered in the reception room. Nylotis told us Uncle Ross had died shortly before we arrived. There was not a lot of grief over his passing, and the family shared some favorite memories of him and then began to plan his funeral service and burial.

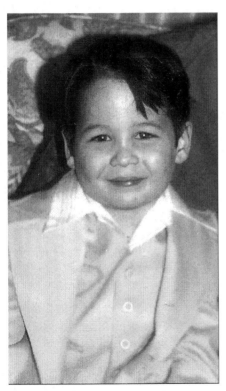

Joel Winston Bean

One treasured memory remains; that night, Joel was the delight of all the relatives. He was adorable, friendly, and inquisitive, and the only baby boy in the Bean family to carry on the name. He eagerly explored the room and spotted Verbal's cousin. Joel's eyes lit up with excitement, and he walked across the room, grabbed the cousin's trouser leg, and began to exchange baby talk with him. Noticing this, Verbal located me in the room and beckoned me over so I could enjoy this remarkable moment. He said, "Look at Joel, Nita. I believe he thinks my cousin is your daddy." As I stood beside him, I felt a wave of gratification, knowing we were sharing something precious.

Nylotis told me a few weeks after all this happened, "I wanted to talk with Verbal that night in the nursing home, but he could hardly take his attention away from Joel." Though this was a small incident, it brought some sweetness to that horrendous night. Verbal's last few remaining moments of time were spent enjoying our beloved son.

Our drive, as we started back to Houston, has never been more than a series of blurred memories and impressions to me. Joel stood between Verbal and me in the front seat; Auntie, again, was sitting in the back. At that time, cars were not required to have seat belts or car seats. I felt sleepy and probably dozed off with my head resting against the back of the seat. I was told later that as we were rounding a curve in the road, we were hit head-on by a man driving a Corvette. The driver and the friend with him had been drinking in a bar down the road a short distance, and both men were killed on impact.

Later, I was told by a doctor that Joel's arm had almost been pulled from his body, causing permanent nerve damage. By this, we know that when Verbal saw the car speeding towards us, he instantly grabbed Joel by the arm, causing the injury but undoubtedly saving his life. Verbal's last act was to protect his son.

An ambulance arrived at the scene, and the attendants were caring for Verbal and Auntie first, as their injuries were critical. Susie, Nylotis's oldest daughter, later recounted that night's events as her mother had shared the details with her.

Nylotis was on the same road we were on but was some distance behind us. She could see a car wreck ahead of her: traffic was stopped, and as she looked more closely, she saw me walking beside a car, which Nylotis then realized was ours. It was in the pile-up, and she was devastated to discover we were in this horrible wreck. She pulled to the side of the road and ran as quickly as she could to try to get to us. She begged the ambulance attendants to tell her what had happened and then was told the heartbreaking news that Verbal had not survived the crash. Auntie was in critical condition, and the paramedics were working to save her life.

When Nylotis reached me beside our car, there was a group of people gathered around, and someone remarked, "I hear a baby crying." They quickly began to search the car and couldn't find Joel. The crying continued, and when they opened the back door, he was lying on the floorboard. He was quickly handed to Nylotis, and she could see he was terribly injured and had a horrible wound over one eye; he was struggling to breathe.

I slowly became aware of flashing lights, confusion, and noise. Our car had stopped, but I didn't know why. I couldn't really focus or see clearly when I opened my eyes. Somehow, I had climbed out of the car and was standing there in a daze. I heard Nylotis talking to a man outside our car door, which was open. The man was shouting, "We've got to take that baby to a hospital! We need to leave now."

Nylotis responded, "You can't drive. You've been drinking."

"You drive then," he said, "But this baby won't live if we don't get him to a hospital."

She agreed and said, "We'll go in my car."

I vaguely remember that someone held me tightly around the waist and held my arm, gently leading me to the other car. I was unsteady and wobbly. My feet felt strange, turning over at every step, and my ankle would almost touch the ground. I learned later that the heel of one of my shoes had broken from the impact of the wreck, and it was a slow, painful journey as I made my way to the car.

I was placed in the front seat; Velda, Nylotis's youngest daughter, and the man holding Joel sat in the back seat while Nylotis drove us to the DeQuincy Clinic as quickly as possible. She could hear Joel struggling to breathe, and she didn't know if he would live long enough to be helped.

When we arrived at the clinic, Nylotis and the man holding Joel rushed into an empty waiting room and shouted for help. A nurse slowly walked in and asked what they wanted. Nylotis tearfully stated, "This is my nephew; he was in a car wreck and needs to see a doctor immediately."

The nurse replied, "The Doctor's not here. We can't help you."

By this time, Joel had begun choking from the blood which was accumulating in his throat. "Couldn't you clear his throat so he can breathe? Can't you use a syringe to help this baby?" the man demanded. "He'll die without help." Nylotis was crying and praying; our good Samaritan was in a panic, trying to save Joel's life.

"Well," the nurse slowly replied, "I guess I could do that." She did take Joel and cleared the blood from his throat. He began to take ragged breaths but was still in a precarious state.

Nylotis and our caring stranger, taking Joel in his arms, rushed back to the car, and we started the drive to the Sulphur hospital. As soon as we arrived, the attendants at the hospital realized they didn't have the ability or equipment to treat the injuries Joel and I had suffered. They put us into an ambulance, and we were taken to the Memorial Hospital in Lake Charles.

The trip to Lake Charles and the next several hours are lost to me. Finally, I began to awaken just a little to find I was in a hospital bed. I was overcome with confusion, and I didn't know where I was or why I was there. I was in severe pain; my back and both feet were hurting terribly. I opened my eyes and saw Sis. O'Brien and Ann Jackson standing on either side of the bed, and although it was a comfort to me to have these loving friends by my side, I slowly understood that this was a dreadful situation. I wanted to ask questions, but before I could form the words, I became unconscious again.

An hour or so later, when I opened my eyes, my friends were still standing by my bedside, and I asked, "Sis, O'Brien, why am I here? Where's Verbal?"

"You all were in a car accident, Nita," she replied, "Please just lie back and rest. We're here with you, and everyone is praying for you all." I wanted to ask again about Verbal but slipped once more out of consciousness.

After a while, I opened my eyes and tried to sit up, and asked again, "Where's Verbal, Sis. O'Brien?"

Again, holding my hand, she quietly said, "Please lie back down and rest so you can feel better." She told me later that she was trying her best to keep me asleep until my parents could arrive from California and be with me when I learned about Verbal's death. I felt something was horribly wrong, but I couldn't put words together and drifted off again into a light sleep.

The next time I awoke, my mind was clearer, and I was determined to get some answers. "Sis. O'Brien," I begged, "Please tell me where Verbal is. I promise you I won't go into hysterics."

Even yet, I can hear the sorrow and heartbreak in her voice when she finally said, "He didn't make it. They've taken him to St. Patrick's Hospital."

When I could finally comprehend what she meant, an endless abyss of grief seemed to open before me. This was crushing news, and I could hardly breathe. I couldn't imagine life without my precious Verbal. He was the absolute center of our lives; we all adored him. Our children, Jana, Jennifer, Joel, and I, depended on him utterly for his unfailing love and endless care. He was our protector and our provider. Verbal was the head of our home, and I looked to him for all the major decisions necessary in daily life. He was never inflexible or dogmatic in his plans for our lives, and I knew his judgment was based on spiritual guidance. How could I even live life without him by my side?

My mind was in turmoil, trying to fathom how I could possibly survive this dreadful night. I couldn't begin to contemplate the future for our children and me. Life without Verbal was simply unimaginable. The enormity of this loss came slowly but relentlessly, rising into my thoughts and emotions, drowning hope and joy.

Slowly, it dawned on me that Greens Bayou Apostolic Church had lost its apostle, spiritual leader, and beloved Shepherd. This crushing loss, combined with the grief our family was contending with, was unspeakable in its sorrow. Words fell short, and no amount of tears could convey the vastness of our anguish.

In addition to the emotional upheaval I was in, I was examined, and X-rays were taken, which revealed my back and both feet were broken. It would be weeks before I could take care of my family. The nurses would turn me from side to side by carefully lifting the sheet where I lay. Feeling helpless when I was desperately needed was one of the most difficult situations I had ever encountered.

My first concern was for our children. Where was Joel? Was he injured or even killed? I knew our daughters weren't with us on that life-crushing trip, and I was grateful they had been spared. Soon, Ann and Sis. O'Brien assured me Joel was still living. He was seriously injured but was alive and being treated here in Memorial Hospital.

I was told the downstairs waiting room was filled with ministers from the area who had come to the hospital when they learned about Verbal's death and sat together in vigil for the rest of the night. Their initial reaction was disbelief. It was difficult to grasp the reality that one of the 'warriors of faith' had abruptly been taken away in such a violent manner. It was also a time of sorrow as these friends came together to offer and receive solace.

Conversations were hushed, filled with somber voices as preachers began to reminisce about Verbal. Then disbelief turned to grief and tears as someone voiced the question that was in everybody's mind, "Who will ever fill Bro. Bean's place in the ministry?"

This was a time of confusion as the news of Verbal's passing swiftly spread around our circle of relatives, saints, friends, and acquaintances. It was difficult, if not impossible, to get an accurate account of all that took place that night. Our Greens Bayou saints were in a state of shock and disbelief when they were told of the accident and the passing of their pastor. It seemed unbearable that he could be taken away from them so quickly. In an instant, the destinies of hundreds of people were irrevocably changed and would never be the same again.

Jana and Jennifer were each with friends that weekend but not together. It was a few hours before I learned what was happening with my precious girls and how they had heard about the death of their father.

When I remembered Jennifer was with Ramona and the Ballestero family, it comforted me. I knew they would shield and protect her as much as possible during this time, but there was no way to soften the blow that would change her life forever. These friends offered all the love and comfort possible, but there were no relatives within reach, and the shock of grief brought about by the knowledge of the loss of her father was overwhelming. Then, she had to deal with learning that Joel was at the point of death himself, and I was in a hospital room, unable to get to them.

Jana was spending the weekend with her close friends, Sherrie and Sandy, in a nearby town. They planned to spend the day with other friends there. During their visit, Sherrie received a phone call instructing her to take Sandy and Jana to the local pastor's home immediately. Upon their arrival, they were ushered into a living room crowded with people. It seemed the church members were there to console each other and pray for the Bean family. These people were strangers to Jana, and she was overwhelmed with a terrible sense of dread about these unusual events. She knew it must be terrible news, but she had no idea what it could be.

The pastor, as kindly and carefully as he could, told Jana about the accident and that her daddy had been killed in the head-on collision. Then, he continued with the description of Joel's injuries and my condition. Jana was devastated but felt awkward and alone in this roomful of strangers. She was taken to a back bedroom in the house and collapsed onto the bed, tears flowing uncontrollably, as the grief too deep to be expressed in words overcame her.

Despite the efforts of her friends to offer support and comfort, the situation was overwhelming. The absence of any relatives compounded her feeling of isolation and grief, and it seemed to her she was left to face these horrible challenges alone.

That Saturday night, the roads were covered in almost impenetrable fog. It would be simply too dangerous to try to drive the girls to Lake Charles. This painful separation from those they loved the most must be endured for the rest of the night.

Internal scars of loss and grief were to be present with both my beautiful daughters for the rest of their lives, and they suffered the turmoil that inevitably followed the adjustments and changes that they faced.

Sunday morning, Uncle James drove from Houston as soon as he could when he learned of the tragedy. He stopped by to see Jana on his way to Lake Charles. Jana was still asleep when he arrived early that morning. He was shown quietly into the room, sat on the edge of Jana's bed, prayed for her, and comforted her as much as he could. Jana was reassured to see family, and she fell into his arms, relieved to finally be able to give vent to her emotions with someone who truly understood her devastating loss.

In the meantime, my parents and other family members had been told of the situation and were overwhelmed with shock and grief. However, they were trying to get to us as quickly as possible. They arranged to fly to Houston on the earliest flight, and most of my family had arrived by Sunday evening. Arrangements were made to bring Jana and Jennifer to me.

It was sometime later before I learned how Sis. Bernice Bean was bearing the knowledge that her son had been taken from her. Her shock when told of Verbal's tragic death almost overwhelmed her. She fell to the floor crying helplessly and begged those present to take her to Verbal. She said, "If I can get to him and lay hands on him, I believe God will raise him from the dead. Please take me to him, please." Bro. Lee and the others tried to reason with her, explaining that driving to Lake Charles while the roads were covered in fog was too dangerous, but she was inconsolable. They carefully and lovingly cared for her the rest of the night.

Chapter 33

But God!

Joel was brought into my room the following day and placed beside me in the bed. He was still very drowsy and quiet, but touching and feeling him close by my side was a source of comfort. No one really knew the extent of his injuries; it was clear he had suffered a massive concussion, but no bones were broken. It was a few hours before we realized he wasn't moving his left arm, but this didn't seem to concern his doctors. There wasn't much to be done for me at this time except to try to keep me comfortable with my pain under control.

That Sunday, my hospital room was filled with relatives and friends. Jana and Jennifer finally arrived, and we hugged and wept together for a long time. Their sorrow broke my heart, but I was grateful they were safe. God had spared them. Early that evening, my parents arrived from California. For the first time, I felt a measure of peace, knowing I was surrounded by people who could help us through this dark labyrinth filled with unanswered questions and difficult decisions.

My family rented hotel rooms in Lake Charles, and Jana and Jennifer stayed with them. When they arrived in my room the following day, my parents discussed the need to bring Joel and me to Houston. They talked with the doctors, who felt we were strong enough to make the trip if we could be transported in an ambulance.

A man in our congregation, Bro. Hebert, a part-time ambulance driver, offered to come to Lake Charles and transport us back to Houston. Mother stayed with me in the hospital that night and rode in the ambulance with Joel and me the next day. It was a painful journey, but thankfully, Joel slept most of the way. I was dropped off at Northshore Hospital, and Joel was taken to Texas Children's Hospital in the medical center of Houston. Bro. Eddie Wheeler met them there and checked Joel into the hospital since none of the family members were available at that time.

The several days I was hospitalized passed in a haze of conflicting images. I was surrounded by an amazing array of flower arrangements in my room, sent by my devoted family and friends, and before long, there wasn't enough room for them all. Each day, I received a steady stream of visitors who came to offer their support, express love, and pray for me and my children. Despite this outpouring of care and concern from others, I remained deeply overwhelmed by grief and the uncertainty of what lay ahead.

I was weighted down with sorrow because Joel was in the hospital across town, and I was not able to see or care for him. However, the body of Christ stood in the gap for me. Along with his nurses and doctors, Joel was looked after twenty-four hours a day by precious people from our congregation and our family. Bro. and Sis. Lee and many other church members spent countless hours holding him, coaxing him to eat, and praying for him. I got many reports daily about his progress, his eating, and whether he was gaining the necessary strength for his recovery. Although his healing was slow, he did seem to be gaining ground as his body became stronger.

While I was still in the hospital, we felt it necessary to begin funeral preparations for my Verbal as soon as possible. Just to discuss these matters would open a floodgate of tears from me, yet I wanted to be involved in every decision. I felt it was the last service I could provide for this man who had filled my life with love and provision, and I was determined each detail would be as perfectly planned as possible.

First, we had to select a church that could hold the crowd we were told would be there. Bro. O. W. Williams, pastor of Stonewall Pentecostal Church, kindly offered his beautiful sanctuary for our use, and we were grateful for this consideration. We also had to select speakers, pallbearers, musicians and singers, flowers, ushers, and numerous other details—too many to list.

Hobert and Daddy were chosen to select the casket for Verbal, and Mother and Sis. Bean chose his burial clothes. These were the most heart-wrenching tasks we could imagine, but everyone worked together to plan the most perfect funeral possible for our precious Verbal.

It was decided to hold a memorial service for the church members in our church building on Tuesday evening, April 5, 1977. The funeral service would be held at Stonewall Pentecostal Church on Wednesday, April 6, 1977, at 1:00 p.m.

Memorial Service

Announcements: Rev. Jimmy Lee

Organ: Sis. Jan Yeats

Master of Ceremonies: Rev. Jimmy Shoemake

Prayer and opening remarks: Rev. Jimmy Shoemake

Song: "Jesus Pilots My Ship": Rev. and Mrs. Jimmy Lee

Prayer and Praise: Congregation

Song: Men's Quartet: "Learning to Lean"

Remarks: Rev. Jimmy Lee

Congregational songs: Rev. Jimmy Lee

Remarks: Elder Eddie Wheeler

Prayer: Rev. Jimmy Shoemake

Message: Elder Carl Ballestero

Song: "After All": Rev. Jimmy Lee

Remarks: Elder F. V. Shoemake

Closing prayer: Rev. Jimmy Shoemake

Funeral Service

Opening song: "Contrast" by Rev. Murrell Ewing

Organ: Sis. Joan Ewing

Obituary and remarks: Rev. Murray Layne

Telegrams read by Rev. James Kilgore

From: Rev. and Mrs. N. A. Urshan

From: Louisiana District Board, Rev. C. G. Weeks

Remarks: Rev. James Kilgore

Song: "Tears Will Never Stain the Streets of that City": Yeats trio.

Remarks: Rev. C. R. Free

Remarks: Rev. H. B. Morgan

Song: "One Day I Will": Sis. Emalie O'Brien and trio

Thanks, and Introduction: Rev. C. R. Free

Message: Rev. A. L. O'Brien

Internment: Brookside Cemetery and Memorial Park

Mother stayed with me in the hospital for both the Memorial and Funeral services. I pleaded with her to attend at least the funeral, but she was adamant that she would remain with me. Understanding her deep love for Verbal, I knew this was a significant sacrifice for her, yet she believed my need for her comforting presence was greater than any other consideration. Susie, Verbal's niece, also stayed in my hospital room during the funeral and was helpful in every possible way.

After each service, the family returned to the hospital to give accounts of all that had transpired. Everyone was gratified but surprised by the number of people who came to pay their last respects and show their love for Verbal. There was standing room only at both services, and the crowd spilled out the doors. Hundreds of ministers came to the funeral, and while this was rewarding, it was also a little bittersweet. I fervently wished Verbal could have known how highly he was esteemed and revered by his brethren in Christ Jesus. I also wondered if any of these precious people wished we had all been more closely knit together before this tragedy occurred.

Chapter 34

From My Heart

When I was finally released from the hospital, it was a relief to be able to go home. However, being almost entirely immobilized, I used a wheelchair. I had to be supported to stand, but somehow, with amazing help, I managed to get by and was surrounded by family and friends twenty-four hours a day.

Joel was still in the hospital for several days after I was released to go home. We believed he was receiving excellent care, but his doctors were concerned because his recovery seemed to be stalemated. They concluded that being separated from his family was the cause of the problem. They arranged to give him a temporary discharge so he could be brought home to us. That day was memorable in several ways. Bro. and Sis. Dees came to visit and pray for me and the family. We were in our living room, and I was sitting in the wheelchair when Bro. and Sis. Lee came into the room. Bro. Lee carried Joel to me and placed him in my arms. When Joel saw me for the first time in many days, he broke into helpless sobs, and I started crying, too. We were both overcome by the emotion of the moment. Joel and I were pushed in the wheelchair back into my bedroom, and we were put in bed together. After a while, we both fell asleep and woke up feeling better. Although Joel had to be taken back to the hospital that evening, he was released two days later. We were incredibly grateful to have him back in the family circle. I have thanked the Lord continually since that time for sparing Joel when he could so easily have been killed.

Mother and Daddy devoted several weeks to our family's needs but were also there for the church congregation. Daddy preached often and strengthened the saints with his encouraging and comforting messages and his watchful care for them all.

Bro. and Sis. Jackson visited us frequently during those days. They had become friends with Mother and Daddy, and we all enjoyed spending time together. One day, Mother and Ann loaded me and the wheelchair into the car and took me to shop for a new dress after we stopped for lunch. It was a refreshing break to leave the house for a while.

Jimmy and Bobby, David and Regina, and Jimmy and Dayna all came to stay and help us at various times, offering their love and care. My brother Jimmy and brother-in-law Jimmy Jones filled the pulpit while they were there, and Bobbie, Regina, and Dayna took care of household responsibilities for us. David paid the bills and helped arrange my financial affairs. Each played a different but valued role in our lives, and they all gave extra time and love to the children.

Those days stand out in my memory as a wall of protection for me and my children. We were literally surrounded by care and support while we were so broken and helpless.

It soon became apparent that I would have to sell off all the equipment and animals on our small holding. I knew I wouldn't be able to remain in our newly built home, but as soon as I was able, we would move to California to be near my family. I felt strongly that I needed to move away from the church with our children so that the people could bond with the new pastor. Later, I would regret that decision.

The following days and weeks were filled with many arrangements and plans for dismantling the life we were leaving behind. Daddy and several of the men in the congregation worked together to get the best price for the things we needed to sell. It was a hectic, difficult time, deciding what would be taken and what would be sold or left when we moved to San Jose later in the summer. We were also responsible for finishing a few projects in the house. But day by day, decision by decision, we finally completed the last of these tasks.

Looking back, I believe there could have been a better solution to the problem of pastoral transition. I wish we had enlisted Bro. Ballestero to be the supply pastor for at least six months. That would have given the congregation and our family time to deal with the grief and upheaval in our lives. My children were uprooted so quickly they were left with wounds that had not even begun to heal. The questions of why their lives were so drastically changed in such a short time were not fully addressed or explained.

With counsel from my family, I tried to make the right choices regarding the future. But I wish with all my heart that I would have understood the importance of allowing enough healing time to pass before irrevocable decisions were made. I believe no one has ever judged me about this, but I have regretted the haste to come to conclusions I was not yet mentally and emotionally equipped to handle. I also know that Jesus Christ is our counselor and guide, and He alone can make our crooked paths straight. He is merciful and my constant companion and understands that while I may have missed the mark at times, I was genuinely seeking the right way for me, my children, and our beloved congregation.

Reflections and memories from those days are seared into my mind and heart. Bobbie found Jennifer in our closet, wrapped in one of Verbal's suit coats. She was crying uncontrollably and told her aunt, "I think my heart is breaking." She explained, "I'm trying to remember how Daddy smelled when he was ready to go to church."

Jana told me later that it seemed to rip apart the fabric of her world as she stood weeping and watched people load up the horses she dearly loved and haul away our livestock and equipment. It created a sorrow that settled into the core of her being, reminding her of the life she was leaving behind, a life she would never be able to revisit.

Susie came to be with us and helped with our many obligations. She kindly volunteered to take Jana and Jennifer to buy new clothes for the funeral. While in the car on the way to the clothing store, Jennifer began to recount, through tears, words people had spoken that hurt and angered her. "People tell me that Daddy's in a better place. That's not true. A better place would be here, with us!"

Nylotis spent many days with us despite her own grief. She came into my room one day, almost unable to speak through her tears, telling me Joel, standing in our bedroom window, was crying out, "Daddy, Daddy," as he saw one of the men in our congregation walking toward the barn. He thought it was Verbal. Hobert, Ruth, and Doll were supportive and loving throughout these uncertain days.

Sis. Bean spent as much time with us as she could. Later, when we moved to San Jose, it was an almost unbearable loss for her. It saddens me even today to recall how she suffered through that time. Verbal had been a constant in her life; he was more than a son to her, but also a spiritual strength through his ministry. Her life would never return to the place of joy she had known before Verbal's passing.

It was almost like another death to think about getting a new pastor for Greens Bayou Church and leaving the people who had become part and parcel of our lives. They supported us in every way imaginable, caring for me and helping Jana, Jennifer, and Joel as much as possible. They cleaned the house and brought in innumerable meals for us all.

Our Greens Bayou saints continued to be faithful to church services under the excellent leadership of Bro. and Sis. Lee and the other young ministers in the congregation. Although carrying their own grief, they did everything possible to hold things together during this unfathomable time. Bro. and Sis. Wheeler spent several days caring for us all. Bro. Ballestero and his family stood like bulwarks against the onslaught of grief and uncertainty we all faced.

Bro. O'Brien and Daddy worked together, along with the church board, to try to locate and install the new pastor. After proper notification, an election was held, and Rev. and Mrs. C. R. Free were chosen as the new pastor and wife of Greens Bayou Apostolic Church.

Although I recognized the necessity of relinquishing our places in the congregation as the beloved family of the pastor, it was almost an insurmountable obstacle, but we did it.

With all this grief engulfing me like a tidal wave, I found that often I only thought about the loss of my Verbal and wondered how we could possibly go on with life. Later, however, I slowly realized how different Verbal would recount that day if we could have heard him speak. He had preached countless messages about Heaven and quoted the powerful scriptures in Revelation about its grandeurs. Verbal's earthly descriptions of the hereafter always brought a high anointing on us all as he would lift his voice and hands in worship, tears flowing freely. But now, as his praise was perfected at his entrance into New Jerusalem, the mortal had put on immortality, and death was swallowed up in victory; what might be unfolding in the heavens? To think of Verbal in the presence of the Savior he had loved and served all his life, surrounded with angelic choirs and with those who had gone on before him, knowing he was experiencing unspeakable joy, provided a respite from grief and sorrow and Heaven became more real to me than it had ever been.

There was a comfort in knowing my separation from Verbal was only temporary and understanding he was in a place where there was no pain, no sorrow, and I could whisper, "You've left this world, but your love remains in my heart, a part of my very soul. And I know you'll be there, waiting for me with that smile I loved so much."

Chapter 35

Revival Testimonials

The Fresno Revival

Bro. Jimmy Shoemake

When Bro. and Sis. Murray Layne took the church in Fresno, there were a lot of things going on that shouldn't have been happening. The church was very troubled. Bro. Layne began to work on the congregation, both with prayer and teaching, and the saints began to come out of their carnal state. Not long after he took the church, they had a church split. It wasn't a big church, but it was a big church split. The disagreement was over purchasing a piano; the disgruntled group got upset and left, which was probably a good thing.

Bro. and Sis. Layne prayed and worked with the remaining saints. I preached a revival for them during this time and saw the church starting to recover. Sis. Layne was a worshipping person, and during the services, she could be very inspirational. The church started doing better, and two families moved in from out of town. They were solid saints, and they contributed to the church's maturity and growth.

Soon, they outgrew their building and purchased a Baptist church which was located on Harvey and Festus. It was there that Bro. Bean preached his revival. This was probably the most powerful thing that had ever happened to the church. It brought the congregation to a new spiritual liberty.

Bro. Bean was completely committed to the revival. Sis. Layne said, "While I was walking down the hall and passed Bro. Bean's room, I could hear him praying. I would stand outside his door and listen; I would weep and pray myself because I knew he knew how to touch God."

There was a couple in the church who had serious issues. Bro. Bean was able to help them get through the problems. He worked and prayed with them until they got their lives on a serious footing. They became established in their walk with God and were a blessing to the church.

The church still needed some cleansing; there were still old spirits trying to hang on. Bro. Bean preached powerful messages, and finally, Bro. Layne felt the church was on a new footing and ready for a mighty influx of souls. Bro. Bean was also gifted with the ability to make people understand the value of freedom of worship.

Bobbie and I were in the services in Fresno during most of the revival. She had been a member of this church and considered Bro. Layne her pastor. We were in full-time ministry ourselves but attended the Fresno revival whenever we could. We often sang with Bro. Bean and helped wherever we saw a need.

I remember one night in particular; I was sitting on the platform with Bro. Layne, and Bro. Bean came in and sat down beside me. A new couple came to the revival that night. Neither Bro. Layne nor I knew them. Bro. Bean spotted this couple in the crowd, bowed his head, and began to intercede. I will never forget his prayer. He prayed, "Oh, God, we've got some people here tonight who need You so badly." Then he started crying desperately. "Oh, God," he prayed, "I don't know if I have prepared myself for this." Just before service started, he got up from his chair, walked down the aisle, and moved into the row behind this couple. Then, he leaned over between them and started talking. I couldn't hear what he was saying, but he talked with them for a good while. He then got up and returned to the platform.

When the service was turned over to him, Bro. Bean walked to the pulpit and said, "God has shown me a couple tonight, and I'm thankful you are here because God is giving you a chance to restore your lives and be saved. If you don't take advantage of His mercy tonight, you will probably never have another chance to do so." He was visibly touched and very passionate. It seemed his heart was breaking to think about somebody who could possibly be lost.

He continued, "I'm giving you an opportunity now to make everything right with God." The couple got up and walked together to the altar, and they prayed through to the Holy Ghost. We found out later that they were backsliders and within six months of that night, both of them were killed in a car accident. They served God until He called them home. There were numerous saints in that congregation whose lives were changed and renewed in the Holy Ghost. Only eternity will reveal the complete story of that marvelous revival.

Throughout the revival, Bro. Bean had been pleading with someone in the congregation to get right with God. Often, God would deal with him about a person with a particular sin or problem but wouldn't always tell him who it was. He kept reaching for this individual, who was a member of the church. He said, "There is a man in this congregation; your heart isn't right with God. You've been out of step with the Holy Ghost during this whole revival, and you've been doing things that are contrary to the laws of God. He is giving you a chance to repent, restore yourself, and save your soul from hell. Please don't turn away from the voice of your Savior." Sadly, no one responded to this pleading.

On the last night of the revival, Bro. Bean again pleaded with that individual. He said, "Tonight is your last opportunity to get your life straightened out and make things right with God. If you reject

God tonight and refuse to hear him, the whole city is going to be made aware of your sins."

The service continued, and the revival closed. Soon after the revival closed, one of the saints called Bro. Layne and said, "Bro Layne, have you read the Fresno Bee today?"

Bro. Layne replayed, "No, why?"

The man replied, "You need to read it."

Bro. Layne picked up the paper from the yard, opened it up to the front page, and saw the headlines: "Foster parent and city custodian has been charged with child molestation, which has continued for several years." The paper carried the name and a picture of the man in the article. He was tried, found guilty, and sentenced to the penitentiary.

It was amazing how God used Bro. Bean and how great the results of his revivals were. When pastors trusted him, turned their pulpits over to him unfettered, and let him follow God, there was always victorious revival. He would go in and clean out iniquity and things that were hindering God's good move. Then, when he closed the revival, the revival continued in the church. This was true in nearly every revival Bro. Bean preached. Those anointed services reminded me of the Scripture:

**"And hath raised us up together, and made us
sit together in heavenly places in Christ Jesus:"
(Eph. 2:6)**

Mother was such a wonderful hostess; it was amazing to know she had been raised in abject poverty. Mother was a Kilgore, raised by my grandparents, C. P. and Ella Lee Kilgore. Granddad was a pioneer preacher of the gospel message. They traveled and evangelized while Mother was growing up and often had to stay with people in their homes. This was difficult for Mother because she was a timid child and often sickly. But I'm sure these memories created a desire in Mother's heart to make sure everyone who stayed in her home was welcomed and treated with the utmost kindness.

While Bro. Bean was preaching the revival in San Jose for my parents, F. V. and Blanche Shoemake, I remember a particular day when Mother was cooking a beautiful steak dinner with all the trimmings for all of us. Before we began to eat, Dad asked Bro. Bean to offer thanks for the dinner. He bowed his head and began to pray; the more he prayed, the more anointing came on him. It was no longer just a prayer for the food but was a prayer for the lost and for the service that night. Soon, he was weeping. I don't think there was a dry eye around the table. He sat there for a moment, then he said, "Sis. Shoemake, you've prepared a wonderful meal, but would you please excuse me? I have to go pray." He then went to his room and prayed until it was time to get ready for church. He was so very committed to the cause of Christ.

Bro. Bean touched many lives, churches, and preachers. He was so very effective in his ministry.

Bro. Bean wanted everybody he considered to be a friend to enjoy the blessings of God as he did. We spent many hours discussing various scriptures, and he always tried to encourage me in my ministry. He was very enjoyable to be with and loved the fellowship he shared with his friends. While he was preaching in San Jose, we decided to take a trip to Los Angeles during our first Monday night off. We drove to Los Angeles, and we had a good time looking at the sights. But along towards evening, Verbal started saying, "Oh God, did we miss you by taking a night off?" We assured him God was not displeased with friends enjoying fellowship occasionally.

Bro. Bean was loyal and generous as a friend, and I've missed that. He was fun to be with around the family and could fill the room with laughter as he told his stories. I don't think you could ask for a better friend.

I've never really understood why God called Bro. Bean home at such an early age. Bobbie and I drove to Mom and Dad's house one day, and Dad met us at the door. He tearfully said, "Jim, I hate to tell you this, but Verbal's just been killed in a car wreck." A kick in the stomach wouldn't have been as painful as hearing this horrible news. I couldn't understand why God would take a man who was so dedicated, so valuable to the Kingdom and had such an anointing from the Lord. I don't question God, but I couldn't understand it. But God knows all things, and I'm sure there was a purpose in that death; there was a reason.

Verbal was forty-four when he was killed, and I would say that in that short span of years, he greatly impacted innumerable people, preachers, and churches with his powerful ministry. People would come to his revivals from every walk of life and were touched by the powerful anointing on his life. His life was not wasted but totally dedicated to the Kingdom of God.

The Madera Revival

Sis. Karen (Toole) Davies

In the spring of 1963, Rev. Verbal Bean came to Madera to hold a revival. He, his wife, Sis. Nita Kay, and their baby girl, Jana, stayed in our home. We had services every night except Monday. The services lasted sixteen weeks, and during that time, it seemed almost one hundred people received the Holy Ghost. Many were not only from Madera but also from neighboring Pentecostal churches.

One night, when Bro. Toole turned the service to him, Bro. Bean began to tell of a dream the Lord gave him. "God showed me in a dream last night that a man who attends this church and seems to be 'in good standing' is living the life of a hypocrite. When I saw him in my dream, he was sitting on a barstool in a bar, drinking alcohol, and smoking a cigarette."

 It stunned the congregation, but he continued. "God is giving you an opportunity to repent tonight. I could call your name, but I won't. I plead with you to confess your sin." The church began to pray earnestly with great heaviness, interceding and wondering who it could be. Again, Bro. Bean pleaded with the man. "The Lord is merciful and is giving you an opportunity to make things right and get ready for His soon coming. Don't hesitate! We're not promised tomorrow."

The church became more fervent, but the man didn't make a move. It was so fearful. Bro. Bean stood with his eyes closed, shaking his head, recounting a similar service at a church in Texas, where he had held a revival. He described a couple he'd felt to reach for that night. They didn't repent. On their way home later that evening, they hit an embankment, were instantly killed, and went out into eternity. "I feel more of the judgment of God tonight than I did in that service in Texas. Would you please repent and make it right tonight? God loves you; the church loves you. Would you come?"

There was a powerful heaviness of conviction. It was a service that arrested every adult, young person, and child. We begged God for the man and prayed that he'd repent that night.

The man didn't repent and eventually walked out of the building, went to his car, and waited for his wife to join him. He never came back to church, never repented, and continued to live the life he'd been living.

There were many other services with powerful, moving conviction in the preaching, but with different results. Many responded by running to the altar. Backsliders prayed through, and new people were filled with the Holy Ghost and baptized in Jesus' name.

Later, the Perocellis, a middle-aged couple, came to the revival. Juanita Perocelli was someone my mother had known when they were both in their teen years. She was a backslider and hungry to get right with God. Touched deeply by the message that night, she repented and sought a renewing in the Holy Ghost but didn't make much progress. After she'd finished praying, Bro. Bean looked her in the eye and said, "I'll tell you what your problem is. It's pride! If you'll get rid of your makeup, the Lord will refill you with the Holy Ghost."

She was a loan officer at a bank and took pride in her appearance. But God used Bro. Bean in the gift of the discerning of spirits and let him know what she needed to do to get victory.

The next morning, at about seven o'clock, the phone rang at our home. Juanita Perocelli was on the line and told my mother, "Would you tell Bro. Bean my makeup is on fire in the burning barrel right now, and I'm coming to be filled with the Holy Ghost tonight." And that's exactly what happened! She never made it to the altar that night because while we were still singing and worshipping God, she threw her hands into the air and was gloriously filled and renewed in the Holy Ghost. The church shouted and danced, rejoicing with her. Her Catholic husband also received the Holy Ghost, as well as her father, who was also a backslider.

These are just a few examples of the mighty move of God we experienced in that revival. God used Bro. Bean to bring about a new dimension of worship, a liberating, exuberant flow of the Holy Ghost in our services. That set the stage for an ingathering of souls even after the revival was over and for years to come in Madera. Only eternity will reveal the true impact of that powerful revival in 1963 with Bro. and Sis. Bean.

The Silsbee Revival

Bro. Tommy Jackson

Bro. Dunn was pastor of the First Pentecostal Church in Silsbee, Texas, at the time of Bro. Bean's revival. He was a personable man and a powerful preacher. The men of the city loved and respected him very much. When he took the church, there were about eighty in attendance. He had done a good work, but at the time, there was a lot of carnality in the church: rings, brooches, and dyed hair. Bro. Dunn had brought the church a long way, and attendance was probably about one hundred sixty at that time.

Bro. Bean came in the fall of 1967, and he started preaching and digging and getting things out of the way that shouldn't have been there. Eventually, he started the church on a twenty-four-hour and seven days a week prayer chain. During that time, the revival was for seven nights a week. Shortly after the revival began, the devil was stirred up, and sinner men were very upset when their wives started taking off their wedding rings. One of the men, Ed Kurt, came with his pistol, prepared to kill Bro. Bean, and he ended up getting the Holy Ghost that night. People started praying through, and the revival spirit spread. They counted eighty-six people who prayed through in the revival, and a picture was taken of them. There were many more who had also prayed through but were not present that night for the picture.

So many young people received the Holy Ghost that it had a profound effect on the high school. I went to the coach and resigned from the baseball team, and that caused a stir. The High School was close to the church, and a big group of us would go there for prayer meetings during our lunch hour. Two of the girls who were at the prayer meeting went back to school and spent the rest of the day speaking in tongues. The school administrators couldn't handle that, and it created a tremendous uproar, and everybody was talking about the revival.

The revival was so effective in Silsbee that it reached the First Assembly of God Church on the south end of town, and they started praying people through to the Holy Ghost. It was sad they didn't understand the doctrine of baptism in Jesus' name; however, they did make some changes in holiness issues.

The revival lasted over three months and continued on into 1968. There are still saints in that church today who received the Holy Ghost during the revival. By the end of the revival, the congregation numbered around two hundred fifty people. That revival truly established the saints; they got rid of jewelry and television sets, women stopped dying their hair, and a lot of worldliness was conquered. A real appreciation of a prayer life was also started at that time.

The revival was the turning point and established a spiritual foundation for the Silsbee Church.

Six of the young men who received the Holy Ghost in that revival were called to preach: Tommy Jackson, the twins Mike and Malcolm Seal, another set of twins Jimmy and Tommy Tomplate, and Marvin Dunn. Derryl Doughty prayed through after the revival when Bro. Bean returned for a series of services.

After Bro. Bean left, the revival continued on for several years. That revival turned the church around and shook the community like never before. People were established in Apostolic doctrine and holiness, and freedom of worship was present in every service. It was truly a work of the Spirit, and eternity will witness: "…The effectual fervent prayer of a righteous man availeth much." (James 5:16)

Pastor Dunn, Verbal Bean, and those who received the Holy Ghost in the revival.

The South Bend Revival

Nila Ballestero Marxer
and Bro. Martyn J. Ballestero, Sr.

During the '60s, Bro. Verbal Bean was an evangelist sought after by many ministers. He was in high demand because of his unique ministry, his ability to pray people through to the Holy Ghost, and his ability to obtain liberty in God.

My father, Bro. Carl Ballestero, was serving as the pastor of Christ Temple Church in South Bend, Indiana, when he spoke with Bro. Bean about holding a revival for us. Although Bro. Bean didn't confirm a date, he responded, "I'll pray about it and get back to you."

Every month or so, Bro. Bean would call Dad and ask how the church was doing. The response was usually, "The church is doing fine." They would continue their conversation, and Bro. Bean would assure Dad that he would come to South Bend and hold a revival soon.

A few months later, Dad hung up the phone after they had the same conversation. Turning to Mom, he said, "I know why Bro. Bean hasn't come for a revival. I keep telling him everything is fine.

When he calls again, instead of giving him my pat answer, I'll tell him how it really is."

After a few months went by, Bro. Bean called and asked the usual question. Dad replied, "The tent is flapping in the breeze, and the stakes are coming loose. If Heaven doesn't help us, the bottom might drop out of this whole thing."

"I'll be right there," came the response.

Dad made arrangements with Bro. Bean to stay for at least three months. Since Jennifer was recovering from an illness, Bro. Bean drove up alone the first week of January 1967, and Sis. Nita, Jana, and Jennifer flew up a week later.

Bro. and Sis. Victor Simon, a couple in our church, had a one-bedroom apartment on the second floor of their house that they would rent out. Dad rented it for the Bean family to use during the revival. It was close by, and our church family had a wonderful time stocking the kitchen with food and the apartment with necessary items.

On the first night of the revival, Bro. Bean instructed the church family not to invite any visitors. "If Momma is sick," he said, referring to the church as Momma, "then the babies will be sick. First, we have to make sure Momma is healthy. We must learn to pray and get our hearts right; we must repent and learn to worship God right."

He called the saints up, one by one, to pray for us all. A lady who had not spoken in tongues for over thirty years was gloriously refilled with the Holy Ghost when he laid his hands on her head.

When the revival started, we had no nights off. Service began at 7:30 p.m. and often lasted until midnight. It was only after the first month of the revival that Bro. Bean announced we could take Monday nights off.

We had prayer meetings at 10:00 a.m. every day except on Sunday mornings. Our church family learned to band together and pray. Christ Temple was hungry for revival.

On Wednesday, January 24, 1967, South Bend experienced a few unseasonably warm days with temperatures reaching 65°F. Rain and snow were forecast for Friday, with the Weather Bureau predicting a fifty percent chance of precipitation and one to two inches of snow.

Bro. Bean was not used to Northern winters. On Friday morning, the temperature hovered at 32°F. He asked Dad if he was concerned about the weather. Dad said, "It's too warm. The snow is too wet to stick." A few hours later, when the flakes started sticking and falling harder, Dad said, "This won't last because the snow is too wet. It will melt."

Little did he know, this would turn into one of the worst blizzards South Bend had ever experienced. The weather forecasters called it the Surprise Blizzard. South Bend is situated on the leeward side of Lake Michigan, and the city experienced massive lake-effect snow. Twenty-three inches of snow fell in just over twenty-four hours, followed by winds over fifty miles an hour. With ten to fifteen feet of snow drifts, this weather brought the revival to a standstill. Although it was difficult for many to dig themselves out from the mountainous drifts and drive through the snow-laden streets, church service reconvened on Tuesday.

The following month, in February, Bro. Bean announced a three-day fast, ending on Sunday morning. He said revival would begin that day, and we could finally invite visitors.

We lived in the parsonage next door to the church. In preparation for the meal that day, Mom prepared a roast with all the trimmings for Sunday dinner and placed it in the oven. At the last minute, someone had put some clothes in the dryer, turned it on, and we all went next door to church. When service was over, my sister, Carlene, slipped out the side door and ran to the house to drink some orange juice, breaking her fast. As she opened the back door, smoke billowed out into her face. Thinking the roast was burning, she ran to the church to get Mom, frantically calling, "Mom! The house is on fire!"

As Mom hurried toward the side door, Bro. Bean was walking down the steps of the platform. She called out, "Bro. Bean, please tell Bro. Ballestero that the house is on fire!"

Bro. Bean, the quiet man that he was, turned and saw Dad standing on the platform talking to a church member. He casually walked over to him, paused, and softly said, "Excuse me, Bro. Ballestero, but I think your house is on fire." Dad loved to tell this part of the story because Mom was extremely emotional while Bro. Bean remained calm.

We later discovered that the roast had not burned, but the dryer had caught fire. The fire severely damaged the basement and filled the house with smoke. For the next month, we had to live in a motel.

Since Bro. Bean felt that the church was revival-ready and told us it was time to invite visitors, he instructed the church family on how to pray for the lost. "God doesn't care until you care," he instructed. "You have to be specific. You can't just say, 'God save, or God heal.' You must be explicit with your request."

Pulling out a rolling chalkboard, he asked the crowd, "Give me the name of someone you've been praying for to receive the Holy Ghost."

Someone called out, "Paul Minton."

He wrote down his name and said, "Now, here is how we will pray for him. We're going to pray for four particular things.

"First, we'll pray for Paul Minton to come to church tomorrow night." He had us all stand, and we prayed that Paul would come to church the following night. "Next, we'll pray that God puts Paul Minton under conviction when he comes tomorrow night." Again, the church family joined in, and we all prayed for God to put Paul under conviction. "Now, we're going to pray and ask God that Paul Minton would come to the altar tomorrow night." We all prayed again. "Finally, we're going to pray and ask God to refill Paul Minton with the Holy Ghost tomorrow night."

After we prayed specifically for each request, he called for the names of others until the board was filled. He said, "We're going to pray for each name exactly the way we prayed for Paul Minton. When these people come to church, and God fills them with the Holy Ghost, we will have them come up to the platform and erase their names from this board."

The following night, service had started, but Paul Minton was not there. We were singing our third congregational song when he walked in the back door. Because he was late to service, our faith was not high. But when he walked in and slipped into his seat, we started believing that if God could answer the first prayer, he could answer all four of them! While the congregation sang "He Set Me Free," tears started streaming down Paul's face. Bro. Bean walked to the pulpit, stopped the singing, and spoke a few words. Within minutes, Paul left his seat and walked down to the altar. No one persuaded him to pray; it was just Holy Ghost conviction that drew him to the altar. He knelt, raised his hands, and God gloriously filled him with His precious Spirit. Then he walked up to the chalkboard and happily erased his name.

The enemy fiercely opposed our church during Bro. Bean's time with us, attempting to hinder the revival. Yet, Jesus stepped in at every obstacle, and countless miracles occurred. This revival transformed our faith, deepened our prayer life and worship, and brought many souls into the Kingdom! I'm not sure of the exact number of people saved at that time, but our church was filled to overflowing, and every person whose name was written on the chalkboard received the gift of the Holy Ghost before the revival concluded. It was the most powerful and life-changing revival I've ever experienced.

Chapter 36

Ministerial Testimonials

A Man of God

Bro. Roy Lawrence

Bro. Verbal Bean, a man of God, was used very effectually in all nine gifts of the Spirit. He was a man who individually filled the role of the five-fold ministry, yet he was not haughty, proud, or egotistical. He was a humble servant of Christ, His church, and humanity, and was very ethical with fellow ministers. Someone from a neighboring pastorate called Bro. Bean to come to the hospital to pray for him. Bro. Bean stated, "I'll call your pastor and arrange to meet him at the hospital, and we will both pray for you." This was always his policy.

Bro Bean was so very kind, considerate, and compassionately Christlike in dealing with those caught in the devil's snare. His objective was not to expose or to ridicule but to express compassion and hold the door open for repentance and forgiveness. As a father gently dealing with an errant child, he worked with sinners. The main objective always was repentance, refilling, and restoration.

Being the masterful preacher that he was, Bro. Bean could preach for two hours or more, and it seemed as if it were thirty minutes.

Verbal Bean was a revivalist. He believed in revival for the past, present, and future. He believed God would give him revival regardless of the times, simply because he insisted that God give him revival. As a basis for his prayers and faith, he used the scriptures concerning the widow and the unjust judge from Luke 18:1-8, and most importantly, the verses following the Lord's prayer in Luke 11:5-13. Verbal Bean not only preached and taught prayer but also practiced prayer and challenged others to pray.

Deeply devoted as a husband and father, Verbal Bean was eager to provide a godly heritage for his children as his mother had for him. He was strong in faith, trusting God completely for his healing and didn't use any type of medicine. He did not ridicule those who did not trust God completely for healing. He was a kind and understanding builder of faith.

Verbal Bean was soft-spoken and kind yet firm in conviction. Though he was often disappointed when others could not see the vision he had for revival, he was not argumentative.

I had the opportunity of serving as president of the *Apostolic Ministers Training Institute* and working 'hand in glove' with Bro. Bean. The tapes on *Prayer* and the *Works of the Holy Ghost* are classic Verbal Bean. He was attempting to pour his experience and knowledge of the workings of God into young ministers. We recorded the sessions on the finest reel-to-reel recorder available, a large, cumbersome Roberts recorder.

During a fellowship meeting in Pasadena, Bro Bean said, "Brethren, I'm hungry to see someone receive the Holy Ghost. Would it be all right if I used my time praying people through to the Holy Ghost?" He asked for two people who wanted the Holy Ghost to come forward, and two responded. He instructed them to repent and expect God to fill them with the Holy Ghost. He laid hands on them, led them in prayer, and God filled them with the Holy Ghost.

Bro. Bean loved to hunt and fish, though he had little time to do so. I had the opportunity to hunt with him on a small acreage he had purchased not far from Bandera, Texas. He had put up a deer stand and feeders, which was legal in Texas. We had set up the tent, made the camp ship-shaped, and gathered the firewood.

We had a fantastic camp and a tremendously successful hunt, bagging deer, turkey, Russian boar, Javelina, and even ducks on the hills of South Texas.

Messages preached by Verbal Bean live on. For example, these are some of the sermons he preached: *Footsteps of the Flock, The Scum Pot, The Necessity of the Holy Ghost, Off Course, and Spiritual Childbirth.*

Verbal Bean knew how to work within the framework of an organization or fellowship. He simply loved fellowshipping those who believed the Apostolic message. He consistently and unapologetically stood for Truth.

A Most Unusual Man

Bro. Ed Wheeler

It is a most difficult task to express one's thoughts and feelings about a man so great as Bro. Bean. At times such as this, words seem to fail, and the vocabulary seems inadequate. However, I would like to mention a few things I knew about him, having been associated with the Houston church for almost twelve years.

When Bro. Bean first took the church in Houston, I immediately saw his unusual burden for the lost. Much of his time was spent reaching the lost. I have not seen anyone carry such a burden more consistently than he did. He always showed deep love and compassion toward us, who were members of his church. It was never too early or too late for him to take time to pray for the sick. Often, that involved hard prayer for hours until Heaven moved, and God answered.

Over the years, my family has had numerous occasions to spend time in Bro. and Sis. Bean's home, sometimes for extended periods of time. There was always a godly atmosphere in his home and among his family. I admired the closeness between him, his wife, and the children. His teachings were also put into practice at home.

Having personally assisted Bro. Bean, for a while, I have spent a good bit of time with him at work and at pleasure, often just the two of us. He was always careful to live up to what he preached. In fact, he had a stricter rule for himself than he did for others.

One must have known him to believe and understand the good things that can be said of this most unusual man. It is a great honor to have crossed his path and heard his ministry.

A Man to Ride the River With

Bro William J. Garrett

Someone once said, "Whatever a man does leaves a trail behind, and in his passing, he leaves an indication of the manner of man he is, of his character, even something of his plan. It requires only the observant and understanding eye to read what the trail can show. Nor does any person stand completely alone in the world, for when he passes, he brushes, perhaps ever so slightly, upon others, and each is never quite the same thereafter."

Bro. Bean came into our lives, passed among us, and is gone. The tangible has become only a memory, but he brushed upon us in passing, and we will never be the same as before.

My earliest memory of Bro. Bean was shortly after my wife and I received the Holy Ghost. He, his mother, and his sister moved to Orange, Texas, and our home church, where Bro. J. H. Stanton was the pastor. Though he was only a young teenager, his prayer life was almost legendary even then.

When he was seventeen years old, they moved to Houston, Texas, and started two churches at once. He started his work in South Houston, and his mother started her work in Greens Bayou. He went to work many a day without lunch and had a fresh piece of cardboard in the soles of his shoes to keep his feet off the ground. He didn't mind doing without and suffering to build a church.

Our early evangelistic work was with them in Orange. We prayed together daily, and many messages God gave me were on my knees praying beside Verbal Bean. We were never really together very much after those days, but the feeling was there, and from time to time, we were in contact. I remember him calling me in the night on the phone to share a burden with me and weeping. He was a man not ashamed to weep.

When it came to preaching, he just always knew he would be a preacher. He wanted God to give him a supernatural call, like a voice from Heaven, which never happened. The anointing was on him just the same. As he preached his early sermons, I remember shyness was in him. He would look up at the ceiling almost all the time. A shyness that God replaced with a boldness to look the Devil in the eye and not flinch. As the old saying goes, he was given "The courage to charge hell with a bucket of water."

He was a pastor's friend. I have heard comments made, "If it had not been for Bro. Bean, there would not have been a church to dedicate a new building or burn the mortgage." Also, "Our church had not had a real revival and was at a standstill until he came, and the weeks he was here produced a mighty revival that kept going on when he was gone." Many pastors will be forever grateful for this man of God who came into their lives, interceded with God, and fought with them until victory was won.

Bro. Bean was a lover of good men, as the Bible says, but he also fulfilled Jesus' words: "Love your enemies and do good to them that despitefully use you." Under no circumstance would he tolerate bitterness in his heart, which he had so carefully sanctified with a prayer life. Neither would he sympathize with it in others. He would carefully investigate whether bitterness was the source of a man's motives before he would ally himself to the cause.

Conviction is defined as "Strong belief." He was a man of conviction. Courage is defined as "Response of facing and dealing with anything recognized as difficult and painful, instead of withdrawing from it." Many have convictions, but Verbal Bean had the courage of conviction. Because of it, he became "A stranger to his brethren and an alien to his mother's children." Painful, yes, but he endured it as a price to pay for what he believed. He was no bargain hunter and never tried to cut the price. If he believed in it, you could count on him. He was what the old timers used to call "A man to ride the river with."

He believed in revival and preached it with vehemence, yet he was unalterably opposed to television as a vehicle to promote it. He felt it would open a far more dangerous and destructive gate than any good would provide.

Yes, he passed our way and brushed our lives, and we are the better for it. The warrior is gone, fallen in battle, but his trail is there to see, and the memory lingers. A tribute to Bro. Verbal Bean was that so many came from far and near to salute him in his passing.

My Pastor

Bro. T J Marshall

In 1969, I was living in Cleveland, Ohio. Mary, my sister, and her husband Buddy invited me to move to Houston to work with them in their salvage business.

I had contacted my former pastor, Bro. C. E. French and told him I was moving to Houston, Texas. He encouraged me to look up Bro. Verbal Bean's church and visit there.

After we arrived in Houston, I looked up Bro. Bean's number and called to get directions to the church. After several rings, Bro. Bean answered, and after a long pause, he said in a deep voice, "Hello." He was very cordial and told me how to get to the church. Hanging up the phone, I told my wife I didn't think we would like that church because the pastor sounded like an old man. Was I ever mistaken!

We went to Greens Bayou Apostolic Church for the first time the following Sunday morning. What preaching we heard, and what a powerful service it was! We went again several times, and each time, it was the same. People were being baptized in Jesus' name and receiving the Holy Ghost. We were hooked and decided to make Greens Bayou our church home, even though it was what we considered a long drive away. What a great decision that was!

After a few years at Greens Bayou, Bro. Bean had a desire to start a Bible training school for young ministers. He named it the ***Apostolic Ministers Training Institute*** and he felt that if he could train young men, they would receive the benefit of his years in the ministry. He also called on other men to share their wisdom, such as Rev. Murray Burr, Rev. C.R. Free, Rev. Ray Majors, and others. I feel as though I have greatly benefitted from the year that I spent at his Bible school.

Bro. Bean was compassionate and loving but did not pull any punches when you were wrong. I remember during a business meeting Bro. Bean said, "Brethren, I need your help. I have found some property on Wallisville Road for sale and would like to purchase it for a new church building. For this, I need your input. I am not a businessman, but when it comes to the doctrine, don't question me."

Son in the Gospel

Bro. Ted Buxton

The first time we went to Greens Bayou Apostolic Church was Sunday, January 10, 1971. While the Yeats trio was singing, "Sheltered in the arms of God," tears rolled down my face. Bro. Bean walked by, laying his hand on my shoulder. He said, "Son, why don't you holler 'calf rope'?" He then walked on. Shortly after that, I went to the altar. We went to church that night and returned on Tuesday night. My wife, Karen, and I received the Holy Ghost that night. Bro. Marshall was praying with me, and Sis. Marshall was praying with my wife.

A few weeks later, I asked Bro. Bean if my wife and I could go visit her brother in Alexander for the weekend. We wanted to share what the Lord was doing in our lives as they were backsliders. He replied, "No," turned and walked away. Approximately three weeks later, he said, "Bro. Buxton, you can go now.

I said, "Where?"

He replied, "Didn't you ask me several weeks ago if you could go and see Bud and Jo?"

I said, "Yes, sir."

He said, "Well, you can go now. By the way, when you asked me before, I saw a trap set for you."

I am so thankful God put a preacher in my life who was sensitive to the moving of the Spirit. As we progressed in our spiritual journey, I began to feel a call to preach. Bro. Bean used me occasionally to minister at Greens Bayou. Later, I was asked to preach out of town. Bro. Bean gave his permission, and said, "Bro. Buxton, you need to go on a three-day fast before you go." He was so right! When I arrived at the church, I entered into a battleground I had never experienced before. Once again, I was so thankful for Bro. Bean's sensitivity and wisdom.

While under Bro. Bean's ministry, he told me to attach myself to Bro. Marshall and go with him on hospital visitation to pray for the sick. He then explained why he asked me to do that; "Because Bro. Marshall is a man of faith." He also asked me to attach myself to Bro. Buford in the prayer room, because Bro. Buford knew how to pray people through to the Holy Ghost.

Bro. Bean suggested that the young ministers spend time with the Sunday school teachers of different age groups. This would help us understand how to teach children so they could learn the things of God on their own level.

During my time at the Apostolic Ministers Training Institute, I was mesmerized by Bro. Bean's knowledge of the Word of God. When asked a question, he would tell us to turn to book, chapter, and verse, and there would be the answer. He did all this while sitting on top of his desk, and not even opening the Bible.

Once, some of us went to a meeting with Bro. Bean. We rode for two hours without him saying a word. All of a sudden, he said, "Oh, brethren, I apologize; I just got caught up in the Spirit."

What a man of God!

We were blessed to have three of our children born while attending Greens Bayou Apostolic Church, and we are so grateful to God for allowing our family to have Bro. Bean as our pastor.

My Spiritual Father

Bro. Marty Gibson

I am honored to share my testimony of how I came to Greens Bayou Apostolic Church, and how God allowed me to be able to sit under the ministry of the greatest man of God I have ever known. Of course, I'm speaking about Elder Verbal Bean!

As a young boy, I was raised in a very impoverished environment as both my parents were unprepared for the hardships of married life and raising children. Small criminal acts to feed ourselves would eventually turn into experiences that would later mold and shape me into a viable illegal force that would have to be reckoned with. At fourteen years of age, I was taken away from my parents and placed in a foster home for three and a half years because of a robbery I committed at a gas station.

I left the foster home and moved back to my parents at age eighteen, and again, I found myself struggling to stay away from the wrong influences.

Before long, I was in trouble for breaking the law and was taken to the Fort Worth County Jail. Because of a suicide attempt, I was put in isolation. But God had other plans!

Isolation was a five-by-seven-foot cell with only a thirty-watt bulb for light. It was miserably cold, and the room had only one book to read, a Gideon Bible. I started reading the Bible, and every word was directed to me. In my heart, I believed every word and every promise as the Word of God kept leaping off the pages and convicting me!

Suddenly, I fell to my knees; my heart was totally surrendered to the God of this Bible! Tears were flooding my eyes, and I started praying words to God; I was asking for forgiveness and mercy, and I lifted my hands toward the ceiling of the cell. Immediately, my English was taken over by a Supernatural Power, and I started speaking in other tongues! No one was there but God and me. The room was filled with angels, and God told me that He had called me from my mother's womb to preach the Gospel.

Just four days later, I was called into court proceedings for my crimes. I had to answer for eight felonies, and I was facing sixty years of imprisonment. The judge dropped all the felonies to misdemeanors, and he reduced the eight misdemeanors to three. I was sentenced to three years in prison, and that was dropped to ten years of probation. Then the probation was reduced to three years; this was all done on the same day in the same court proceedings with one requirement. I was to go to Elmwood Sanatorium for a three-month treatment.

While at the Elmwood Sanatorium, I met a beautiful young woman, Brenda, who later became my wife. We were married fifty years ago, in December. After we were discharged from Elmwood Sanatorium, we moved to Houston, and we visited a non-denominational coffee house for young Christian seekers. There, we met Jim and Ronda Forgey. They were saints from Greens Bayou Apostolic Church, pastored by Bro. Verbal Bean. They explained to us there was a more perfect way to serve God, and we immediately went to church and had a prayer meeting. We were established in that church, and Jim and Rhonda Forgey made it their mission to make sure we were in every service and maintained a dedicated prayer life.

During this time, we were becoming established in the Word of God under Bro. Bean's ministry. Six years later, we would launch out to evangelize for almost twenty-three years in thirty-eight states for some of the most wonderful churches in the Apostolic movement. We were blessed to see thousands of people converted and baptized in Jesus' name.

Thank you, Bro. and Sis. Bean and the Greens Bayou Church, for believing in these two young people who wanted to do something for God!

The Most Fruitful Evangelist

Bro. Donald E. Haymon

It was my privilege to share under his ministry in the inception of the South Houston United Pentecostal Church which he pioneered. We were as brothers in those early years of his ministry. Often, he would whimsically declare, "You're my companion in tribulation!" However, the tribulation soon passed, and we were both happily married.

I can't recall that his preaching ever improved from those beginning years. As then, it has always been pertinent and wise. I always enjoyed and rejoiced in the message. The most striking thing about his ministry is that he preached to us. None could leave a service in which he ministered without feeling that he personally had been indicted. Never high-sounding phraseology, his ministry was just solid, practical, down-to-earth preaching. This ministry is needed so badly and will be missed greatly from the godly lips of Verbal Bean.

We'll miss him again, as we did so sorely in South Houston when he gave up that pastorate. He then became perhaps the most fruitful evangelist of his day. Though we must adjust to his homegoing, we may be called to join him. Let us live that we, too, may die the death of the righteous. I only hope he knew how much I loved him.

About Verbal Bean

Bro. Nathaniel J. Wilson

How often I have wished I could articulate the impact of the one life of Verbal Bean, first, upon myself, and second, on the Apostolic Movement. I know of no other individual impressed in my generation who has left such a deep and lasting mark on so many—a solitary man who, alone, literally lifted an entire movement onto his back and set it in the rarefied air of new life. His ministry was nothing less than iconic and literally changed the shape of hope for generations to come. Like a spectacular comet, he sped across the sky at supersonic speed for forty-four years.... then disappeared in death equally violent and spectacular, never to be heard from again. However, even now, the Spirit that anointed him can be felt resonating generations later.

Verbal Bean exemplified ministry wherein his existence was a pure manifestation of His essential, infinite self, as seen by God, as the image of God. Without guile, deceit, ulterior motives, hidden personal ambitions, small and cheap goals, he lived solely for God. He was rather possessed of tremendous spiritual power and gifts of wisdom, knowledge, and faith, coupled with a strong preaching and teaching ministry, a ministry of both judgment and blessing with many signs and wonders following. Usually holding two services a day, at times his ministry was splendid, grand, magnificent. The fruit of his ministry speaks for itself and needs no human validation.

His grasp of life was focused, deep, and balanced. It was not just his preaching—although he was an excellent and moving preacher. His secret was finding the path of the Spirit for those to whom he was ministering and walking therein. This might mean preaching, singing, walking around, praying and exhorting, correcting, or ministering in the gifts of the Spirit. His ministry rooted out sin and brought repentance or judgment. Thousands of people received the Holy Ghost through his ministry. He almost single-handedly broke repressive spiritual strongholds across America, which had prevented people from receiving the gift of the Spirit.

Today, leading Apostolic Pentecostal churches continue to be those upon whom the imprint of his ministry rests. Virtually, every contemporary of mine who rose to great things, at one time or another, in one way or another, had an intersection experience with the ministry of Verbal Bean. His passion to create great spiritual leaders burned bright. In turn, he would be mortified to see those who remain camped around the firepits of those 1960s revivals, never moving forward and bringing that power to bear on today's world.

At times, in order to make his point, he was very funny. To this day, I still use things that came directly from him over fifty years ago. A gifted and articulate teacher, in an unusual fashion, he would teach the church and the new converts. Many of the personal guidelines I live with today came out of those teaching sessions when I was a fourteen-year-old boy. These include my prayer life, my appearance, my attendance to Bible reading and study, my consciousness of the holy, an unwillingness to accept "no" as an answer when seeking revival, holding my ministry in a reserved and sacred place, and never mixing the sacred and secular...and... many ...more.

In ways mysterious, pieces of His anointing continue to live on amongst us today. His ministry was epochal and continues to stand tall, towering over the riff-raff world, beckoning us on. May the Spirit which imbued him imbue us likewise.

Assisting Bro. Bean

Bro. Jimmy Lee

In 1967, Dad took me to meet Bro. Bean and Bro. Joe Duke. Bro. Duke was preaching a revival for Bro. Bean at Greens Bayou, Texas. During the service, Bro. Bean came and stood behind me and prayed for me to be blessed of the Spirit. A friend came to me and asked me to run the aisles with him. At first, I was somewhat reluctant, but as the Spirit began to move in my soul, I wanted my friend to get out of my way. I still remember the freedom I felt that night.

In 1968, I attended *Texas Bible College*. Since it wasn't far, I went home nearly every weekend. During the week, I attended church in Greens Bayou. This was when I began to know Bro. Bean a little better. After one year there, I started to evangelize. That summer, I saw Bro. Bean at Topeka, Kansas, and he informed me he was starting the *Apostolic Ministers Training Institute*. From the first, I knew that I wanted to attend. After trying to preach revivals, I was beginning to realize just how little I knew about evangelizing and my ministry.

In the fall of 1969, I was among the students who were privileged to attend the first year of the school. Several ministers from the area and some from a long way off taught us that year. All of the lessons were great, but I could never forget those wonderful sessions when Bro. Bean shared with us the knowledge and burden of a lifetime following after the Holy Ghost and of successful prayer.

When the lessons on prayer started, we were to be at the church at 6:00 a.m. for a prayer meeting. About the third morning, I was awakened by the gentle hand and voice of Bro Bean saying, "Bro. Jim, aren't you going to pray this morning?" It didn't take long for me to get dressed and go over to the church for prayer that morning. We were eager to put to use the wonderful dimensions of prayer to which we were being introduced. Those three weeks passed so very quickly. It was from these lessons on prayer that the tapes and the book on *Prayer* were birthed. I feel very privileged to have been present when these were taught.

Bro. Bean had a way to help take the mystery out of the works of the Holy Ghost. I had heard of the gift of tongues, interpretation of tongues, prophecy, and discernment. After that, all the gifts of the Spirit seemed to just fade away. Even in the late sixties, Pentecost was just getting over the negative effects of the Latter Rain Movement. While teaching on the *Works of the Holy Ghost* one night, the Spirit of God moved in, and class stopped. We started praying, and travail came into the room. God spoke through Bro. Bean in prophecy to the men that were there. I felt that God had put His sacred sanction on what we were learning from the elder.

After my time in the school, Bro. Bean approached me and asked me to pray about coming to Houston to be his assistant pastor. It took a few weeks before I was finally convinced that would be the will of God for my family and me. We moved to Houston and became a part of Greens Bayou Apostolic Church.

The very first Sunday that I was there, Bro. Biscamp, the Sunday school superintendent, came to where I was sitting and said, "Bro. Bean has asked that you come and sing a few choruses to start the service." This was the beginning of a wonderful year of training for me. I was to start and lead every service, knowing that if Bro. Bean wanted something special, he would let me know. If something went wrong, he was there to set it right again. This was such a comfort to me. I had the liberty to follow God to the best of my ability, but still had the comfort that Bro. Bean was there watching and helping me learn more about following God.

The year and a half that I was Bro. Bean's assistant was a bright spot in my life. There was a lot of physical labor, but it was like going to college and being paid while learning. There were times when we worked with cows, built various building projects, and traveled together. Sometimes, Bro. Bean would be in a quiet mood, and there was no use trying to get him to talk. Other times, he would just pour out knowledge straight from his heart. Those times were invaluable to me.

I sometimes think Bro. Bean kept cows on his place to see the city boys try to play cowboy. Every time someone was chased out of the pen, the elder would laugh and enjoy watching the look of terror on their faces. This was therapy for him. The barn was one of his favorite places to pray. Only Heaven knows how many battles were won in that hay loft.

Several times, Elder Bean would share some burden of his heart. While driving across Houston one day, he asked out of the blue, "Bro. Jim, what are we going to do about Chile?"

Taken completely off guard, all I could think about was Mexican food, and said, "I don't know." He was thinking about the need for a missionary for the country of Chile. He wanted to know if I had felt a burden for the country, and I assured him that I hadn't felt anything but would help him pray for God to supply the need.

Sunday nights were very special at Greens Bayou. We always came with expectancy for God to work in a special way. People were receiving the Holy Ghost and being baptized regularly. God continued to use Elder Bean right up to the very last. I shall always remember the last message he preached on Wednesday night. His subject was "The Tribe of the Praisers." He was happy to tell us that the sun rose first on the tribe of Judah. God has special blessings for those who will praise Him.

On Friday, April 1, 1977, the elder and I went into central Texas to pick up a load of hay for the feed store he had purchased. We made it in late that night, and I promised to come out the next morning and unload the hay for him. When I came the next morning, I brought my wife and son with me. Bro. Bean said for us to sit down and visit. It was one of those rare times that he shared his heart with us. He spoke about some of the people we were working with in the church and gave some special insights as to their progress. Finally, he told me to go home and rest for a while. After the feed store closed that night, he wanted me to lay tile on the floor. He came by, laid his hand on my shoulder, and told me he was going to Louisiana to pray for his uncle, who wanted the Holy Ghost. He continued, "I plan to be back tonight. If, for some reason, I don't make it back for the morning service, Bro. Carl Ballestero is to preach. Carry on as if I were there. I will be back for church tomorrow night, Lord willing." This was the last conversation I ever had with him. As he was leaving, he waved goodbye to our small son as he drove out of sight.

The first call I received was from my dad. He had heard of the accident and wanted to know if it was correct. Next, a brother from the church called and said, "Tell me it isn't true! Tell me my pastor isn't dead!" My father-in-law lived in Sulphur, Louisiana, and we called him and asked him to check on the details of what happened at the time. While we were waiting to hear from him, Bro. Bean's mother came to our home. She wanted to return to Louisiana right then and pray for her son. The weather had turned very foggy, and I persuaded her to wait until we heard an accurate account. Soon, Bro. and Sis. Ballestero came to my home, also. Oh, what a God-sent blessing they were on that night. From then until about two the next morning, my phone was busy receiving and sending calls. This is one night that I shall never forget.

The next morning, Sis. Lee and I went to Sulphur, Louisiana, to check on Bro. Bean's wife and son. There was nothing we could do for the elder; God had called him home, but we felt a strong obligation to do what we could for his wife and children. I shall never forget the great character that showed forth from Sis. Nita on that extremely hard morning. She was doing very well, considering all she had been through.

That Sunday night, I arrived at church as Bro. Ballestero started service. As I walked in, Bro. Ballestero invited me to the pulpit to take over the service. It seemed a very long walk down the aisle that night. The atmosphere was heavy with grief. On the way down to the front, God dropped a thought into my heart. As I took the pulpit, I said, "Nothing we can do tonight will bring our pastor back. Let's have church like Greens Bayou knows how to have Sunday night church." At that point, about six of the good men of the church took off around the building, running for the Lord. The Holy Ghost fell in a great way. What a comfort the Holy Ghost always is in hard times.

Much of the memorial service is a little fuzzy by now. I remember that we were in the middle of a remodeling project. The carpet was out, the church was being repaired, and there was standing room only that night.

Many people may remember the funeral. There seemed to be preachers everywhere. I felt the loss of my pastor, my friend, and my mentor. There is still a vacant place in my heart that only time has been able to ease.

I would like to say a "Thank you," to Bro. Voar Shoemake for his help in the days that followed. His wise counsel to the church was such a blessing. He was there to help in the services and encourage us to stay together. His constant stability was truly a blessing to the church there in Houston.

It would be redundant to say that I still miss our precious Bro. Bean. So many times, in the last several years, I would have loved to call or just sit down and unload my burden to him, again. So many of us depended on him and his prayer life. When Bro. Bean said, "God told me…." everyone listened. Some may not have liked what was said, but all took notice. I certainly feel my life has been made much richer because I knew Bro. Verbal Bean.

Eulogy

Bro. Murray Burr

Harold Bell Wright, in his hauntingly beautiful story, *The Shepherd of the Hills*, wrote, "Here and there among men, there are those who pause in the hurried rush to listen to the call of a life that is more real. How often have we seen them jostled and ridiculed by their fellows, pushed aside, and forgotten as incompetent or unworthy? He who sees and hears too much is cursed for a dream, a fanatic, or a fool, by the mad mob, who having eyes, see not, ears and hear not, and refuse to understand."

Such, in a measure, had been the story of the life of Verbal Bean, but now, he has gone from the world in which he had never really belonged nor had been at home. Do not tell me that this was by accident. Those who know will not believe you. Accidents do not happen to men like Verbal Bean. Almighty God, who shapes the destinies of men, called him home, and we are the poorer for it.

Verbal Bean was a prophet, and strangely, God never makes two alike. Coming fresh from the hands of the Master designer, each is an original. God fashions His prophets, distinct and individual; then He breaks the mold.

In the presence of grief and bereavement, we grope for words of comfort and consolation, but mere words are so inadequate. To his grieving wife, whom he loved dearly; to his children, who were so precious to him; to a mother whom he cherished; and to his family and friends in general, I address these few personal observations.

"Of all the men that I have ever known, Verbal Bean was the purest; of all the prophets I have ever known, he was the most dedicated; of all the ministries I have ever known, his was the most nearly Apostolic."

STILL, HIS SHADOW FALLS

BY MURRAY BURR

He finished his course; he's claimed the crown.
The image looms stark and tall;
When Giants stalked the brooding land,
He stood above them all.

The seasons came, and the days have fled,
And memories grow frayed and dim:
Yet his awesome shadow towers still,
And across our pathway falls.

The Pigmies stride, they oft have tried,
To match his ten league steps,
Of lofty intellect and stately form,
Hopelessly, they stand bereft.

Only noble men and tall, receive such call,
To walk along beside;
Spirit chosen and qualified,
Heaven delights to point with pride.

Let us lift our sight to loftier heights,
 And follow the plain path he has blazed
The more his great life unfolds before us,
The more we are amazed.

Critical little men stand appalled,
Their vision so mean and small;
Yet the seasons come, and the years have fled,
Still, his awesome shadow falls.

The Memorial Service

Bro. Martyn J. Ballestero, Sr.

The organ played softly as the ministers made their way to the platform, one by one. The church was already full, and still they came. Saints and friends from all over lined the back wall and completely filled all the entrances. Many were not able to get inside at all but contented themselves with the fact that they could hear.

Silent cries went up to Heaven from the church as a whole. The sanctuary was filled with saints who had been salvaged by his ministry, sheep who had been guided by his counsel, and backsliders who had ignored him. Also attending were young ministers who owed an unrepayable debt to him for his patient molding of their young ministry. Older ministers and pastors whose respective churches had been helped and blessed beyond words or measure were there as well. All came to honor Bro. Verbal Bean, and to thank God for the benefits of having known him.

The church quartet and Bro. and Sis. Jimmy Lee sang songs that Bro. Bean loved and often requested. A free spirit of worship flowed across the audience as the congregation joined in and sang unto the Lord through their tears.

Bro. Jimmy Shoemake was the Master of Ceremonies and led the congregation in worship and in prayer for Sis. Nita Bean, little Joel, the girls, Jana and Jennifer, and Sis. Bernice Bean, and family.

Bro. Ed Wheeler represented the local church. In eulogizing his pastor, Bro. Bean, Bro Wheeler likened him to many Biblical characters: men who walked with God, men who lived by faith, men of purity and honor, men above reproach, men used of God, and men who loved God.

Bro. Carl Ballestero preached the memorial service, using for a subject Ezekiel's words' "There hath been a prophet among you."

Bro. Ballestero said, "If you didn't believe in prophecy before you met Bro. Bean, you did afterward." Without a prophet, the people of God suffer, and sin remains unmolested.

It is indeed a great honor to have sat and listened to Bro. Bean, as the Holy Ghost used him to break the bread of life. What a great privilege it was to have felt the warmth of his friendship, the white heat of his message, the strength of his love, but most of all, to have known and loved the prophet that was among us.

A Prophet Has Been Among You

Bro. Carl J. Ballestero

"And they, whether they will hear, or whether they will forbear... yet shall know that there hath been a prophet among them." (Ezek. 2:5)

The word *prophet* means "To bubble up, to announce; one who utters a God-given message." A prophet is, as others are not, a man of God.

The ministration of the priest was to take the burden of God and make it known to the people. He represented God to man.

In the Old Testament, God used a ministerial system incorporating "checks and balances" to preserve the purity and sacredness of both His message and His people. In the event one of these representatives did not function properly, then God promoted the other to do so. Israel's survival depended on their faithful witness and representation of a man of God.

Ordinarily, the prophet was not sent to the heathen but to the people of God. It seems he came into prominence when apostasy ruled or at least threatened. He became the voice of God to the people. It became Heaven's design and the prophet's desire to turn divided hearts back to the God of their covenant, to turn straying feet from wayward trails. Such a ministry is seldom popular and sometimes successful.

The ministry of the prophet appears to have been one of restoration. He warned, instructed, and attempted to rebuild the moral and spiritual fiber of the people. The priesthood might officiate, rituals might become elaborate and over-emphasized, but without proper communication and a clear voice of God in their midst, the nation only degenerated. Then, as now, the letter killed, but the Spirit gave life.

As bad as the Babylonian captivity was, there was something infinitely more tragic to happen in Israel. At least there, they found some of God's greatest prophets. But it became a dreaded day and time when, for four hundred years, the voice of the prophet was stilled.

Note that trial and tragedy are often associated with the prophet. Other men might live well into old age, but this man of God might be removed when it seemed his usefulness was indispensable. Others might live and die in harmony with all and may never know the lonely depths of intense pressure and prolonged trial. The faith of the prophet would be tested to the limit, and he would become a favorite of the enemy.

The childhood of Bro. Verbal Bean gave evidence of God's touch on his life. People came from afar to hear the young boy pray. His pastor loved to mention how he would spend the day alone in church, praying and singing.

His remarkable ministry became known while he was yet a young man. He came to the pulpit at a time when churches needed a challenge and faith needed strengthening. His faith set him apart from the ordinary preacher. He could pray people through that other folk had given up. He could do many things well, whether it was to preach, pray, worship, sing, play an instrument, or administer spiritual therapy. Sometimes, he was an artist in painting spiritual therapy, and at other times, he was a soul surgeon. He would set a church in order and instruct saints in righteousness. He was an advocate of holiness, a contender for worship, and had a true compassion for those needing deliverance. He was at his best in prayer and consecration. We found his words weighty, his life practical, his advice sound, his life and labors an example, and his character above reproach.

I have often known him to be a peacemaker and friend to those in need. One felt he could go to him, tell his heart, and trust the judgment he gave.

I admired the way he avoided senseless arguments. I noted that he kept himself from the forefront. He often walked away from the crowd. He was a lonely man. He fled from those tainted with bitterness. He refused to seek an office.

I appreciated the way he could make a vow and then stand by it. When in the pulpit, if he felt God would have him minister in a channel other than in preaching, the urging of hundreds could not change him. He strove to please his Master. He was no man's man but was a friend to every man.

I liked the way he contended for those missing essentials in our midst. Years ago, when the gifts of the Spirit were not in abundant evidence and seldom sought after, we heard his voice urging the revival of them.

His success as an evangelist was outstanding. His ministry was often imitated but never duplicated. I liked the way he laughed when God slayed proud church members with His power. He ever advocated liberty and freedom for the saints. He refused to put up with a dead service.

Strong conviction was much in evidence while he ministered. He exposed hypocrites and troublemakers. When it became known that he was coming to hold a revival, people paid up their back tithes. God often showed him the lamentable condition of many in an assembly. He would "pick up" a bad spirit or troublemaker the first night of the meeting.

I found him to be always firm but fair. He was a protector of the good and a friend to the weak. If you did not believe in prophecy before, you did when you heard him.

Those many people who have been converted, delivered, or strengthened through the efforts of his ministry are the proof of his calling. This is especially so for those members of his church in Houston. They can allow his ministry to continue through their proper spiritual deportment and life of faith. It becomes an evil day when saints and ministers neglect the labor and tears of a burdened ministry by changing their prayer life, their worship, their standards, their doctrine, and their manner of living. Continued faithfulness would mean an acknowledgment of a minister's God-ordained effort upon assemblies or individuals and their holding fast to those sound words and examples; then can it be said that "He being dead, yet speaketh."

We are made to thank God for the life, labor, and love of Bro. Bean. It has been our good fortune to have known him, and our privilege to have companied with him. Peace be to his memory.

In the perfecting of His people, God uses men of different abilities, gifts, and temperaments. Some men seem to fit into a pattern, while others stand apart. Some types are given to us quite often, while certain kinds come along only once in a while. Moses had a Joshua ready to follow him. Elijah gave his mantle to Elisha. Replacement for Samuel was to take a little longer. In the instance of Bro. Bean, as with other anointed and singular ministries, we can only pray, "Do it again, Lord!"

His Promotion Came at Last

Bro. Robert C. Cavaness

The battle he fought is now over,
And all his pains are past;
Awaiting now, the trumpet sound,
His promotion has come at last.

We think not in our memories of him
Having victories just in the past,
For a new body, he now awaits,
His promotion has come at last.

It left us all shocked and stunned,
When his sudden death came to pass.
Though long, dreary moments of grief
remain
His promotion has come at last.

And so, to a faithful man of God
Whose ministry remains steadfast;
Apostolic Ministers bid this final salute:
You've obtained the grandest promotion
at last.

"Blessed and holy is he that hath part in the first resurrection ..." (Rev. 20:6)

Verbal Bean Quotes

1. You can no more live for God without praying than you can stay alive without eating.

2. I was a bachelor for years, but I would be lost as a goose to go back to being a bachelor tonight.

3. I am talking to people today who have fallen into a spiritual coma.

4. I will not move until Heaven speaks to me.

5. As far as I'm concerned, there is no divine truth, there is not a more golden truth, there is not anything richer and more blessed handed to me, a divine revelation, than that which declares there is but one God.

6. Tonight, I know what the name of God has always been and will always be; it is the name Jesus.

7. I'm glad someone influenced my life to want to go to a prayer room.

8. I've got a list of scriptures that would fill up a typewritten page which say that men in the Bible wept. Every man God has ever used was a weeping man.

9. Evangelism is making friends for God.

10. If I'm wrong, you won't hurt my feelings by telling me I'm wrong.

11. While the tares are growing, let's do something about the wheat.

12. Pursue peace; it's worth running after.

13. Harness me up to whatever I can do, and I'll do my best to pull the load.

14. I'm so slow. Slow to get started and slow to stop.

15. Shortcuts can be dangerous sometimes.

16. You can never be who I am, and I could never be what you'll become.

Epilogue

Verbal's death, the move from Houston to San Jose, Joel's injury, and Jana and Jennifer's sorrow were devastating. My girls not only lost the daddy they adored, but they also had to leave our newly built home, lifelong friends, and the only church congregation they had known. I look back on our little family and marvel at how we survived. Although wounded and anguished, we made it from day to day; days became weeks, and weeks became months. It was always surprising to me to find we not only lasted through this seemingly endless season but also found pockets of joy that carried us through another day. We certainly could not have endured this period of grief without the love and support of our family and friends.

Life was never the same without Verbal, but through the lonely days and nights, God was faithful as I endeavored to put our lives back together again. Stephen Wilson Jr. wrote, "Grief is simply love with nowhere to go."

When we moved to San Jose, it was only a few months before I bought a house, and until that time, we stayed with Mother and Daddy. It was comforting for us to be with them, and the rest of the family were in and out most days. There was always something going on and certainly delicious meals to enjoy.

Daddy found a house in our price range about three blocks from the church. I bought it, and we moved in with help from friends and family. This proved to be a great choice; my cousin and his wife, Harrell and Barbara Shoemake, lived across the street, and Lonnie and Norma Smelser, one of the foundational families of the church, were next door. From the day we arrived until we moved away, Lonnie Smelser put my garbage can out and brought it in for me every week. I was surrounded and cared for by these wonderful people.

Mother and Daddy moved in with us for several months while they were building a new home, and their presence was a comfort. My family and the children of God were ever-present. They embraced us spiritually and carried us in their prayers and concerns. We received dozens of cards, letters, flowers, gifts, phone calls, visits, meals, money, and much more.

For a long period, after the brutal loss of so much I had loved and lived for, I found it difficult to pray. I could, if I conquered my emotions, say prayerful words. I had to hold my feelings under a tight rein to do this. Prayer is an emotional experience for me, and it seemed, in my weakness, that if I gave myself to heartfelt prayer, I might never be able to stitch my heart and feelings back together again. I feared a total breakdown. But God, in His infinite mercy, provided a safety net for me and my children by putting a burden for us in the hearts of our many friends, family, and acquaintances.

It seemed everyone I encountered wanted to reassure me I was not carrying this load of grief and sorrow alone. Countless times, I heard words like these:

>"I'm praying for you."

>"I'm praying for your children."

>"Our church is praying for you."

>"My family and I prayed for you all last night."

I am convinced this wealth of prayer and intercession kept us from complete desolation.

When I arrived in San Jose, Jimmy told me they would want to include me in church ministry. He said, "Nita, I know you'll need time for healing, but when you're stronger and feel able, you'll be a part of the church team."

After a time of adjustment, I became involved in church activities. I joined the choir, taught the Singles Class with my cousin, and enjoyed the revival the church was experiencing at this time. I was able to purchase a new Oldsmobile, and Jana and Jennifer were enrolled in the church school. It became a period of healing and restoration for me and my children. Although grief was at the forefront of our lives during those years, the memories I hold are cherished.

After being in San Jose for three years, one day, I brought in the post and found a most interesting letter. Bobbie happened to be with me that day, and after reading the letter, I handed it to her. She had hardly finished the letter when she stood up, smiled at me, and said, "We have to let Jimmy see this!"

We found him at their house, and I gave him the letter and said, "What do you think about this?" The return address on the envelope listed Arthur Hodges, Jr. as the sender, but I noticed he signed the letter as Johnny. I soon found out Johnny was his nickname. He had written to invite me to share dinner with him on Valentine's Day.

Jimmy was smiling by the time he finished reading the letter, and I asked him, as my pastor, as well as my brother, what he thought about it. Jimmy and Johnny had been close friends for years, and I was very interested in his opinion of this invitation. Jimmy was very careful when he replied, but finally, he said, "Nita, I think you would enjoy getting acquainted with Johnny Hodges. He's a good man and a successful pastor. We've been friends for a long time, and I believe he's a man of integrity." With my pastor's blessing, I replied to Johnny's letter and told him I would be glad to join him for dinner.

Johnny sent me a return letter and explained that he would fly from his home in San Diego to San Francisco, rent a car, drive to San Jose, and take me back to San Francisco for dinner. After dinner, he would drive me back home and return to San Francisco for his flight home. This seemed to be a very complicated date, but he had carefully planned every detail, and it worked.

He rang my doorbell that fateful evening, and I met him at the door. It was a little awkward initially, but we both did our best to appear relaxed. As we started the thirty-minute drive to San Francisco, we began talking, and I found we had a lot in common. I already knew his wife, Elaine, had died in a terrible car accident. She was riding in the back seat of the car with their son, Brent, while he delivered newspapers on his early morning route. He fell asleep at the wheel and ran into a barrier on the side of the road. The car crashed through the barrier; Brent was uninjured, but Elaine was killed instantly on impact.

We continued talking about many things during the ride to San Francisco, all through dinner, and on the way back to my home. It seemed as if we had been friends for a long time, and the evening ended all too soon. It wasn't love at first sight, but we made a connection that night, which was surprising but reassuring to me.

Johnny called me each night from that time forward. We spoke for hours, sharing concerns about our children, how we were dealing with our loneliness and grief, and what this friendship meant to us both.

After a few weeks, Johnny asked me to fly to San Diego and meet his family. When I landed there, I promptly fell in love with the city, even before I fell in love with him. It was a perfect city for a courtship, and there wasn't enough time to experience all the sights San Diego had to offer.

Meeting Johnny's family during that first visit was a highlight of the trip. His son, Arthur Edgar Hodges III, or Art, as he was called, was married to Rosalinda, and their only child, Amber, was a beautiful toddler. Art, Rosa, and Amber lived with Johnny and his other two children, Jonathan Brent and Cami Dawn. Rosa kept the family going by cooking, cleaning, and caring for Brent and Cami, while Art took over most of the pastoral responsibilities as Johnny tried to get his life back together.

I attended church with Johnny during that first visit. It was a fervent revival church blessed with a great pastoral team. George and Roseanne Nobbs oversaw South Bay Christian Academy as well as preaching, teaching, and helping wherever there were needs in the congregation.

Johnny also visited San Jose several times during our courtship and stayed with Jimmy and Bobbie in their home. Johnny and I would drive over the mountain to the beautiful coastal town of Santa

Cruz, one of our favorite places to visit. He spent time with my children, who soon became comfortable with him. Joel was especially happy to have this kind man visit with us. Soon, they were all laughing and talking together like old friends.

Unless you have experienced the type of tragedy and grief Johnny and I had suffered through, it would be difficult to understand what we were feeling as we became better acquainted. I have described it like this: When you have been extremely ill for a very long time with a high fever, aching bones, and nausea, it seems you will never recover. Then, one morning, you wake up, your fever has broken, the nausea and pain have subsided, and you are ready to eat breakfast. It's wonderful just to feel hopeful once more. This resembles the emotions you go through after you have felt grief and sorrow as a constant companion for many months. You meet someone who brings happy anticipation to your life, and it occurs to you that maybe this is a time of restoration. You wake up in the morning with a smile and know this day will be good. Those were my feelings when Johnny and I fell in love.

When I was convinced that ours would be a lasting romance culminating in marriage, I discussed what this would mean to our family with Jana and Jennifer. Shortly after arriving in San Jose, Jana and Calvin Bass were married, so they would remain there when we moved to San Diego. This change wouldn't affect Jana's life as it would Jennifer's. It would be difficult to uproot her again after living only three years in San Jose. I knew it wouldn't be a problem for Joel; he was already calling Johnny 'Daddy' and loved to be with him. However, there were some real advantages to our move. We would be living in one of the most beautiful cities in California–San Diego. South Bay Pentecostal Church also had a Christian school, which Jennifer and Joel would attend.

It would be a real blessing to have Johnny looking after us all. I knew there would be difficulties blending two families, and there were, but it would also be a wonderful benefit to my children and me to be active and involved in ministry once again.

After spending time with Johnny, I discovered he was a loving, caring father to his children. I explained it like this to my girls. "I know Johnny can love another man's children because Brent and Cami were adopted, and he loves them with all his heart. I know he will love you all, too." Those proved to be prophetic words. My children soon bonded with Johnny, and he gathered them together in his heart with his own children. His capacity for love was unique and treasured by me. He is the only father Joel can remember, and he is so very grateful that Johnny came into our lives when he desperately needed a Daddy. Jana and Jennifer often talk about Johnny and what he meant to us all. He had a zest for life and an unending sense of humor.

We were married on August 9, 1980, in a lovely afternoon ceremony at the San Jose church. Jimmy officiated, and all our children stood with us on the platform as we took our marriage vows. The weather was perfect, and a crowd of family and friends surrounded us. After spending two nights in San Francisco, Johnny and I flew to Hawaii to share a splendid three-week honeymoon.

When we returned to San Jose, Johnny loaded a moving van with our furniture and belongings. While he drove the van, Jennifer and Joel rode with me in my car on the trip to San Diego.

Jennifer, Joel, and I moved into Johnny's house with the understanding I was free to make it into 'our' home. It was lovely, but the outstanding feature was the view through the wall of windows in the family room. We would watch the sunset over our beautiful Pacific Ocean, drink coffee, and count our blessings.

Jennifer, Joel, and me

The merger of two families was challenging, to say the least, and had some sobering moments. It was also a great comfort to know I had someone by my side to share all the good and bad elements of bringing our families together.

Johnny proved to be a loving, caring companion to me. He was patient, funny, and devoted to us all. He loved my children, and they fervently returned his affection. I, too, loved his family and doted on our beautiful granddaughter, Amber. In retrospect, I was so busy during those first few years with a husband, three teenagers, and a five-year-old to care for that it seemed our life was a blur. But those were happy days. I laughingly told friends, "I think there are more rooms in the house than just the laundry room and kitchen, but I'm not sure."

Once, while Mother was visiting with us, she asked, "Nita, are these cookies in the pantry fresh?"

I said, "Mother, everything in this kitchen is fresh. Keeping enough food in the house is the problem."

Getting to know Johnny's parents and siblings was a real pleasure. They were devoted, godly people who loved each other totally. Johnny was especially close to his only brother, Jack. Jenelle Durrance, Johnny's youngest sister, was a member of the church, and we had wonderful times with her and her family. These were busy but golden days, and we were totally immersed in life.

After living in San Diego for four years, Johnny felt a call to take the pastorate of Moss Bluff Pentecostal Church of Lake Charles, Louisiana, which was Johnny's birthplace. The hot, humid summer months could be trying, but we loved the people of the congregation and discovered that Cajun food is some of the best in the world. We lived there for fourteen years until Johnny resigned because of age and health issues and returned to our beloved San Diego. We purchased a home there and were happy to lay aside the responsibilities of ministry and try to be the best saints possible at South Bay Pentecostal Church.

We had several years of retirement in San Diego and enjoyed those days immensely. One of our favorite pastimes was to drive down the coast from La Jolla to Pacific Beach. La Jolla is a beautiful city with exquisite views of the Pacific Ocean. A cove on the coast was initially designated a children's pool but was soon overtaken by seals. They recognized this would be a protected place to birth their pups, and it became our favorite place to visit. Our out-of-town guests always enjoyed these coastal tours.

I thank the Lord for the years we spent together. Our children were in and out of the house, bringing the grandchildren to spend time with us. Christmas dinner was shrimp gumbo, potato salad, and banana pudding for dessert, as requested by the family. These are precious memories for all of us.

When Johnny entered his late seventies, his health issues became very serious. He had been a diabetic for several years, and his cardiologist told him he needed a heart valve replacement. He had the surgery but never fully recovered. The next few years were spent mainly trying to strengthen Johnny and deal with his declining medical condition.

Sadly, the year 2015 brought more and more serious health problems for him, and by April, he was failing rapidly. I'm very thankful that many of Johnny's family and friends visited during this time. Bro. and Sis. T J Marshall arrived and said they were there to help with Johnny's care; it was a blessing to Johnny and me both. He lapsed into a coma after several days of distress, being unable to sleep or rest. Our children stayed in our home with us during this final vigil, and on April 17, he was ushered into the presence of the Lord, never to suffer again.

The family prepared a beautiful going-away service for Johnny, and the building was filled with loving saints, friends, and family. He had served his congregation and community with unwavering devotion. As a faithful shepherd, he profoundly impacted the lives of hundreds, and these grateful individuals gathered to honor his memory and pay their final respects.

Art and Rosa Hodges and the South Bay Pentecostal Church continued to provide their care and love for me after Johnny's passing. I have cherished this church and consider it one of the precious benefits of my life to sit under the leadership and ministry of Art Hodges. Rosa has been like my daughter, and her devotion has filled my heart with gratitude.

Jana and Calvin, Jennifer, Joel and Sheree are held closely in my heart. As I have aged, I have lost confidence in making the right life decisions. This is puzzling because I have been a decisive person all my adult life. Still, often, I find myself calling them, explaining I need advice. I trust them implicitly; they always have my best interests at heart. Joel patiently explains passages of scripture, which I am convinced have a deeper meaning than I have found and helps me rightly divide the Word more clearly. Sheree and I spend treasured hours in the kitchen, cooking, talking, and laughing together.

My girls prop me up in more ways than I could describe. They instinctively know what type of clothes I should wear, and with unerring sight, they kindly tell me I might consider changing my hairstyle. I tell friends, "No matter how old my daughters get, they'll always be my mother." I can't imagine life without Jana and Jennifer by my side. Neither has said an unkind word to me their entire lives, and I depend on their love more than they could ever know. Calvin has become a chef unparalleled, and he patiently explains how he creates his culinary masterpieces to me.

I am wealthy with children, grandchildren, and great-grandchildren who fill my life to the brim. Their presence and love are my greatest treasures, giving me the strength to face the long days ahead.

This book would have been impossible without the help and encouragement my family has given me. There were days I was convinced I could never adequately describe Verbal and his ministry, and my children would remind me that no one else could tell this story. They also wanted everyone to get a glimpse of the man behind the ministry: he was kind, considerate, patient, and always loving. Verbal cared deeply and fervently for his mother, Jana, Jennifer, Joel, and me. His personal life is one to be followed, as well as his life of prayer. I am a living witness of how blessed life was with Verbal, the man–the minister, and though my loss was profound, I wouldn't trade anything for experiencing life with Verbal Bean.

While writing this manuscript, countless times I have wept with the knowledge that Jesus Christ has been with me, bringing events to my memory and allowing me to feel the touch of His glory while telling the story of my Verbal and his ministry. In some ways, while I have relived the loss of Verbal's passing and experienced that heart-rending grief it brings, it was well worth it to me because I again felt the Shekinah glory that covered Verbal's walk with God. Thank you for reading this story. Verbal's ministry was greater than could be contained in one book, and I trust you have been blessed by not only gaining knowledge of the awesome minister he was, but also by getting to know the man who loved and cared for us all.

Our last picture

Verbal's artwork

"Boyhood Memory"

"Boyhood Dream"

Made in the USA
Columbia, SC
09 January 2025

51576849R00233